CHILDHOOD, WELL-BEING
AND A THERAPEUTIC ETHOS

CHILDHOOD, WELL-BEING AND A THERAPEUTIC ETHOS

Editors

*Richard House
and Del Loewenthal*

KARNAC

First published in 2009 by
Karnac Books Ltd
118 Finchley Road
London NW3 5HT

British Library Cataloguing in Publication Data

A C.I.P. for this book is available from the British Library

ISBN-13: 978-1-85575-633-5

Typeset by Vikatan Publishing Solutions (P) Ltd., Chennai, India

www.karnacbooks.com

CONTENTS

THE EDITORS AND CONTRIBUTORS

Christopher Clouder, FRSA is Chairman of the Steiner Waldorf Schools Fellowship for the UK and Ireland, and the CEO of the European Council for Steiner Waldorf Education. He is a co-founder and a leader of the Alliance for Childhood. He writes and gives public lectures internationally on educational matters, contemporary social issues, and cultural evolution. He has produced books and articles on education and childhood, his most recent publications being on creative play for parents of young children. He has recently been appointed Director of the International Platform for Educational Innovation for the Fundación Marcelino Botin of Santander.

Dr Kathryn Ecclestone is Professor of Education and Social Inclusion, University of Birmingham. Kathryn worked in post-compulsory education for 20 years, in youth employment schemes, further education, and as a researcher. She has recently researched and published on the growing 'therapeutic ethos' in subject content, pedagogy, and assessment throughout Britain's education system. Kathryn is writing two books from a project on formative assessment in vocational education, and adult literacy and numeracy programmes. A co-edited book from an ESRC-funded seminar series

'Transitions through the lifecourse' is due in October 2009. She currently directs an ESRC-funded seminar series on 'Changing the subject: interdisciplinary perspectives on emotional well-being and social justice'.

Ricky Emanuel is a Consultant Child and Adolescent Psychotherapist and Adult Psychotherapist trained at the Tavistock Clinic, London. He is Head of Child Psychotherapy Services for CAMHS at The Royal Free Hampstead NHS Trust, and also Clinical Lead for CAMHS working for the Children's Commissioning team in NHS Camden. Ricky has sat on a number of Government bodies, including, amongst others, the Expert Working Group for the CAMHS module of Children's National Service Framework, and on the CAMHS Review. He has also chaired the Child Psychotherapy Strategy and Steering group for NHS London, which commissions pre- and post-registration training for child psychotherapists.

Sue Gerhardt is a practising psychoanalytic psychotherapist based in Oxford. She is the co-founder of a charity, the Oxford Parent Infant Project (OXPIP), which provides psychotherapy for babies and parents, and has worked part-time as an infant–parent psychotherapist for over 10 years. Previously a documentary film-maker and community worker, she is also the author of *Why Love Matters: How Affection Shapes a Baby's Brain* (Brunner Routledge, 2004) and of the forthcoming book *The Selfish Society* (Simon and Schuster, 2010).

Richard House, Ph.D. is Senior Lecturer in Psychotherapy and Counselling in Roehampton University's Research Centre for Therapeutic Education, a publishing editor with Hawthorn Press, and a trained Steiner teacher. A campaigner for childhood with the 'Open EYE' Campaign, he writes regularly on childhood and psychotherapeutic issues. With Sue Palmer, Richard co-initiated the Open Letters on 'toxic childhood' and play to the *Daily Telegraph* in September 2006 and 2007 respectively, which have precipitated a global media debate on the place of childhood in modern technological society. His books include *Therapy Beyond Modernity* (Karnac, 2003) and *Against and For CBT* (edited with Del Loewenthal, PCCS, 2008).

Oliver James has a Social Anthropology degree (Cambridge University) and trained as a child clinical psychologist (Nottingham

University). Oliver was Research Fellow at Brunel University and worked in the Cassel mental hospital, before becoming an author, journalist (with columns in six national newspapers), TV producer, radio broadcaster, and television presenter. He is the author of *Britain on the Couch* (1997), *They F*** You Up...* (2002), *Affluenza* (2007), *The Selfish Capitalist* (2008), and *Contented Dementia* (2008). Oliver has also contributed articles to scientific journals in recent years, including the *Journal of Epidemiology and Community Health* and *The Psychologist*. He has acted as an adviser to both New Labour and the Conservatives.

Del Loewenthal is Professor of Psychotherapy and Counselling at Roehampton University where he directs the Research Centre for Therapeutic Education and the Doctoral Programmes in Psychotherapy, Counselling and Counselling Psychology. He is also a Chartered Counselling Psychologist and Analytic Psychotherapist in private practice. His books include *Against and For CBT* (with Richard House, PCCS, 2008), *Case Studies in Relational Research* (Palgrave, 2007), *What is Psychotherapeutic Research?* (with David Winter, Karnac, 2006), and *Postmodernism for Psychotherapists* (with Robert Snell, Routledge, 2003). Del is currently interested in the development of post-existentialism, and is founding editor of the *European Journal for Psychotherapy and Counselling* (Routledge).

Sue Palmer, a former primary headteacher, has written many books, articles, and TV programmes about primary education, and acted as a consultant to the Basic Skills Agency, the National Literacy Trust, the former Department for Education and Skills, and the BBC. Since her 2006 book *Toxic Childhood* helped spark a debate about modern childhood, she has been involved in many campaigns around education, outdoor play, screen-based entertainment, and the commercialization of childhood. Sue is Chair of the Scottish Play Policy Forum, Fellow of the English Speaking Board and the English Association, and President of the Montessori Association AMI UK. In 2008 the *Evening Standard* listed her among the twenty most influential people in British education. Her latest book is *21st Century Boys* (Orion, 2009).

Bob Reitemeier, in his six years as Chief Executive, has led the transformation of The Children's Society's work to focus on improving the lives of all Britain's children. Since 2006, he has overseen the highly successful Good Childhood Inquiry, strengthening The Children's Society's position as a thought-leader in the sector, dedicated to ensuring every child has a good childhood. Before this, Bob had over 20 years' voluntary-sector experience, mostly in Africa. He moved to The Children's Society as Operations Director in 1998, working closely with national government to improve children's and young people's lives. Bob is co-chairing the Social Work Taskforce, and is also a member of the Youth Justice Board.

Andrew Samuels has an international reputation as an influential commentator on politics from a psychological perspective. He is Professor of Analytical Psychology at the University of Essex, and holds Visiting Professorships at New York, London, and Roehampton Universities. He is a Jungian Psychoanalyst in private practice in London, and was elected one of the first group of Honorary Fellows of the United Kingdom Council for Psychotherapy. Andrew was co-founder of Psychotherapists and Counsellors for Social Responsibility and works internationally as a political consultant. His books have been translated into 19 languages, and include *The Political Psyche* and *Politics on the Couch*.

Eugene Schwartz has served as a Steiner Schools teacher, author, and consultant for over thirty years. He has been awarded a Fellowship by the Carnegie Foundation for the Advancement of Teaching and he presently serves as a Fellow of the Waldorf Research Institute. He has created Discover Waldorf Education, a YouTube.com channel, to air a series of videos introducing Steiner education to a wide viewing audience. Eugene's commentaries, articles, and podcasts are available on his web site www.millennialchild.com. His children's story, 'Dragonsblood: An Eco-Fable', will be published in 2010. He lives in Kimberton, Pennsylvania, USA.

Sami Timimi is a Consultant Child and Adolescent Psychiatrist in the National Health Service in Lincolnshire and a Visiting Professor of Child and Adolescent Psychiatry at the University of Lincoln. He writes from a critical psychiatry perspective on topics relating to mental health, and has published many articles in leading journals and chapters in books. He has authored four books, including *Pathological Child Psychiatry and the Medicalization of Childhood* and

Naughty Boys: Anti-Social Behaviour, ADHD and the Role of Culture; and co-edited three others, including *Liberatory Psychiatry: Philosophy, Politics, and Mental Health* and *Rethinking ADHD: From Brain to Culture.*

Elizabeth Wood is Professor of Education at the University of Exeter. Her research interests include the role of play in early learning; progression and continuity in play; teachers' professional knowledge and practice; and curriculum, pedagogy, and assessment in early childhood. She was consultant to the National Union of Teachers on developing their play policy in 2007, and has an international reputation for her research on play and pedagogy. Her publications include *The Routledge Reader in Early Childhood Education* (2008), and (with Jane Attfield) *Play, Learning and the Early Childhood Curriculum* (Paul Chapman, 2005). Correspondence: e.a.wood@ex.ac.uk

Biddy Youell is Head of Child Psychotherapy at the Tavistock and Portman NHS Trust. A former teacher, she retains a particular interest in the application of psychoanalytic ideas to educational theory and practice. In her book *The Learning Relationship: Psychoanalytic Thinking in Education* (Karnac, 2006), Biddy re-emphasizes the centrality of the emotional experience of teacher and learner, illustrating how psychoanalytic theory can help in understanding many of the issues which help and hinder the educative process.

FOREWORD

No-one can now ignore the fact that a serious debate about the welfare of children has at last begun in our society. And, appropriately, it has started to open up a wider debate about the nature of learning and even the nature of human maturity. The essays in this collection are significant not only for what they say about childhood but for what they invite us to think about human growth and well-being in general.

So in this volume you will find some searching reflections on what we do to the growing human consciousness by certain styles of education. Several contributors make a powerful case for resisting the pervasive drift towards measurable skills and tightly defined goals for (especially) primary schoolchildren. Richard House, in a very challenging piece, appeals to Rudolf Steiner's theories to underline the dangers of treating the child's consciousness as simply a limited and inadequate version of the adult's, and argues that the best way to keep therapists in work indefinitely is to perpetuate this error. And whether or not the reader will share the Steinerean perspective, it seems undeniable that one of the roots of the expanding and well-documented unhappiness of children and young people in our culture is the sheer impatience we exhibit with the long period of latency that characterizes the human animal. We want to supply a storehouse of useful skills and to measure their acquisition at every step. But what if that biologically unusual latency is in fact itself a treasury for human well-being? What if hurrying children through it is one of the most effective forms of deprivation we could devise?

If 'therapy' is one of the key words in this collection, the other is 'play'. Therapy, so the editors argue, is not a matter of damage limitation—nor does it necessarily imply that we begin by assuming a state of 'victimage' or diminution on the part of all young people. Rather, it is to do with attempts to heal an entire social climate that is unduly obsessed with outcomes and panicky about wasting productive time, focused overwhelmingly on fantasies of individual success and damagingly clumsy in most of what it seems to think about relationships. And in this light, the connection of therapy with play becomes clear. Play (as the essays in Part IV particularly show) allows the growing consciousness to establish a very particular kind of relation with the world of physical stimuli: it allows you to think that it might be different. It develops the 'what if…?' function in the mind—the function that in the long run permits art, science, and even politics, and a bit paradoxically, strengthens our awareness of what is specifically in front of our noses by challenging us to think it away and 'remake' it. This is not a matter of acquiring skills that will enable us to solve problems, but of nurturing the imagination that will make us constantly wonder if we are asking the right questions of our world. And it is in this imaginative maturity that we discover what is distinctive in our humanity and why our humanity, with all its pain and frustration, can be an opportunity for joy.

The freedom of the imagination, the freedom to ask whether we are asking the right questions and to reconstruct the world in speech and image and vision, is of course an essentially spiritual thing. For the Christian believer, 'spiritual' is not a word that designates simply some distinct quality or 'territory' in the individual subject; it is a word deeply imbued with resonances to do with connection or communion. A spiritual education is not one in which we are shown how to cultivate certain highly satisfying and even useful private experiences, but one that exposes us to connections, possible and actual, with other subjects, with the material world we inhabit and ultimately with its source. The discussion in these pages of spirituality in education assumes, refreshingly, that the capacity to rethink the world, to see it differently through the imagination, is bound up with the capacity to see yourself as connected in ways you did not choose with a whole environment, human and non-human. Behind the back of the conscious ego lie all sorts of links, life-giving and also at times frightening, which make us who we are; imagination allows us a glimpse of that rich and elusive hinterland, and without it we shall both wreck our own selfhood and ravage our environment and our human relations. Whether or not all this opens on to the wider horizon of relatedness to the ultimately mysterious life of the creator is something about which these authors will not agree, any more than readers will. But it is important that the question be recognized for what it is, a serious one that asks about the framing of our whole imaginative life.

Kathryn Ecclestone casts a sharp and sceptical eye on an approach which, disturbed by all that we have identified so far, comes to see education and nurture as fundamentally problem-driven—so much so that it casts children in the light of helpless and shrunken souls who require endless therapeutic attention. Education, she argues, is thus distorted into a constant struggle to make the world easier for its injured and hyper-sensitive subjects. It is, as the editors acknowledge, a salutary warning. Talk about 'emotional literacy' *can* turn into a recipe for emotional illiteracy if it refuses to deal with the challenges of managing the reality of others, the inevitability of frustration, and the tough edges of choice. But the concern of other authors here is certainly not to collude with the idea of a 'diminished' self or to propose that the ideal educational process is one in which individual emotional states are to be cosseted or indulged. Properly understood, there is much in common between a good deal of what Ecclestone argues and the rest of the book: education is how we equip children for transforming their thinking and acting and for relating with both celebration and critique to the world they inhabit.

Sue Palmer and Sue Gerhardt summarize their invaluable researches in their contributions here, showing in different ways the complex interweaving of patterns of imaginative and affective deprivation with neurophysiological problems and behavioural disorders. For those who apparently want to trivialize the question of children's well-being (young people have always said they're unhappy; children just *grow* up however you bring them up; we can't over-protect our children by going along with their complaints; and so on), the concrete evidence, medical and statistical, represented in these as in many other chapters ought to give pause.

But the resistance to such evidence suggests the uncomfortable conclusion that quite a lot of commentators in the UK at the moment are still reluctant to approach these issues with care and openness—and that this is sometimes expressed in terms that imply a positive dislike or fear of children and young people. Why this should be is a question that deserves a whole series of further essays. But here is one way into the issue. Our uneasiness with our children—that is to say, the uneasiness over-represented in public comment and media rhetoric, if not corresponding very exactly to how any one of us is likely to feel with particular young people—is rooted in our own uneasiness as to what it is we want to communicate to the next generation. The presence of the young reminds us painfully that we have little or no 'wisdom' to transmit. As a culture, we are individualistic and focused on short-term gratifications—or at least that is the public rhetoric we allow and indulge in advertising or entertainment. But not to have any clarity about what we believe worth transmitting is a sobering and unpleasant condition. The threat that so many claim to see in the young is in fact, as much as anything else, the threat of the void we suspect in ourselves as modern or postmodern adults, unclear as to whether we really have anything to *value*.

Which may mean that we ourselves, modern and postmodern adults, have been deprived of some of that spiritually serious playfulness that allows us to approach the world as if it were a place of possibilities and unexpected affinities, as well as a place of profound challenge and potential pain, to be reworked through the imagination. If this excellent collection helps us think through not only the needs of our children but our own often unacknowledged needs, it will have achieved a very great deal. But meanwhile we owe much to the authors and editors of such a varied, engaging, and outspoken guide to our ills and puzzles, and to what we might need to address them, at last, with greater honesty.

Dr Rowan Williams
The Archbishop of Canterbury

ACKNOWLEDGEMENTS

We would like to thank, in no particular order of importance: Karnac Books for their confidence in this project, and for their patience and flexibility with its preparation and production—and particular thanks to Oliver Rathbone, Karnac Books' Managing Director; to the Archbishop of Canterbury, Rowan Williams, for taking the time to read the manuscript and to write a foreword amidst his very busy schedule; to Sue Palmer for her path-breaking work on popularizing the notion of 'toxic childhood', from the seed of which this volume essentially springs; and to the seminar participants at the Roehampton University 'Childhood, Well-being and a Therapeutic Ethos' Seminar of December 2006 (and to our Dean of School, Michael Barham, for his support with the latter)—including Professor Richard Layard and MPs Annette Brooke, Tim Loughton and Anne McIntosh (and arising from which event, many of the chapters in this book derive).

Further thanks are also due to those who took part in the 'Play and Playfulness in Children and Adults' conference, which we ran at Roehampton in November 2007; and our thanks also to the staff and students from our own Research Centre for Therapeutic Education, through which all these events were organized, including our series of Policy Forums; whose contributors included James Park, Dennis Hayes, Helen Penn, Ricky Emanuel, Andrew Cooper, Chris Woodhead, Debbie Epstein, Heather Geddes, Kathryn Ecclestone, Fiona Carnie, and Mike Davies, thus further informing our thinking; and thanks most especially to Rhiannon Stamp for her invaluable help with all of these events. Additional thanks to the publisher Routledge, for their kind permission to reproduce three papers, the original versions of which appeared in the *European Journal of Psychotherapy and Counselling*; to Bloomsbury Publishing PLC and Vermillion for kind permission to reproduce excerpts from Oliver James's books *They F*** You Up* and *Affluenza*, respectively; and to Dr Brien Masters, former editor of *Child and Man*, for permission to quote extensively from the journal. And last but not least, our warm thanks to the esteemed contributors to this book, whose wisdom and care for the deep needs of children shine through, throughout the book. Thank you to every one.

Richard House and Del Loewenthal
London, July 2009

CHAPTER ONE

Editorial introduction: 'Therapeutic ethos' in therapeutic, educational and cultural perspectives

Richard House and Del Loewenthal
Research Centre for Therapeutic Education, Roehampton University

> [T]he protection of the imaginative space of childhood ... needs a background of security, adult availability and adult consistency ... — the safeguarding of a space where identities can be learned and tested in imagination before commitments have to be made.
>
> (Williams, 2000, pp. 61, 31)

Introduction: Is modern society really bad for children?

It is something of a truism of many, if not most, psychotherapy and counselling modalities that adult emotional difficulties are to a significant extent rooted in, or at the very least influenced by, childhood experience. On this view, it follows that we surely need to pay particular attention to childhood experience if we are to minimize the extent to which today's children will need therapy as adults, and maximize levels of emotional well-being across society. Put differently, and culturally speaking, the aim of a society should perhaps be that of reducing the need for psychological therapies—in the sense that an emotionally mature, virtue-centred society which minimized noxious childhood experiences of all kinds, and which also had culturally and community-sanctioned means for 'holding' and supporting people's 'difficulties of living', would have far less need for therapy as a culturally legitimated healing practice.

The burgeoning increase in mental-health and 'emotional literacy' initiatives and support for children in both schools and in the wider community suggests that all is not well with childhood experience in Late Modernity (but for a rather different, cautionary view, see Kathryn Ecclestone's Chapter 9, this volume). Traditionally, and certainly starting with the early, 'seduction theory' of Freud, the focus of psychoanalysis and psychotherapy was upon childhood trauma, and the way in which it can affect and severely disrupt ordinary human functioning (for moving case material on this theme, see Ricky Emanuel's Chapter 6). Yet for some commentators—some of whom are represented in this book—modern technological society, and all that goes with it, is responsible for generating very particular kinds of distress and anomie which are in danger of becoming normalized, and even so taken for granted that, as one of us (DL) puts it in Chapter 2, we are so thoroughly alienated that we're quite unable even to perceive our own alienation.

It is not insignificant that in times of increasing financial uncertainty, Karl Marx's critical works on capitalism are coming back into fashion, with incredulous (political) economists returning to Marx as an incisive critic of capitalism. Certainly, Marx's theory of alienation and commodity fetishism (e.g., Ollman, 1971) and his trenchant critiques of technology (especially when put alongside the work of the much-neglected Frankfurt School) seem as prescient and insightful today as they were a century and a half ago. With the so-called 'commercialization of childhood' becoming a major theme in current critiques of Western society (e.g., Compass, 2006; Linn, 2005; Schor, 2004), this is perhaps an opportune moment to bring to the foreground the theme that is central to this book—namely, the culturally fashionable notion of 'toxic childhood' (see Sue Palmer's Chapter 3, this volume), where this book's story really first begins.

A central axiom of the 'toxic childhood' theme might be that it is the moral responsibility of everyone, including academics, to consider just how we might counter the unintended and negative side-effects of modern technological culture on children's well-being and being-in-the-world. And far from being new, this modern cultural theme is merely expressing—albeit in a different way—a deep question that has preoccupied many great philosophers of technology and its vicissitudes over the millennia (Plato himself, Heidegger, Adorno, Habermas ...), and more recently, cultural commentators like Postman, Lasch, Chilton Pearce, and so on. Touching again on the commercialization theme, it is no coincidence, and has great relevance to the concerns of this book, that in recent years we have seen the emergence of cogently argued critiques of materialistic values from both academic and more culturally activist standpoints (see, for example, James, 2007; Kasser, 2002; Kasser and Kanner, 2004—and see also the former's Chapter 15, this volume); and this in turn leads us inevitably into deep ideological and even spiritual questions (Wiliams, 2000) about the kind of society, and its associated values, that we are creating for our children, and for ourselves.

Notwithstanding the considerable methodological difficulties entailed in attempting to measure well-being cross-nationally and cross-culturally, and the associated methodological shortcomings of the UNICEF report which placed Britain's children at the bottom of a league table of children's well-being (UNICEF, 2007), and of the more recent report from the Child Poverty Action Group, showing that, based on data for 2006, the UK ranks 24th in a list of 27 European Union countries plus Norway and Iceland (Goddard, 2009), these dramatic findings are clearly picking up on something that is, at the very least, significant, and which at worst might appropriately call forth an urgent and comprehensive investigation into children's well-being, like that recently brought to fruition in the UK by the Children's Society (Layard and Dunn, 2009; see Bob Reitemeir's Chapter 5, this volume). Kate Green, chief executive of Child Poverty Action Group, was quoted as saying: 'We need to rethink the place of children in today's Britain and ensure [that] the right to a good childhood is central to our national culture. We cannot afford a "do nothing" budget for our children' (Goddard, 2009)—a statement which would form a very fitting *raison d'être* for the current book.

The childhood field has generated a very strong campaigning zeal and associated cultural commentary amongst a number of writers and academics who, besides empirical research, are also interested in intuition, wisdom, and 'ideology critique' self-reflexively founded in the primacy of personal experience (Reed, 1996); an approach which we could perhaps loosely term *research through phenomenology* and which one of us (DL), through exploring meaning in the context of post-existentialism (which can include the implications of psychoanalysis and other developments in our cultural practices) has termed 'post-phenomenological' (Loewenthal, 2008b). We would like to invite the reader to engage with the arguments as they unfold.

Propelling children's well-being on to the media agenda: Some 'toxic childhood' origins

It was widespead concerns about children's well-being that led writer Sue Palmer (Palmer, 2006; see her Chapter 3) and Richard House (see his Chapter 10) to compose, and seek widespread endorsement for, two Open Letters to the national press on the state of modern childhood, which were signed by hundreds of professionals and academics (Palmer, House and others, 2006; House, Palmer and others, 2007; see also Fenton, 2006). The letters highlighted the many challenges of being a child in a world transformed by several decades of rapid social, cultural, and technological change. In galvanizing and focusing 'like minds' across a wide range of professional and academic fields, and although at least some academics made it clear that they were less than comfortable with these initiatives, these letters seem to have played a key part in precipitating a discernible sea-change in the British policy-making agenda since the first of our Open Letters appeared in September 2006—with, for example, the British Government announcing its Children's Plan in December 2007 (Department of Children, Families and Schools, 2007; see also BBC News, 2007), and approaching £400 million of new public spending having been allocated to creating and improving children's play spaces (Paton, 2007). Children's well-being has now become—thank goodness—a topic of increasing concern in political and policy-making circles.

The first Open Letter, published in the *Daily Telegraph* on 12 September 2006, drew attention to what many believe to be the increasing incidence of children's mental health problems, and propelled the terms 'toxic childhood' and 'junk culture' into the public realm, in what quickly turned into a quite unprecedented news story centred on children's well-being, with a media 'fire-storm' quickly spreading across the globe. In that letter, to which this book's editors were both signatories, we wrote that

> As professionals and academics from a range of backgrounds, we are deeply concerned at the escalating incidence of childhood depression and children's behavioural and developmental conditions. We believe this is largely due to a lack of understanding, on the part of both politicians and the general public, of the realities and subtleties of child development.
>
> Since children's brains are still developing, they cannot adjust—as full-grown adults can—to the effects of ever more rapid technological and cultural change. They still need what developing human beings have always needed, including real food (as opposed to processed 'junk'), real play (as opposed to sedentary, screen-based entertainment), first-hand experience of the world they live in and regular interaction with the real-life significant adults in their lives.
>
> They also need time. In a fast-moving hyper-competitive culture, today's children are expected to cope with an ever-earlier start to formal schoolwork and an overly academic test-driven primary curriculum. They are pushed by market forces to act and dress like mini-adults and exposed via the electronic media to material which would have been considered unsuitable for children even in the very recent past.
>
> Our society rightly takes great pains to protect children from physical harm, but seems to have lost sight of their emotional and social needs. However, it's now clear that the mental health of an unacceptable number of children is being unnecessarily compromised, and that this is almost certainly a key factor in the rise of substance abuse, violence and self-harm amongst our young people.
>
> This is a complex socio-cultural problem to which there is no simple solution, but a sensible first step would be to encourage parents and policy-makers to start talking about ways of improving children's well-being. We therefore propose as a matter of urgency that public debate be initiated on child-rearing in the 21st century and that this issue should be central to public policy-making in coming decades.

Several months after the Open Letter appeared, we organized a one-day seminar at Roehampton University in December 2006, under the auspices of the Research Centre for Therapeutic Education, to which the hundred or so signatories to the Open Letter were invited, and at which a number of the eminent signatories gave presentations. This path-breaking seminar was unique in also attracting the attendance and active participation of shadow ministers Anne McIntosh, Tim Loughton, and Annette Brooke, government spokesperson Naomi Eisenstadt, and Professor Richard Layard, with the latter giving considered responses to the day's proceedings at the end of the seminar. Nine of the speakers at that seminar are represented in this book, with their talks being reproduced in updated form for the book. We have also added several new chapters on the theme of play, which was the focus for the second Open Letter which appeared in September 2007.

It can be argued that all of us (and many less than consciously) seek out reparative experiences which will help to heal lacks or abuses from our developmental histories, and the importance of play can certainly be seen in this light. In the summer of 2007, Sue Palmer and Richard House resolved to repeat the successes of their 'toxic childhood' Open Letter of September 2006, by collecting signatories to a new Open Letter on play. To their astonishment, approaching 300 signatories were quickly collected from right across the globe, and with such high-profile public names like Steve Biddulph, Dame Susan Greenfield, Oliver James, Penelope Leach, Michel Odent, Susie Orbach, Sir Jonathan Porritt, Dorothy Rowe, and Professors Andrew Samuels, Ernesto Spinelli and Brian Thorne, all enthusiastically signing this modern 'manifesto' for the defence and advocacy of play and its central importance in modern life—especially for children.

Many other aspects of children's lives were perceived as highly concerning, not least, the medicalization of children's experience (e.g., House, 2002–3; Timimi, 2002; Timimi and Maitra, 2005), and the way in which the 'high-stakes' testing and managerialist 'audit culture' values have swamped educational experience (House, 2008a), and have deprived children of their birthright—the right to enjoy and be empowered by a developmentally appropriate learning environment. Indeed, an increasing number of commentators believe that the various 'symptoms' of distress colloquially labelled 'toxic childhood' are more accurately interpreted as children's insightful commentary on just how badly we adults are doing, rather than some kind of child 'psychopathology' that needs to be medicalized and 'treated'.

The theme of play has been taken up in recent years by education policy-makers of many a hue, and it is currently a hotly contested notion in the passionate debate about the fundamental nature of early childhood experience (House, 2002a, 2008b). Play and playfulness have also long been alive and, to some extent, influential within the field of psychotherapy—most notably in the play therapies themselves, but also within some humanistically incined therapies, and of course within psychoanalysis—and most notably, perhaps, in the work of the great paediatrician Donald Winnicott (e.g., 1971). We should by no means assume that the ascendency of play within policy-making discourse (and rhetoric) is straightforward and unproblematc, for as Powell (2009) has pointed out in an assessment of the impact of national policies on children's opportunities for play in England, systematic analysis of policy documents and interviews reveals that the Government has not been promoting a consistent conceptualization of play in England, with some policy documents emphasizing play's instrumental value and potential contributions to the priorities of government departments, and others referring to its intrinsic value. This confusion is perhaps symptomatic not only of the impact of politicization on policy discourse, but also of the subtle nature of play and its (welcome) reluctance to be pinned down in, or by, rationalist discourse.

The 'play' open letter

With almost 300 signatories from across the academic and professional world, the letter duly appeared in the *Daily Telegraph* of 10 September 2007, accompanied by a front page report (Paton, 2008), a substantial editorial, and a comment piece by Bob Reitemeier, Chief Executive of the Children's Society (cf. his Chapter 5, this volume). Subsequent press reports were to indicate support for this initiative from both Prince Charles and the Archbishop of Canterbury, Rowan Williams, who has contributed the Foreword to this book.

The open letter can be seen as highlighting the need for 'a wide-ranging and informed public dialogue about the intrinsic nature and value of play'. For whilst we all routinely *talk about* play, do we really understand its deep nature? Might the utilitarian, 'instrumentalist' mind-set and 'development-obsessiveness' that tend to so dominate modern children's learning unwittingly make play into 'a thing'—an object to be manipulated by adults which, in turn, fatally compromises the essence of truly authentic playing? (cf. Heaton, 1978). Perhaps there is a need to explore just what authentic, unintruded-upon playing might consist in, and how we might begin to think and speak about it, so that we are more able to preserve its intrinsic reverence, rather than betraying or destroying it through the coarse bludgeon of 'modernity'.

In the open letter, we wrote,

> Play—particularly outdoor, unstructured, loosely supervised play—appears to be vital to children's all-round health and well-being.... It [encourages] the growth of self-reliance, independence and personal strategies for dealing with and integrating challenging or traumatic experiences. [Yet] many features of modern life seem to have eroded children's play. They include ... the ready availability of sedentary, sometimes addictive screen-based entertainment; [and] a test-driven school and pre-school curriculum in which formal learning has substantially taken the place of free, unstructured play [the testing regime, of course, being a defining *leitmotif* of the burgeoning 'audit culture'—eds.].

As already mentioned, it certainly seems no coincidence that hot on the heels of this high-profile media coverage on play, in December 2007, the British government unexpectedly announced a major new 'play strategy' as part of its new Children's Plan, with some £385 million new government spending on children's playgrounds (Paton, 2007). As clear evidence as there could be that concerted engagement with the media in this way can galvanize professional and public opinion, and thence have discernible impacts upon government policy-making.

Concerns about what is happening to play in the modern technological age have certainly been gaining increasing prominence in recent times. There are parallel concerns, discussed elsewhere in the book, about the ways in which a control-obsessed 'audit culture' and 'managerialist' ethos (e.g., London Society of the New Lacanian School, 2007; Power, 1997; Strathern, 2000) are generating a crass instrumentalism right across the public sphere, which is, we maintain, the very antithesis of what truly authentic play consists in. Such cultural, psychodynamic, and even spiritual questions, in all their complexity and subtlety, are rightly commanding our concerned attention and thoughtfulness at this time.

The October 2007 Roehampton University conference on 'Play and Playfulness'

Arising from the Open Letter on play, again House and Loewenthal, through the Research Centre for Therapeutic Education, organized a further one-day international conference in October 2007—under the title 'Play and Playfulness in Children and Adults: educational and therapeutic perspectives'—aiming to facilitate a major cross-fertilization of educational and psychotherapeutic thinking about play in the modern world. Prominent speakers were chosen to offer educational and psychotherapeutic insights into the nature of play—what it is (and isn't); why it is so important in human experience and development; why it is becoming distorted and degraded in 'Late Modernity'; and what we might do about such degradation. Approaching 200 people attended the conference, with psychologist Oliver James launching an engagement of the therapeutic and the educational with his introductory keynote speech (see his Chapter 15, this volume). The psychotherapeutic and educational worlds certainly have their own particular insights into the phenomenon of play, with the latter being concerned with children's play, and the former often encountering adults' painful *inability* to play. There are major issues in all this about just what adults and children have to learn from each other; and play offers a powerful relational framework through which such educational reciprocity might be fruitfully explored.

The conference was introduced with the following memorable quotation from phenomenological psychotherapist and philosopher John Heaton:

> Play has an essence which is completely independent of the attitude of the player. If this is not realized, then *play becomes*

> *distorted by being cultivated*, as is commonly done in both
> educational and psychotherapeutic circles ... All playing is a
> being played ... [It] does not allow the player to behave towards
> it like an object ... Play does not point to purposes beyond itself,
> it *celebrates* itself ... *Its nature is completely distorted if it is consid-*
> *ered psychologistically as a known thing about which assertions can be*
> *made and which people then set forth to cultivate.* [our emphases]
>
> (John Heaton, 1978, *passim*)

In Part 4 of this book, 'Play, playfulness and well-being', we present
a number of chapters that focus on play that are based on papers
given at the conference by Oliver James, Eugene Schwartz, Elizabeth
Wood, and Biddy Youell.

The book's contributions

With regards to the other chapters in this book (though at least some
of them have already been tangentially referred to): In Chapter 2,
Del Loewenthal puts the case for the importance of Therapeutic
Education both at a societal and individual level, in combating the
problematic aspects of individualism. He attempts what we consider
to be a crucial act of resuscitation, to illustrate the place that Plato's
much neglected notion of 'therapeia' might have in these debates
and discussions, and particularly its implication for psychological
therapies and education.

In Chapter 3, **Sue Palmer** shares the background to how she fell
upon the 'toxic childhood' syndrome. We believe that the academic
world—and certainly that section of it that aspires to influencing
government policy—has a great deal to learn from the extraordinary
impact that Palmer's writings and campaigning have had in the
childhood sphere. This chapter gives the reader a window into the
process through which Palmer has managed to have such an influence in high-profile areas in which more timid academics sometimes
fear to tread.

In Chapter 4, **Christopher Clouder** of the Alliance for Childhood offers a detailed commentary on the malaise that is manifest-
ing in manifold ways in the childhood experience of the developed
West. The Alliance for Childhood has championed a holistic, 'post-
technological' approach to children's experience, strongly informed,

but by no means exclusively so, by Steiner Waldorf pedagogical thinking and praxis; and Clouder is a very effective spokesperson for those perennial values, representing an organization that succeeds in foregrounding enduring values in a way that is progressive rather than reactionary or sentimental.

In Chapter 5, **Bob Reitemeier** of the Children's Society sets out in some detail the rationale behind, and the way in which his organization implemented, its path-breaking Inquiry into Good Childhood, the final report of which was published in 2009 (Layard and Dunn, 2009). In this ongoing inquiry, which promises to continue for a number of years, the Society has succeeded in 'operationalizing' and investigating many of the core concerns that 'toxic childhood' campaigners have been highlighting for a number of years, yet in by no means an uncritical way, as the report takes care not to take for granted at least some of the headline quarries of the 'toxic childhood' perspective.

In Chapter 6, child psychotherapist **Ricky Emanuel** makes a strong case for the term 'toxic' being treated with far more circumspection, and for its perhaps being confined to those children whose early experience is at the extreme end of (de)privation and abuse. Emanuel gives some detailed and moving case material to illustrate all too graphically the hugely challenging intra- and inter-psychic issues with which severely abused children have to contend and struggle, and how a sensitive psychoanalytically informed approach offers hope for healing and change.

In Chapter 7, **Sami Timimi** looks at the question of narcissism (Lasch, 1979), giving us long pause for thought in his convincing claim that 'amongst those more stable and rooted cultures across the world, sophisticated discourses on childhood and child-rearing spanning millennia exist (including within Islam), with many anthropological and other studies confirming that such communities do not share the same magnitude of problems with anti-social behaviour, anxiety states, and so on, amongst the young'. This perspective in turn leads us to think very carefully about a Western technological 'modernity' and its cultural-historical specificity, and what it might be about specifically Western values and practices that seem to be so 'toxic'.

In Chapter 8, **Sue Gerhardt** develops her celebrated work on the neuroscience of early experience (Gerhardt, 2004) to look at early childhood, and why love matters in early childhood experience. Gerhardt's work has made a major impact on the fields of attachment studies and the dynamics of early experience, and it is particularly welcome to have her perspective on the vicissitudes and challenges of children's early lives, and why anyone concerned with children's well-being really needs to start from here.

In Chapter 9, **Kathryn Ecclestone** strikes a controversial and thought-provoking note in her critical perspective on resisting images of 'the diminished self' in education, and specifically in education policy and practice for emotional well-being. In true postmodern deconstructive spirit, we welcome Ecclestone's work, along with her colleagues Dennis Hayes and Frank Furedi, in causing us to pause and think more deeply about what the unintended effects might be of privileging the emotional over the rational-cognitive in children's educational experience (Ecclestone and Hayes, 2008). Certainly, if we are to reach a mature and sufficiently subtle understanding of these complex questions, we need to embrace the kinds of challenges to the New Orthodoxy around the emotional that Ecclestone and her colleagues are developing and presenting.

In Chapter 10, **Richard House** draws upon the work of paediatrician and psychoanalyst D.W. Winnicott's notion of the 'mind-psyche' to argue that Winnicott's work provides a clinical rationale for the pathological effects of children finding themselves prematurely awakened intellectually and cognitively because of failures in the (in this case *non*-facilitating) environment. Mention is also made of the spiritual rationale that Rudolf Steiner offers, to reach essentially identical conclusions to those of Winnicott. If it can be shown that there are new norms of modern techno-experience that are leading to children's premature growing-up becoming the cultural norm rather than the exception—which House attempts to argue—then childhood experience, certainly in the West, is surely in very serious trouble indeed.

In Chapter 11, **Andrew Samuels**, writing from the perspective of Jungian analytical pychology, offers us a typically insightful and provocative foray into, first, the question of 'who or what is the child that we have in mind when bemoaning the advent of toxic childhood?'; secondly, whether therapy can really make a difference to whatever educational malaise Britain is currently suffering from; and thirdly, whether it is possible that our educational discussions have become too 'heady' and abstract, and whether this imbalance could be more effectively managed by more of a focus on the body. Like several other of our contributors, Samuels by no means buys into the 'toxic childhood' arguments uncritically, and his contribution is all the more provocative and telling for that.

To continue with the topic of play, which is a central and recurring theme throughout the book, in Chapter 12, child psychotherapist **Biddy Youell** looks at the psychodynamic roots of play(fulness) in children's early relational experience. As with Ricky Emanuel's contribution (Chapter 6), Youell cautions against too reductionist and simplistic an approach to 'toxic childhood' arguments, maintaining that current political and media debates about outdoor play space, and about the dangers of a preponderance of televisual/ digital entertainments and technologies, are in danger of missing the *developmental achievement* that play(fulness) entails. Youell also argues that there are considerable variations in children's capacity to make use of whatever opportunities children might have in their lives. One clear implication is that we should at least pause before reaching for over-generalized and possibly simplistic conclusions about the malign influence of broad cultural trends, which can so easily miss the particularities of individual children's experience.

In Chapter 13 academic educationalist **Elizabeth Wood** explores the idea of play activities as everyday therapeutic and pedagogical encounters. Wood develops the interesting notion of play as a 'stretching towards', and as creating the possibility of what she refers to as 'co-construction', and 'intersubjective, relational spaces and possibilities' contributing to well-being. Wood also helpfully highlights the very diverse theoretical perspectives that are adduced to make sense of play, and argues for an unromanticized awareness of the changing nature of children's play in young people's lives in an era of rapid cultural and technological change. In her discussion of 'dark play' or cruel play, we begin to see the extent to which there can be a significant cross-over of interest in educational and psychotherapeutic perspectives on play.

Then, in his engaging Chapter 14, **Eugene Schwartz** draws upon Rudolf Steiner's developmental ontology to illustrate just how, in early play, the totally absorbed child is developing flexible, imaginative thinking, completely at one with her surroundings. A young child is all-sensitive and highly impressionable (or 'wholly sense-organ', as

Steiner termed it), reflecting his innate capacity to develop language in his inner play. On this view, then, in health, capacities naturally arise in the soul of the young child which only mature much later in childhood, and even later life—or as in Schwartz's example, in the capacity for scientific thinking about the world.

In his Chapter 15, celebrated media psychologist and cultural commentator **Oliver James** offers a panoramic perspective on play and its place in modern culture. His chapter is based in part on the keynote address he gave to the Roehampton University conference on Play and Playfulness, mentioned earlier.

We do hope you enjoy the book, and find it helpful and stimulating in reappraising what we might need to do in order to enhance the well-being of our children and ourselves.

References

BBC News (2007). Play and learning children's plan. 11 December; retrievable at: http://news.bbc.co.uk/go/pr/fr/-/1/hi/education/7136564.stm.

Compass (2006). *The Commercialisation of Childhood*. London: December.

Department of Children, Schools and Families (2007). *The Children's Plan*. London: HMSO.

Ecclestone, K., & Hayes, D. (2008). *The Dangerous Rise of Therapeutic Education*. London: Routledge.

Fenton, B. (2006). Junk culture 'is poisoning our children'. *Daily Telegraph*, 12 September, p. 1; retrievable at: http://www.telegraph.co.uk/news/1528642/Junk-culture-is-poisoning-our-children.html

Gerhardt, S. (2004). *Why Love Matters: How Affection Shapes a Baby's Brain*. London: Routledge.

Goddard, C. (2009). UK near bottom of child wellbeing table. *Children & Young People Now*, 21 April; retrievable at: http://www.cypnow.co.uk/Archive/899658/UK-near-bottom-child-wellbeing-table/

Harvey, D. (1973). *Social Justice and the City*. London: Edward Arnold.

Harvey, D. (1989). *The Condition of Postmodernity: An Enquiry into the Origins of Cultural Change*. Chichester: WileyBlackwell.

Heaton, J. (1978). The ontology of play. In B. Curtis & W. Mays (Eds.), *Phenomenology and Education* (pp. 119–30). London: Methuen.

House, R. (2002–3). Beyond the medicalisation of 'challenging behaviour'; or protecting our children from 'Pervasive Labelling Disorder'

(3 parts). *The Mother* magazine, issues 4–6 (Issue 4, 2002, pp. 25–6, 43; Issue 5, 2003, pp. 44–6; and Issue 6, 2003, pp. 44–6).

House, R. (2007a). Schooling, the State, and children's psychological well-being: a psychosocial critique. *Journal of Psychosocial Research*, 2(2): 49–62.

House, R. (2007b). Research must fight the status quo. *Times Higher Educational Supplement*, 9 November: 15.

House, R. (2008a). 'Audit culture' and play. *Early Years Educator*, 9(10) (February): 16–18.

House, R. (2008b). Let us play. *The Mother* magazine, 26: 32–3.

House, R., Palmer, S., & 270 others (2007). Let our children play—Open Letter. *Daily Telegraph*, 10 September; retrievable at: http://www.telegraph.co.uk/comment/letters/3642594/Letters-to-the-Daily-Telegraph.html

James, O. (2007). *Affluenza*. London: Vermillion.

Kasser, T. (2002). *The High Price of Materialism*. Cambridge, Mass.: MIT Press.

Kasser, T., & Kanner, A.D. (2004). *Psychology and Consumer Culture: The Struggle for a Good Life in a Materialistic World*. Washington, D.C.: American Psychological Association.

Lasch, C. (1979). *The Culture of Narcissism*. New York: Norton.

Layard, R., & Dunn, J. (2009). *A Good Childhood*. London: Penguin.

Linn, S. (2005). *Consuming Kids: Protecting Our Children from the Onslaught of Marketing and Advertising*. New York: Anchor Books.

Loewenthal, D. (2008a). *Case Studies in Relational Research*. London: Palgrave Macmillan.

Loewenthal, D. (2008b). Introducing Post-Existential Practice: An approach to well-being in the 21st Century. *Philosophical Practice*, 3: 316–21.

London Society of the New Lacanian School (2007) Special issue: Regulation and Evaluation. *Psychoanalytic Notebooks*, May.

Ollman, B. (1971). *Alienation: Marx's Conception of Man in Capitalist Society*. London: Cambridge University Press.

Palmer, S. (2006). *Toxic Childhood*. London: Orion.

Palmer, S., House, R., & 110 others (2006). Modern life leads to more depression among children. *Daily Telegraph*, 12 September; retrievable at: http://www.telegraph.co.uk/news/1528639/Modern-life-leads-to-more-depression-among-children.html

Paton, G. (2007). Ministers in £1bn U-turn over playgrounds. *Daily Telegraph*, 12 December; retrievable at: http://www.telegraph.co.uk/news/uknews/1572321/Ministers-in-1bn-U-turn-over-playgrounds.html

Paton, G. (2008). Modern life 'is destroying children's play'. *Daily Telegraph*, 10 September: 1; retrievable at: http://www.telegraph.co.uk/news/main.jhtml?xml=/news/2007/09/10/nplay110.xml

Powell, S. (2009). The value of play: constructions of play in Government policy in England. *Children and Society*, 23: 29–42.

Power, M. (1997). *The Audit Society: Rituals of Verification*. Oxford: Oxford University Press.

Reed, E.S. (1996). *The Necessity of Experience*. New Haven: Yale University Press.

Schor, J. B. (2004). *Born to Buy: The Commercialized Child and the New Consumer Culture*. New York: Scribner.

Strathern, M. (Ed.) (2000). *Audit Cultures*. London: Routledge.

Timimi, S. (2002). *Pathological Child Psychiatry and the Medicalization of Childhood*. London: Routledge.

Timimi, S., & Maitra, B. (Eds.) (2005). *Critical Voices in Child and Adolescent Mental Health*. London: Free Association Books.

UNICEF (2007). Report Card 7, Child Poverty in Perspective: An Overview of Child Well-being in Rich Countries. Innocenti Research Centre, Unicef.

van Manen, M. (1990). *Researching Lived Experience: Human Science for an Action Sensitive Pedagogy*. Albany, NY: State University of New York Press.

Williams, R. (2000). *Lost Icons: Reflections on Cultural Bereavement*. London: T & T Clark/Continuum.

Winnicott, D.W. (1971). *Playing and Reality*. Harmondsworth: Penguin.

PART I

CHILDHOOD IN CONTEMPORARY PERSPECTIVE

CHAPTER TWO

Childhood, well-being and a therapeutic ethos: A case for therapeutic education

Del Loewenthal

It is argued in this chapter that we first need to consider what it might mean for our society to have an appropriate therapeutic ethos, and how we might achieve this. Only then can we consider what we might take to be meant by the term 'well-being', and how we can provide an enabling, dynamic environment both for our children and, through our children, for ourselves, which in turn potentially enables us to make a better world.

Plato suggested that 'therapeia' is of vital importance to our societies. He posited that whilst scientific and technical knowledge are important, they should always be secondary to the resources of the human soul (Cushman, 2002). Yet a glance at our educational system, with the increasingly central importance given to positivistic auditing, together with the peripheral place of the arts, suggests that we are increasingly in a society where technology comes first, science second and the resources of the human soul a poor third. So, assuming that we want to, how can we change the emphasis so that technology can help develop the potential of our children? Audits could return to being seen more as a rule of thumb, and not as something by which we are systematically governed. It is as if being subject to audit technology gives some a false sense of control. In contrast, it is argued here that it is sometimes better to be subject to that which we can never fully explain, and by being able to stay with such inabilities we can be more open to our potency and potentiality. Otherwise, in the deadness of technical 'thinking', we can only be less alive in terms of what some have variously described as a false self (Winnicott, 1965), inauthenticity (Sartre, 1956) or alienation (Marx, 1844).

At the Research Centre for Therapeutic Education, Roehampton University, United Kingdom, we are particularly interested in exploring the psychological therapies (including psychoanalysis), as enabling a return to learning through experience. Yet, this is so often only once the damage has already been done. If one considers health in terms of primary, secondary, and tertiary (World Health Organization 2001), then primary health, in respect of the psychological therapies, could be seen as attempting to reduce those aspects of our culture which harm our souls, and which do not enhance the development of a culturally facilitative environment. Regarding the distinction between psychotherapy and counselling (which I do not think necessarily has to be made), counselling could be seen as secondary—in its attempt to deal with immediate problems—and psychotherapy could be seen as being also tertiary in reducing the possibility of the problem re-occurring. It is therefore argued here that Therapeutic Education must be considered, not only in terms of the consulting room, but in terms of influencing our wider culture, and thus calling for a greater emphasis on therapeutic education as primary health.

In both the Reports of the Children's Society (Layard & Dunn, 2009) and in Ecclestone and Hayes' book *The Dangerous Rise of Therapeutic Education* (2008), grave concern is raised, in different ways, about the rise of individualism. For those such as Ecclestone and Hayes, counselling and psychotherapy are very much part of the problem rather than the solution. Whilst agreeing with them that a self-centredness can be reinforced by some therapeutic approaches, and that our need to be there for each other can be wrongly taken out of our hands (including the teachers'), it is possible for psychological therapies to encourage a culture which helps us to consider others more rather than less. Also, very fortunately, we have Plato's concept of 'therapeia', which will be introduced here at length as he was concerned that without it, we were 'surely destined to disintegrate under the corrosive force of *rampant individualism*' (Cushman, 2002: 35, original emphasis).

I think it is true that ego psychologists, along with many behaviourists, existentialists, psychoanalysts, and humanists, do attempt to create a situation where the client/patient is led to think they are the centre of the world, and can have reflected back to them the self-image they think they would like to have (and which most likely never existed). Yet Freud, for one, wrote on our soul—which, not by chance, Anglo-Americans failed to translate into English (Bettelheim, 1984). Most importantly, Freud suggested that we are subject-to our unconscious. It could be argued that Freud, and certainly post-Freudians, brought in technology in the name of science which subsequent psychological therapists and their patients/clients have been subject-to in a different sense, and, some would say, to their detriment. Subsequently, with the help of structural linguistics Lacan added that we are also subject-to language, one consequence of which is that words speak us rather than being spoken by us. This perhaps shows more clearly how we are always subject-to. Lacan, in changing Descartes 'I think therefore I am' to 'I am where I do not think', can, for one, be seen, in its de-centring, to reopen therapeutic potential, in contrast to a modernistic notion of individualism (Lacan, 2001; Loewenthal & Snell, 2003).

Yet once again there is the danger, as can be explained by, for example Hegel's dialectic, that through the emerging synthesis, yet another psychological therapeutic technology emerges (in this case 'Lacan-ese') in an attempt to fight what is seen as the current dominant theology. And consequently becomes less effective in awakening our souls.

Audits can be fine if they enable us to think, but not if they restrict the essential human basis of our thinking and acting, which is what happens when we have an 'audit culture'. Audits can have implications that should not be applied as the basis of our well-being (the same could be said of psychotherapeutic theories). Thus, I think, we can consider the implications of how, as a society, we might remedy our horrendous situation as indicated by UNICEF (2007) where Britain is ranked bottom out of 21 countries in terms of children's well-being. The report highlights how the UK lags on such indicators as the time children spend talking or eating with their parent(s). It seems to suggest that the overall quality of life of the majority of children in the UK and USA is worse than that of much of the rest of the developed world. There are probably many causes of this, but how we explore them is vital. For one, as has been mentioned, there is the greater Anglo-American emphasis on a form of empiricism that reinforces modernism. As Cushman (2002), in exploring virtue and knowledge, describes:

> ...in the *Sophist* ... Plato undertakes to show that crude empiri-
> cism is in error since it confuses true reality with that which is
> not true Being ... . It is Plato's intention to show that the Sophist
> is not talking nonsense but is confounding inferior with supe-
> rior reality.
>
> (Cushman, 2002, p. 80)

Can't the same be said about the current strenuous attempt only to consider as evidence that which can apparently be empirically measured?

Another major factor in the potential demise of the quality of children's (and our own) lives can be seen as the effect of the Protestant ethic which has been argued to fuel individualism, in contrast to many of those Continental countries in which, though not without their problems, Catholicism has retained a greater influence. (Though, here as well, beseeching people to 'love thy neighbour as thyself' can have a downside when it comes to enabling difference!) The need to counter such a Protestant ethic was potentially provided in the twentieth century in terms of the ethics of the relational developed by both Buber and Levinas. Buber (1971) attempted to get us to re-think the other as 'thou' rather than 'it', and through this re-enabled the magic of the relational which seems so seriously unacknowledged in our educational systems, not least in the training of teachers.

Levinas also emphasized that we are subject-to, for he defined ethics as being subject-to putting the other first (Levinas, 1969). This privileging of heteronomy over autonomy therefore would be a far greater influence through a therapeutic ethos, both in the consulting room and in our societies. It would counter the very cult of individualism which the Children's Society and others are so concerned is ruining the lives of our children.

Here, therefore, we have Jerusalem versus Athens, the book versus the look (though in the former case both Jews and Arabs may not always be taken as the best example of being able to put the other first!). So is it possible that Schools of Education might give a greater emphasis to heteronomous rather than autonomous learners, and that Chief Executives might no longer talk in terms of 'vision statements' in a way that attempts to ensure others are visionless and incorporated? Also, is it possible for psychological therapies not to speak of people as subjects in a way that makes it more likely that others are objects? For is it possible for two subjects to really meet?

In considering well-being, societal and individual perspectives need to be considered. This calls for something other than what we currently understand as the psychological therapies. For example, whilst it is important to consider health as being individually defined (Heaton, 1998), preventative policies are argued here also to be vital. In a National Health Service, one doesn't want to put all one's resources into hospitals if one has not got clean water or hygienic sewage systems, and, as we seem to be slowly realizing, endorsing and encouraging smoking and excessive alcohol consumption and unhealthy eating. Similarly, one doesn't want to put all one's resources into counselling and psychotherapy when one's very education system may be acting against human relationships, with our personal behaviour becoming alienated. Perhaps we are now so alienated that we no longer realize that we are experiencing our alienation.

I think Plato's concept of therapeia is of vital importance when considering the case for Therapeutic Education, both from the perspective of the individual and the State. In attempting to re-open this question, I am particularly grateful for the work of Robert Cushman (2002). From Socrates, therapeutic education can be seen to be about awakening thought rather than instilling knowledge. Plato can be regarded as understanding Socrates as the best example of somebody who abounded in the consciousness of well-being—making the soul as good as possible. Furthermore, for Plato, both the way in which Socrates lived and died was evidence that virtue and well-being are inseparable. For Socrates, the danger is that we are doing the opposite of what we ought to be doing. Rather like today, it is as if good was more to do with the goods we purchase, thus well-being is seen not as primarily about making one's soul as good as possible, but rather based upon the 'unexamined supposition' (Cushman, 2002, p. 13) that good is defined by consumption. Thus, Socrates was against a well-being in terms of 'sensuous satisfactions, together with the largest attainable measure of affluence and personal prerogative' (Cushman, 2002, p. 13).

For Socrates, the soul is our greatest treasure, so we must first seek virtue. Thus, to Socrates, 'we ought neither to requite wrong with wrong, nor to do evil to anyone, no matter what he may have done to us' (as quoted in Cushman, 2002, p. 24). In Plato's time, there was already a popular tradition in 'dispraise' of learning. For Plato, it was important for both the individual and the state to give a primacy to seeking wisdom. Plato considered, therefore, that politicians should engender love of virtue and the elimination of injustice in order to make citizens as good as possible. Thus, Plato is pointing out that we can seek the wrong type of education, and with it the wrong type of well-being. In order to counter these unhelpful ways of being, Plato further suggests that we cannot rely upon religion or the traditions of the elders, but what we must be most wary of is the use of rhetoric when it is taught and practised in order to subordinate 'truth to mere persuasiveness' (Cushman, 2002, p. 36)— as practised by Greek spin doctors, the Sophists, who codified the art of rhetoric, which we have increasingly taken up right the way through to manualized psychotherapies. Yet for Plato, such Sophistry always attempts to accommodate itself to the prevailing ethos, leaving 'human life unexamined and unchanged' (Cushman, 2002, p. 36). Importantly, the Sophists, as is so much the case today, 'were not interested in questioning the current fashion of life, only in implementing it' (Cushman, 2002, p. 36). Eyres (2009) has reminded us, through taking Montaigne (1993) as an example of developing a self-consciousness which may not be about narcissistic individualism, that as with Cognitive Behaviour Therapy, this is something that gets applied in the mind rather than within the person.

Interestingly, Plato did not believe that knowledge which constituted virtue was to do with technique, nor did he believe that it could be acquired by practice or direct impartation. Knowledge which makes for virtue appears not to be transmissible and therefore cannot be directly taught or obtained through instruction. This then raises the question as to the nature of the knowledge of those who are virtuous; and if this is obtained by more than just one's nature, what form of learning is entailed? For Plato, 'learning … is something like recovering knowledge out of oneself. This recovery of knowledge under the stimulus of dialectical examination is a case of recollection' (Cushman, 2002, p. 81). Plato suggests that we go from cognition to re-cognition through a dialectic:

> Man, then is a dispossessed possessor of truth about Being. He is half-blind to his own legacy. Although awareness of reality in truth is the mark of his humanity, awareness commonly fails to crystallize and formulate itself into articulate comprehension.
>
> (Cushman, 2002, p. 84)

For Plato, 'knowledge cannot be put into "a soul that does not possess it"… Knowledge does not begin with a blank space' (Cushman, 2002, p. 86). Thus, all cognition is really re-cognition. 'If knowledge, in the last resort, is insight, it manifestly cannot be conveyed even if its condition may be induced' (Cushman, 2002, p. 88). This implies that 'conventional notice of instruction had to be replaced' by a way 'which would make room for recovery of knowledge out of the self. For such knowledge alone is virtue' (Cushman, 2002, p. 88).

> By means of recollection, true reality begins to be discerned … . (Such) [c]atharsis is more than clarification of the mind to itself. Although [c]atharsis requires the articulation of the presentiments of truth which lie as an unexplored deposit in the human soul, it also involves increase in virtue. Additionally, it is purging of unrighteousness from the soul but [c]atharsis is always something positive, namely replacement of vice by self-restraint, justice, courage and wisdom. Wisdom replaces 'folly' in the soul and is itself the summit of virtue.
>
> (Cushman, 2002, p. 57)

I am hopeful this very much speaks to at least psychotherapists and counsellors. Furthermore, those influenced by psychoanalysis may be interested in further parallels:

> Of the two ruling and determining principles in the soul, one leads through intelligence toward what is best. The other is bent upon pleasurable satisfactions. The two are sometimes in agreement within the individual; but with most men, they are in perpetual strife.
>
> (Cushman, 2002, p. 64)

Therapeutic education therefore needs to be considered both on a micro and macro level. (The micro-level might be seen in terms of working with individuals, couples, and therapeutic groups.) Therapeutic education does not have to be provided in terms of an individualism where the person can be made to believe that they are like a god returning to situations which in actuality never existed (Borch-Jacobsen, 1989). Anthony Elliott puts the case as to how psychoanalysis can possibly correct inappropriate individualism through us being 'subject-to ourselves' (Elliott, 1996). Yet interestingly, Richard Layard talks of the importance of involvement in something greater than yourself (Layard & Dunn, 2009). Here, unlike Layard's insistence on focusing on happiness (Layard, 2006a) and evidence-based psychotherapeutic practice (Layard, 2006b), I am in agreement with him.

For those who are atheist or agnostic and do not see themselves as subject-to a god, is it not still possible for them to be subject to such notions as beauty, love, wonderment, spirituality, the infinite, and to have a therapy which might include some of these considerations—for example, through being subject to an unconscious, language and/or heteronomy? I have previously written about one approach which I termed 'post-existential' but which could enable a search for meaning in a way that we could be subject-to such aspects without being caught in a theoretical strait-jacket of the wrong sort of knowledge (Loewenthal, 2008a,b).

On a macro-level, hopefully the last thing being suggested here is some single policy measure with a rule-of-thumb indicator posing as science (any change perhaps should be seen as an accumulation of many different influences). Nevertheless, as the Archbishop of Canterbury, Rowan Williams, suggests in his Afterword to the report on Childhood (Williams, 2009, p. 169), we do need to consider 'what makes for long-term well-being otherwise, the educating of a new generation is hamstrung from the start'. These macro forces include the emphasis on consumer relations rather than human relations, and educational systems which favour the advantaged over the disadvantaged, ensuring that, increasingly, our socio-economic systems are generated more by competition than cooperation. As suggested at a recent OECD conference (September 2007) I was involved with organizing, university systems are being developed that encourage greater competitiveness. This is on the assumption that academics do not like teaching, and will not like to do the type of research required for tenureship and promotion.

We no longer consider what a university might be there for; instead, bland mission statements are issued which seldom seem to consider what a good education might be, or what it might mean for a university to be encouraging thoughtfulness, independent yet serving its communities. Such macro developments involve a managerialism, one aspect of which is the development of systems which both encourage individualism and which simultaneously bind the individual as a small cog in a large wheel. It is the choice of these systems which increasingly determines the, so-called, quality of our lives.

This systematic move away from personal, *human relations* to *market relations* can be seen to have influenced our culture in general. For example, in countries such as the UK there has been the demise of trade unions, where a history of fighting for our human rights has almost been forgotten and has been replaced by market relations where the trade union is regarded by members as little more than another service industry. Again, in the UK, the National Health Service no longer considers people working together to provide a service by encouraging each other to work for the greater good of humanity through what calls to them. Instead, attempts to foster the idea of a hospital and hospitality, where we look to welcome a stranger and diminish our own hostile feelings, replacing them with the offer of shelter—traditionally, for some, the breaking and sharing of bread and offering wine—is replaced by competitive systems. We see systems of, for example, foundation hospitals where people in the same town can be paid different salaries for the same job and where the introduction of such notions as 'purchasers and providers' means that where research is carried out, often with the help of a university, it need not be published if it gives away a local competitive advantage either in terms of showing a good way of doing something, or that an existing way is not succeeding as previously hoped. Here, for example, the whole ethos of our university and public health systems has radically changed to encourage a competitive individualism, and where previous checks and balances such as trade unions, health service professions, and academics have been systematically sidelined.

Whilst I would not disagree with those who claim that there did need to be some limits to the power of trade unions, the professions, and academia when they may have been abusive and not in the 'public interest', the multi-headed movement of managerialism, consumerism, and individualism destroyed, and is still destroying, a collective sense, a therapeutic ethos, which is fundamental to the public interest.

There is a prevailing culture whereby universities through control by central government are rapidly losing their independence, and public service management is adopting a private-sector model that, again, encourages an individualistic competitiveness over collective action, which is perceived by those in power as a threat rather than an enhancement of democracy. Indeed, in the UK, the marketing of such changes is such that the re-organized National Heath Service is replaced by a series of organizational systems that are given the public misnomer of 'Trusts'.

Another, more personal illustration of the demise of everyday human relations is that whilst being brought up in the suburbs of London, I can remember as a family that we knew the name of the cashier of the bank; and when he asked after other members of the family, this was reported at the dinner table. Yet now I am forever being asked to talk to my unknown 'personal banker' whose name I do not know.

A final example of how, particularly in a UK context, the assumptions underlying the very language we use to experience being with each other is being systematically changed is with regard to 'de-mutualization'. Mutuals, or building societies, are not-for-profit organizations whereby people in the community can save and borrow money at interest rates which are usually more favourable than a bank that would require profit to pay dividends to its shareholders. Unfortunately, a legal way was found around the mutuality originally intended, whereby for short-term gain, the members of a building society could receive a lump sum if their building society was privatized as a bank. One of the consequences of such deregulation was the replacement of competition through a mixed economy (Public, Private, and Mutual/Co-operative), with a banking system that subsequently went bankrupt to the profit of a few, and the long-term detriment of the majority. But what we can see from banking in other countries in Continental Europe is that whilst there are large global, cultural shifts, it is possible to have some agency in our responses to them, and it is not inevitable that we have to destroy so much of what are good aspects of our heritage that we have painstakingly built up to enable how we are with each other.

Therapeutic education through counselling and psychotherapy can therefore take on the values of individualism and autonomy, but this is not inevitable. It can, for example, give a primacy to heteronomy whilst not ignoring issues of autonomy. However, therapeutic education can also be seen as an additional way of taking responsibility for considering how the therapeutic ethos is affected through economic, social, political, and technological changes.

'Well-being' is the second term in the title of this chapter (and this book). Here I find useful Heidegger's notion of Dasein, or 'being in the world with others'. Yet again, the way our society is developing is to ensure that there is less opportunity to dwell on what we might mean by well-being. Not untypically, when I asked some researchers presenting at a recent Economic and Social Research Council (ESRC) conference how they defined well-being, I was told they no longer focused on this, but, instead, on how it might be measured. Indeed, increasingly, my experiences of academia are that what was previously a standard conceptual exploration is now often dismissed as 'philosophy', and that the philosophy department has often been closed down. Similarly psychology, particularly in the UK and USA—which, as previously mentioned, are countries doing so poorly in international comparisons of childhood—focuses again on the empirical, forgetting that its founders, such as Wilhelm Wundt (1904), suggested that the key task of psychology was to marry the empirical with the cultural and the historical. Similarly, schools of education are increasingly caught up with pseudo-quantification of aspects of quality that are often in danger of bringing about an ethos which may be more detrimental than beneficial.

Social anthropology, because of the influence of multi-culturalism and the relative demise of sociology, together with the study of literature, perhaps provides some of the few remaining places where relationships can be thought about in a social context (though positivism also appears to be creeping in here). Certainly, programmes in counselling and psychotherapy rarely seem to provide a significant critique of their own gurus, let alone considering individual therapeutic interventions within a broader socio-economic context; and attempts to set up, for example, organizations like Psychotherapists and Counsellors for Social Responsibility (Samuels, 2003) have not as yet entered mainstream thinking.

It is even rarer for any university course to consider what impact policy changes might have on how we experience each other. Our higher education system therefore is not strong enough to allow the questioning, socio-economically, of the government which funds most of it, and it could be seen that the ideological control is such that we can not allow thought to come to us, not only in terms, for example, of a Freudian unconscious, but also in terms of Marxist notions of aliena- tion. It's as if the fall of the Iron Curtain and the knowledge of the hor- rors of communist totalitarianism have undermined other notions of working together for the common good. We therefore do not see the potential damage we are doing in establishing perhaps a more subtle ideological totalitarianism, where knowledge is seen in terms of com- petencies which can always be explicit and measured, and Polyani's notion of 'tacit knowledge' (Polyani, 1966) recedes even further.

Perhaps it is the relationship which is the greatest educator of them all. Yet in some ways will it always be mysterious? Here, something rather than just being taught and learnt is imparted and acquired, and might well be a key aspect of how psychotherapy and counselling works (should we ever find out!). It is perhaps impor- tant to remember here what Merleau-Ponty warns—that sometimes if we try to take away what is mysterious, we end up taking away the very thing itself (Merleau-Ponty, 1956, p. 70).

Speaking of a relationship finally brings me to the first term of this chapter, 'Childhood'. It is suggested here that the relationship between the child and the adult is not only of vital importance to the child but also to the adult. And consequently in our society and in the very world in which we are bringing up our children and living our lives, there is a wonderment about childhood—an almost magi- cal space where not only can we enhance their lives, but through which adults can gain a dimension that may never be made explicit, but which can nourish human well-being. Yet what we find are con- ditions developing which produce a dramatic reduction in the time spent between adults and children. Parents in the UK spend less time with their children than most other Western societies (virtually all have the technological changes such as central heating, enabling more individual members of families to be in their own rooms, with the proliferation of personal TVs, video games etc.), and we see the shocking statistics of how very few male teachers now work in primary schools. It is this last statistic that may provide a clue as to how the changing therapeutic ethos leads to an impoverished sense of well-being for our children and ourselves.

Deregulation has also taken part in the more complicated area of censorship. I rarely watch television, but I have heard a Friday evening prime-time chat-show host saying 'I'm going home for a family wank (whatever that is)', and on another programme I have heard young adults being asked in what ways they thought their parents enjoyed sex best. Their parents then gave, in turn, the 'true answer' etc. Once again, sex is made explicit and measurable, but it perhaps leaves us to being even less thoughtful and more frightened of ourselves. It's not only male teachers who are frightened of being paedophiles but in an overtly and increasingly sexually explicit world, parents can not so easily play with their children or spend time with them, perhaps with the fear that the thoughts that may come to them cannot be shared with anyone.

Through Plato can be seen the importance of play, and how the child can uniquely develop through it. Both children and adults need to be able to be trusted, and to trust themselves to play with each other through being subject-to play. We need both to allow time for each other and not let unspeakable anxieties get in the way. The danger is that we become less thoughtful as we become less able to learn through the relational and play. One detrimental effect of this is that we become less playful, not only with each other, but with ideas; for example, our preoccupation with increasingly narrow notions of 'evidence', where it is almost as if we try and believe that if it can't be measured, it doesn't exist. Science, and particularly technology, increasingly rule our lives, and in so doing we become less thoughtful of such developments.

Many children and adults, through the psychological therapies, are able to return to becoming more playful and hence more alive. But could more be done preventatively? It is not only people who have been sexually, physically, and particularly verbally abused who may find it difficult to learn in an ordinary healthy way through play; but because of increasing cultural concerns such as 'stranger danger' in an increasingly sexualized world, we are becoming a more frozen society and unable to play with our children, who in turn may become less playful in their own and our lives. Mayo & Nairn

(2009) warn us that child's play has become manipulated through the consumer culture, leading to children whose resulting materialistic output is, they suggest, correlated with lower self-esteem. This is in contrast to free play, where children can let play emerge with other children. However, whilst our audit culture is potentially robbing us and our children, it would be wrong to end without also mentioning Fletcher's work (2008) on growing up in England 1600–1914 with its high infant and child mortality and tough social conditions for the majority, to warn us not to be too nostalgic about the past.

In summary therefore, whilst exploring what makes a good counsellor or psychotherapist is significant, such considerations of our practice, in terms of the good, may well be healthy, but it is suggested in this chapter that therapeutic education is a necessity, not only on an individual level but, more importantly, on a societal one. If this does, for some, smack of social engineering, then it has been argued here that this can still be open to the wonderments of an unknown. Notions of transforming our potential hostility to the stranger into hospitality cannot be left solely to professional therapists. As a profession, we will surely fall short unless such notions of 'meeting' are more part of our culture. This is perhaps more akin to what Plato termed 'therapeia'.

A growing trend in Europe is, for example, a narrower reading of evidence-based practice, which in turn is significantly changing the provision of psychological therapies. This apparent acceptance of science over wisdom has significant consequences for the quality of our lives. If we are to be in with a chance of leading a good life, it is essential for therapists to consider how they can influence education in general. Plato intended that if we are to avoid the disastrous consequences arising from the distortion of our souls, then virtue must be a precondition of knowledge.

To Plato, the highest form of knowledge was wisdom, and education is required to revolutionize the mind. Therapeia is therefore the therapy of the soul, and Plato regarded a conversion to be necessary in order to tackle the ignorance of corrupt minds. As psychological therapists, we need to look at therapy as an educational practice not only as part of what is now increasingly termed 'continuous professional development', or possibly in the consulting room, but in terms of educating our societies to see the wisdom of locating scientific, technical thinking as secondary to the resources of the human soul.

For Plato, as for Socrates beforehand, a key question was, 'Can virtue be taught?'. Cushman (whose book *Therapeia* is now, sadly, out of print) details that Plato thought his educational schema was only barely a sufficient antidote to cope with our desperate human plight. For Socrates, the aim of teaching (and this may be familiar for some psychological therapists) was not that it was possible to impart truth, but what others could be led to apprehend as their own discovery. Therefore, such a therapy can be seen not as about knowledge but instead about awakening thought. Plato thus saw Socrates, as some of us might see current psychological therapies, as a physician of souls by means of dialogue.

All this raises a number of questions: perhaps most importantly, can we put the resources of the human soul first, so that audits and empirical research become its servant rather than the other way around? Should a psychological therapist's responsibility be to make each soul as good as possible, or would this be too much of an agenda? Do we not in some way always imbue our clients/patients with our own value systems? Is therapy about resolving into virtue 'the warfare between the conflicting impulses of the soul'? What if therapy only seems to do this, where 'word juggling' may inappropriately transmute irresponsibility into integrity?

Building on the work of Gadamer (1975), therapy with individuals could be seen as a way of enabling an interrupted process of education, facilitating the return to learning from experience. But this can only really take place, and consequently be sustained, in a society where learning from experience is for the good. We might then examine more healthily what part those in such professions as management and education should undertake with regard to those souls for which they have a responsibility (without reducing this to either a manualized set of counselling skills or the non-sequitur of 'an ethical code', as if either could be a basis of training), regardless of whether this includes formal psychotherapy/counselling.

Then we could consider more the training of 'good' teachers, supervisors, and researchers of counselling and psychotherapy in a different way. But in the first instance, we need as psychological therapists to do everything we can to educate our society as to questions about the 'good', otherwise we will be at best marginalized, and at worst part of the 'bad'.

References

Bettelheim, B. (1984). *Freud and Man's Soul*. New York: Random House.

Borch-Jacobsen, M. (1989). *The Freudian Subject*. Stamford, CT: Stamford University Press.

Buber, M. (1971). *I and Thou*. New York: Free Press.

Cushman, R. (2002). *Therapeia: Plato's Conception of Philosophy*. New Brunswick and London: Transaction Publishers.

Ecclestone, K., & Hayes, D. (2008). *The Dangerous Rise of Therapeutic Education*. London: Routledge.

Elliott, A. (1996). *Subject to Ourselves: Social Theory, Psychoanalysis and Postmodernity*. Cambridge: Polity Press.

Eyres, H. (2009). Within you, without you. *The Financial Times* ('Life and Arts' section), 11–12 July: 20.

Fletcher, A. (2008). *Growing up in England: The Experience of Childhood, 1600–1914*. Yale, CT: Yale University Press.

Gadamer, H.-G. (1975). *Truth and Method*. New York: Seabury Press.

Heaton, J. (1998). The enigma of health. *European Journal of Psychotherapy and Counselling*, 1: 33–42.

Lacan, J. (2001). *Ecrits*. London: Routledge.

Layard, R. (2006a). *The Happiness Report: Lessons from a New Science*. London: Penguin.

Layard, R. (2006b). *The Depression Report: A New Deal for Depression and Anxiety Disorders*. Centre for Economic Performance, Mental Health Policy group, June.

Layard, R., & Dunn, J. (2009). *A Good Childhood: Searching for Values in a Competitive Age*. London: Penguin.

Levinas, E. (1969). *Totality and Infinity*. Pittsburgh: Duquesne University Press.

Loewenthal, D. (2008a). Introducing post-existentialism: an approach to well-being in the 21st century. *Philosophical Practice*, 3: 316–321.

Loewenthal, D. (2008b). Post-existentialism as a reaction to CBT? In: R. House & D. Loewenthal (Eds.), *Against and For CBT: Towards a Constructive Dialogue?* (pp. 146–155). Ross-on-Wye: PCCS Books.

Loewenthal, D., & Snell, R. (2003). *Postmodernism for Psychotherapists*. London: Sage.

Marx, K. (1844). *Economic and Philosophical Manuscripts of 1844*. California: International Publishers, 1969.

Mayo, E., & Nairn, A. (2009). *Consumer Kids: How Big Business is Grooming our Children for Profit*. London: Constable.

Merleau-Ponty, M. (1945). *Phenomenology of Perception*. London: Routledge, 1956.

Montaigne, M. (1993). *The Complete Essays*, trans. by M.A. Screech. London and New York: Penguin.

OECD (September 2007). *Supporting Success and Productivity: Practical Tools for Making your University a Great Place to Work*. OECD Directorate for Education.

Polyani, M. (1966). *The Tacit Dimension*. New York: Doubleday.

Samuels, A. (2003). Psychotherapists and Counsellors for Social Responsibility (UK). *Journal for the Psychoanalysis of Culture and Society*, 8: 150–153.

Sartre, J.-P. (1956). *Being and Nothingness: An Essay on Phenomenological Ontology* (trans. H.E. Barnes). New York: Philosophical Library.

United Nations International Children's Emergency Fund (UNICEF). (2007). Report on 'Children in Industrialised Countries'.

Williams, R. (2009). Afterword. In: R. Layard & J. Dunn, *A Good Childhood: Searching for Values in a Competitive Age* (pp. 167–178). London: Penguin.

Winnicott, D.W. (1965). Ego distortion in terms of true and false self. In D. Winnicott, *The Maturational Processes and the Facilitating Environment*. London: Hogarth Press.

World Health Organization (2001). Mental Health: New Understanding, New Hope (The Health Report, 2001). Geneva: World Health Organization.

Wundt, W. (1904). *Principles of Physiological Psychology* (trans. B. Titchener). Cambridge, Mass.: Harvard University Press.

CHAPTER THREE

What is toxic childhood?

Sue Palmer

> In the early years of the twenty-first century, the people of Planet Earth discovered they'd been poisoning their offspring. The food they'd fed children for several decades had damaged both bodies and brains, making the next generation less healthy, less able to learn and more emotionally disturbed every year ... .

It reads like a science fiction story, doesn't it? Now that the UK media have latched on to the 'obesity time-bomb' and the contribution of junk food to behavioural problems, it seems impossible that everyone could have been so stupid for so long. But, as has been apparent for many years to specialists in child development across a range of disciplines, diet is only the tip of the iceberg. According to scores of experts I've interviewed over the last decade, many other aspects of twenty-first century life are seriously damaging children's physical and mental health.

In September 2006, a letter to the *Daily Telegraph* organized by Dr Richard House and myself[1] was signed by 112 experts in children's health, education, and well-being, as well as many well-known children's writers, indicating their growing concern about contemporary childhood in Britain. At a conference for signatories to that letter held at Roehampton University in December 2006, I was asked to talk about my own involvement in this issue, and my book *Toxic Childhood*, in which I attempted to sum up expert concern. This chapter tells how I, as a specialist in primary literacy, found myself in the middle of the 'toxic childhood' debate.

Language, listening, and literacy

It began in response to concerns among primary teachers around the UK. Back in the 1970s and early 1980s I was a primary teacher myself, but somehow transmogrified into a 'literacy specialist', meeting thousands of teachers every year on speaking tours. It was in 1995, whilst running an in-service course about phonics on the Devon–Cornish border, that the alarm bells about childhood began ringing for me.

A group of teachers were telling me that (contrary to all government and press reports at the time) they were perfectly happy to teach phonics, but they didn't know how ready the children were to take the information on board. 'They're changing', one of them said. 'Their language development doesn't seem as good as it used to be.' 'They can't listen as well as they once did', added another. 'Too much TV, probably.' 'But it's more than that', someone else said. 'They don't come in with the old repertoire of nursery rhymes we used to expect. Parents don't seem to be talking and singing to them as much.'

It seemed reasonable to assume that, if children aren't able to talk and listen when they arrive at school, if they haven't been sensitized to the sounds of language through songs and rhymes, you can teach phonics till you're blue in the face—but many of them won't catch on. At the time, I wondered whether their concern was just 'Golden Ageism'—the traditional conviction of the older generation that summers were summery in the good old days and 'young people are going to the dogs'. But as I travelled around the country, exactly the same concerns seemed to be echoed by teachers everywhere. From Cumbria to Kent, from Aberdeen to Swansea, from Birmingham to Newcastle, they were *all* worried that something was happening to children, even young entrants to the profession. These were people who'd chosen their career because they *like* children, who spend all day in children's company, and who can compare classes year on year. And they thought something was wrong.

So I started looking for people who might be able to throw light on the question, and was fortunate to stumble on a speech and language therapist called Dr Sally Ward. In a long-term research study during the 1980s and 1990s,[2] she'd found that an increasing number of 9-month-old children could not single out a significant foreground sound from background noise. When she started screening children in 1984, the number experiencing difficulties was 20 per cent. When she stopped in 1999, it had doubled, to 40 per cent.

I interviewed Sally for the educational press, and remember standing in her kitchen as she said, 'It seems to me that in the early years of the new millennium, about half the children in this country won't be able to attend to their mother's voice above the noise of the television—and that's going to have an impact on their language development.' As she pointed out, when the TV is on, parents don't need to talk to their children, and children would find it difficult to listen to their parents, and therefore to learn to talk themselves.

There was clearly more to it than TV, of course. Our conversation that afternoon ranged from the effects of traffic noise (human beings gradually learn to screen this out, but for tiny children the increasing din must be more disconcerting every year), through the trend for working mothers to put their babies in day-care centres where opportunities for adult–child interaction are limited, to the fact that modern pushchairs generally face *away* from the parent so that conversation as one pushes a child along the street is impossible.

But we kept coming back to electronic media. Until the arrival of video in the 1980s, there was really only one way for parents to soothe their fractious infants—or, indeed, entertain the contented ones. Mums or dads had to pick their children up, look into their eyes, and talk or sing to them. A sort of universal parental behaviour seemed to apply on these occasion—rhythmic rocking movements, high-pitched sing-song tone of voice, exaggerated facial expressions, simplified language that scientists now call 'parenteze'. And, of course, the age-old repertoire of nursery rhymes that emphasizes, through repetitive rhythm and rhyme, the tunes and sounds of the children's native tongue.

However, once screen-based entertainment became available on demand, this behaviour changed. Parents could now pick up their children briefly, then flick a switch and settle them down in front of an electronic babysitter. The baby was being tuned not to the human voice, but to rapidly changing visual images. This seemed to us, standing in Sally's kitchen in Chiswick, a very significant change: something completely new was happening in terms of human child-rearing habits, and most of the world seemed completely unaware of it.

Too much too soon

Sally Ward died tragically in 2003, so she didn't live to see her gloomy prediction come true. In 2006, the speech and language charity I CAN collated the findings of English local education authorities on children's language ability on entry to schools.[3] In disadvantaged areas of the country, just as Sally expected, upwards of 50 per cent of children were now arriving in the reception class with significant language delay.

My meeting with her at the end of the 1990s, however, propelled me towards another speech and language specialist, Clare Mills, who was interested in another aspect of contemporary culture on the development of listening, language, and attention skills. She had just spent several years working with her husband David, a TV producer, on a programme for the Channel 4 *Dispatches* series on the damage begin done to English children by our schools' increasingly early start on formal teaching.[4]

Until the 1990s, most children started school when they were five. The first year—or for some younger children, part of a year—was a settling-in time, for finding their way around the classroom and playground, and learning how to get along with a teacher and lots of other boys and girls. It was a time for learning through play (sand, water, making things, dressing up, role play), listening to stories, and getting used to school. Though there was a little gentle preparation for the 3Rs in this reception year, formal learning didn't start till children were six, in Year 1.

But then, a series of unfortunate events happened in England. One was the appointment of a Chris Woodhead as Chief Inspector of Schools. Woodhead was obsessed with starting formal education much earlier, and during his reign of terror at Ofsted, school inspectors demanded much more literacy and numeracy teaching—not only in reception classes but in nurseries and pre-school playgroups.

The second was something called Bums on Seats. Due to changes in funding arrangements, schools increasingly welcomed four-year-olds into the reception class. (Some parents didn't like this at first, but for their child to be guaranteed a place in their chosen school they had to put up with it.) The floodgates into reception opened when the government offered a free nursery place for every four-year-old but didn't actually provide any more nurseries.

The third unfortunate event was that, when two national strategies were established to raise standards in literacy and numeracy,[5] they fell under Chris Woodhead's early-start spell. Reception teachers were required to introduce a Literacy Hour, coralling children on the mat while they tortured a big book for half an hour. They were given a long list of sight words to teach, and instructions to crack on with phonics as soon as children tottered through the classroom door. It didn't take long for parents to be conned into thinking an early start is a good thing. Since our new educational rat-race is similar to the competitive ethos of big business, it fed their fear that a beloved child might be 'left behind' or 'held back'.

So, just as children began to miss out on first-hand interaction at home due to the arrival of the electronic media, they also began to miss out at school because the time for settling in, playing, learning to get along, and so on had been hi-jacked by literacy and numeracy specialists. Clare and David Mills' *Dispatches* film contrasted our early start culture with the kindergarten curriculum of other European countries where formal teaching didn't begin until children were seven. Their influence led me as a literacy specialist increasingly to challenge government policy—and I wasn't alone. The following letter to *The Times*, which I organized several years later,[6] was signed by professors of human communication, linguistics, neuropsychology, and early education, as well as another prominent literacy specialist and the country's foremost expert on dyslexia:

> In a multi-media world where children increasingly arrive in nursery or primary school with poorly-developed speech, attention and social skills, the development of oral language is of even greater importance. Many have had few life experiences beyond watching TV, and there's much groundwork to be done before these children are able to read and enjoy books, wield pencils and understand what writing is about.

However, despite the best endeavours of early childhood specialists and government advisers, our extremely early start on formal education (the earliest in Europe) leaves little time for early years practitioners to develop children's speaking and listening through the sort of first-hand experience and child-friendly structured activities used in other European countries.

While children elsewhere follow a 'kindergarten curriculum' until they are six years old (indeed, in Sweden and Finland, the two countries that do best in international studies of literacy, until they are seven), children here are often required to start on more formal approaches to reading and writing when they are five, four and sometimes even three years old. Many therefore fall at the first fence in literacy learning and, sadly, catch-up programmes do not seem to work. We believe this is a key reason behind our country's inability to reduce the 'long tail of underachievement', especially in areas of deprivation, despite the huge investment of recent years.

It was becoming very clear that the changes those infant teachers had noticed in children could not be traced to a simple cause. The world was changing in all sorts of ways, and children seemed to be caught in the middle of the changes.

The cradle of thought

By the beginning of the new millennium, I'd become obsessed by the problem of language, listening, and attention skills. If, in a fast-moving, multimedia world, children weren't developing these skills in ways previously taken for granted, the repercussions could be much wider than difficulties with early literacy. Perhaps these changes in parental behaviour could also contribute to behavioural problems in schools and the wider world beyond. Children who can't listen have trouble attending to the adults in charge, so don't know what's expected of them. Children who can't express their needs are more likely to resort to pushing and prodding to get what they want. Once this sort of behaviour has begun, it's all too easy to spiral down into disaffection and underachievement.

This was when *The Cradle of Thought*, a book by the developmental psychopathologist Professor Peter Hobson and published in 2002,[7] gave me another perspective on early communication. I was directed to it by Professor Margaret Donaldson, whose own book *Children's Minds*[8] had fired interest in child development in a generation of primary teachers (including me) a quarter of a century before.

Hobson argues that the human capacity to think requires a certain amount of nurturing. He doesn't deny that infants are born hard-wired for thought, just as they're hard-wired for language—to that extent, thinking is genetically predetermined. But he maintains that, like language, this aspect of nature also needs nurture before it can take its course: adults must provide some input. If babies get that input in the first year or so of life, they'll be able to understand, think, communicate, learn. If they don't, their human potential is damaged.

The cradle in which Hobson claims thought begins is the deep emotional attachment that exists between parent and child. This allows them to form what he calls the 'triangle of interrelatedness'—parent at one corner of the triangle, child at another, and the outside world at the third. Secure in the parent's presence, the child looks out at the world, then back at the parent; the parent looks at the world, then back at the child; their mutual gaze acknowledges a mutual experience—they've both seen the same bit of world. Often the parent goes one step further: 'Can you see that doggy? Look at the doggy. Isn't it lovely?'

Hobson argues that, through taking part in this emotionally embedded triangle of interrelatedness, children acquire three key insights. First, there's the dawning realization that they and their parent are separate beings, looking at the same bit of world from different viewpoints—the child is simultaneously attached to and separate from the parent. This is a supremely important insight, because it's the beginning of empathy. If the mind-blowing discovery that other people have their own points of view is rooted in emotional security and pleasurable communication, the chances of the child later extending empathy to a widening range of people are much greater.

The next vital insight is the infant's recognition of his own personal perspective, different from the parent's ('She's looking at it from there, and I'm looking at it from here—this is *my* point of view). The child thus becomes conscious of himself as a thinker, an intellectual self-awareness that underpins rational thought and behaviour.

Think of it: millions of little minds throughout the millennia, experiencing their own amazing Cartesian moments.

Finally, the realization that it's possible to have more than one perspective on an object points children towards symbolic play ('If I can look at this box in different ways, I can *pretend* it's a car … *brmm, brmm!*'). Soon they'll delight in using dolls as symbols for babies, sticks for horses, cardboard boxes for cars. As Vygotsky pointed out,[9] symbolic play lays the foundation for understanding the many systems of symbols used in our culture, including numbers and letters. It's also critical for the development of imagination and creative problem-solving abilities.

Hobson's journey towards *The Cradle of Thought* was via his long-term research into autism. He believes children with a genetic predisposition towards autism do not naturally acquire these three insights: if an infant's genetic make-up prevents him from sharing in the triangle of interrelatedness, he's trapped alone, unable to fly. But perhaps, if opportunities to participate in an emotionally satisfying 'triangle of relatedness' are missing in their first eighteen months, even children *without* such a genetic vulnerability may have difficulty in acquiring one or more of the insights. He cites the example of the unfortunate babies raised with little human contact in Romanian orphanages under the Ceauşescu regime—many more than would be expected in a normal population developed 'autistic-like' behaviour. Similarly, blind children, unable to make eye-contact with their parents, are at greater risk of such behavioural traits.

Hobson doesn't take the argument any further, but after my conversation with Sally Ward and the concerns of all those teachers, I couldn't help it. What if a normal child isn't exactly neglected, but the 'triangle of interrelatedness' isn't as good as it could be? What if opportunities for shared gazing and communication are limited? What if parents don't have time, or are too busy, or too distracted by electronic entertainment to interact with their babies? Or if the babies themselves are so attracted to looking at screens that they lose interest in interacting with people?

Friends in special-needs teaching pointed me towards the a growing body of neuroscientific research connecting successful early attachment with the development of neural networks in the prefrontal cortex of the brain—the area associated with rational thought, decision-making, social behaviour, and self-control. It seemed to me that, if Hobson was right, the way we look after tiny children is profoundly important, not only for the children themselves, but for all of us.

The elephant in the house

At around the same time I read *The Cradle of Thought*, I had another alarming encounter. While checking up a news report about the vast increase in prescriptions for Ritalin (the 'chemical cosh' prescribed for children with ADHD), I met another 'child development expert' from the special-needs field, who was investigating the same story.

'I've got a theory about ADHD', I told her. 'In some children it may be because they're not interacting with their parents so much in the early years.' I explained about Sally Ward and Peter Hobson, and how unintended side-effects of cultural change might be affecting early attachment and communication. 'Good Lord', she said. 'I'd never thought of that!' Then she outlined her theory: that—for various reasons, again connected with recent social changes—contemporary children aren't getting enough activity, especially outdoor play. This could be affecting the development of bodily coordination and control. 'Boys especially don't have opportunities to run off excess energy', she explained; 'so not unnaturally, they act up. We're pathologizing normal childhood behaviour.' 'Good Lord', I said. 'I'd never thought of *that!*'

This was when I began to feel really guilty about my career trajectory. The problem with being a specialist is that you get to know a great deal about your own specialism, and less and less about everything else. Over the years, I'd developed into an 'expert' on children's literacy, and my attention had gradually focused on the specific skills and concepts children needed to read and write. I might have widened my scope to take in early listening and language development, and then the significance of attachment to early communication and learning—but that was still only a fraction of children's day-to-day experience. Here was someone reminding me that they had to move about as well!

And it was perfectly obvious when I looked about me that children were not moving very much at all—indeed, they seemed always to be strapped into things: car seats as their parents drove them from place to place; baby seats or 'bouncers' or 'baby-walkers' in the home; pushchairs (facing the wrong way, of course) on the dwindling occasions when they left the shelter of vehicle or building. How many more unintended consequences of cultural change were impacting on contemporary childhood?

A week or so later, while doing a literacy in-service course for a small group of teachers in Portsmouth, I asked them during the lunch break to brainstorm a list of all the things they thought might be affecting children's capacity to learn and behave well in school. They came up with the following:

unhealthy food	poor emotional bonding
couch-potato lifestyle	lack of interaction / communication
lack of sleep	emotional instability
lack of play	competitive educational ethos
lack of first-hand experience	manipulative marketing strategies
consumer-driven lifestyle	morally relative society
too much TV	poor parenting skills

We could all see straight away how changes over the last 25 years or so had contributed to each aspect of this rather terrifying list—the explosion of communications technology, the rise of consumer culture and aggressive marketing, the growth in working mums, the increasing fragility of marriage. It was clearly a tribute to the amazing resilience of children that, living in such a toxic environment, they managed to adjust and cope as well as they did. But surely, unless society got a grip on all these 'unintended consequences', the chances of educational failure and behavioural problems would steadily increase?

This was the moment, in 2003, that I decided I wanted to find out more about the whole damn toxic mix. Trawling press reports and the internet, there seemed no shortage of evidence of significant social and cultural change affecting each of the areas we'd identified. But the specialists involved in research appeared to be proceeding like the blind men and the elephant in a poem I used to read with my Primary 6 classes.[10] They were all digging away at their own little section of childhood, but no one was looking at the whole elephant.

Toxic childhood syndrome

So it was time to stop excavating my own personal trench, and start researching into childhood in general. This wasn't an easy decision—I'm a teacher, not an academic, and the area is so massive I didn't know where to start. I also had to do the research alongside my day job—although in many ways that was an advantage, because every group of teachers I met gave fresh insights, and in-service travel also allowed me to hunt down experts all over Europe.

After dividing the research into ten sections (see Box 1), I interviewed at least two experts in each section—to get an overview of

Box 1
1: Food for thought How twenty-first century food affects brain function and twenty-first century eating habits affect behaviour
2: Out to play How parental anxiety damages children's development by restricting access to unstructured, loosely supervised outdoor play
3: Time for bed Why sleep is important for thinking, learning, and behaviour, and the damage wrought by putting TVs in children's bedrooms
4: It's good to talk The significance of attachment and communication, particularly in the early years
5: We are family How changes in family structures and stability have affected children's well-being
6: Who's looking after the children? What children need in terms of childcare at different stages throughout childhood
7: Best days of their lives Why twenty-first century education fails many children, and what effective primary education might look like

8: The word on the street
How the consumer culture and aggressive marketing damage children's well-being

9: The electronic village
The effects of growing up in a fast-changing multimedia global village

10: Manners maketh man
The problems of rearing children in a morally relative society.

the field, some help in understanding the technical aspects (I'm not
great at science) and directions for further reading. It was an amazing
experience. I'll always treasure memories of walking on a Scottish
beach with the psychologist Colwyn Trevarthen while he told me
about the significance of music in young children's development;
sitting in a lab in Oxford while the physiologist Alex Richardson
railed passionately about the effects of junk food on children's brains;
and climbing to the top floor of the London School of Economics
to discuss contemporary ethics with Lord Richard Layard, world-
renowned professor of economics! Me—Mrs Palmer of 3B!

It didn't take long to discover that the 'further reading' could
keep me busy for several lifetimes. That led me to two research
assistants—brilliant young men with forensic minds, access to their
university databases, and absolute confidence at working the internet. They helped sift through the vast amount of research papers
appearing almost daily in our ten areas of interest, and found more
exciting interviewees. John, who spoke German, tracked down a
German university professor doing cutting-edge research into the
effects of sleep on learning; James, who became fascinated by the
effects of divorce on children's development, netted a high court
judge. It was heady work. But the more widely I read and travelled,
the more convinced I was that these diverse experts' research added
up to something worth worrying about.

In the tumult of change, many parents seemed to have lost sight of
age-old truths about child-rearing. This isn't surprising, as their own
lives were very different from those of previous generations, and
many of the old reference points—lore from the extended family,

cultural, and religious traditions—had been swept away. But simultaneously, the toxic mix of unintended consequences of change had made the task of rearing children more difficult than ever before. Today's parents haven't had the time (or the clarity of information) to make adjustments for these side-effects.

They need to know that, though our culture may have been evolving at a fair old lick, human beings haven't. Children are still born the same small, vulnerable creatures that they've always been; and although they are astoundingly resilient, they still need adult help to develop into bright balanced citizens.

- They need physical nurturing (a healthy mind in a healthy body)—the sort of thing that across generations and cultures, parents have usually tried to provide: nourishing food; freedom to move and grow; adequate sleep.
- They need emotional and social nurturing, rooted in love, time, and attention from the adults closest to them, especially when they're very small. But they also need to play with other children, and opportunities to learn and grow away from an adult gaze.
- For healthy cognitive development, they need first-hand experience of their world; then as they grow older, they need adult help to initiate them into the culture of their time, which in our society starts with the 3Rs.
- And throughout childhood they need moral guidance, to help them navigate through the increasingly complex web of contemporary ethics.

It seemed to me, trying to pull together the insights of all the experts, that children's development in every one of these areas—physical, social, emotional, cognitive, and moral/spiritual—is threatened by the side-effects of technological and cultural changes. A great many (probably a majority) of our children have developed a taste for unhealthy food and a couch-potato life-style, and have related problems with sleeping. An unacceptable number also suffer from inadequate early emotional bonding, lack of interaction with their parents, and a high level of emotional instability. Opportunities for the unstructured loosely supervised play that has hitherto been almost all children's birthright have practically dwindled away. Instead of these stimulating, real-life experiences, contemporary children have TV and computer games at home and, all too often, a narrow test-and-target driven curriculum at school. In a secular and confused society, spiritual and moral guidance is often lacking, while children are constantly exposed to manipulative advertising and the excesses of celebrity culture.

Any one of this vast array of unintended consequences would be enough to trigger developmental delay in a genetically vulnerable child; perhaps the whole toxic brew could trigger it even in the most genetically robust of individuals. This is the 'elephant' at the heart of the experts' deliberations, an elephant now standing full square in the living room of every family home.

Detoxifying childhood

Since the publication in 2006 of my book *Toxic Childhood*, evidence that all is not well with contemporary childhood—particularly in the UK and USA—has continued to mount. The 2006 letter to the *Daily Telegraph*, mentioned earlier, caused a flurry of media attention and the response from around the country (and indeed the English-speaking world) indicated widespread public concern. When a UNICEF report about childhood well-being in early 2007[11] showed that out of 21 nations of the developed world, the UK came 21st, the concern turned into alarm. Politicians finally began to connect huge increases in teenage disaffection and depression with 'toxic childhood syndrome' (UK teenagers are, according to surveys, the worst behaved in Europe, and probably the unhappiest)—and the major political parties began looking for quick-fix policies to wave before the public.

So far, however, none of them looks likely to acknowledge the connection between the toxicity of childhood and our 'winners and losers' culture. My interview with the economist Professor Layard convinced me that many of our problems are due to a loss of social capital, driven by competitive consumerism. As mentioned earlier, rapid social change—especially women's movement from the home to the workplace—has meant the loss of much ancient lore about child-rearing. But something else has now insinuated itself into the vacuum left behind: the jungle law of The Market. It takes a village to raise a child, and today's children are being raised in the electronic global village of mass communications, driven by consumer culture.

Market-driven competition now informs child-rearing methods and educational provision. Everything—from learning to read to dressing up like an adult—has to happen sooner and faster every year. Childhood has become a sort of race, and the glittering prizes are consumer durables. Our culture tells parents that anything freely available (love, smiles, talk, play, sand, water, trees to climb) is clearly worthless. 'Don't waste time just Being with your children: work longer hours so you can Buy Them More Stuff! To play properly today, your child doesn't need friends he needs a Play Station.'

What's more, the Market passes its messages on to children as soon as they can press the 'ON' switch. So even when parents realize something's wrong and try to return to biological necessities, the children don't listen. A harassed mother offering a choice between carrots and peas is on a hiding to nothing when a marketing man in the corner of the room drowns her out with adverts for pizza and coke.

Parents have been kept too busy (and too frightened) to prevent their children's lives being taken over by tests and targets in school and second-hand, screen-based activities at home. Indeed, in many cases they're also exhausted from earning the money to feed their children's fast-growing consumer habits. As a society, we have to tackle this problem if we're going to make any headway in detoxifying the next generation's lives. Will any politician be far-sighted enough to help millions of economy-friendly families out of servitude, and instead create a family-friendly economy? Or to shut down the tests and targets treadmill and admit that there's more to childhood and education than a clutch of Level 4 passes at the age of eleven?

Since we could wait for ever for that sort of political top-down solution, it seems more sensible to seek grass-roots action, and several non-political initiatives are at present raising parents' awareness of the issues involved. There's the Good Childhood Enquiry,[12] commissioned by the Children's Society (see Chapter 5, this volume); an independent review of primary education organized by Professor Robin Alexander of Cambridge University;[13] a House of Lords enquiry into the effects of contemporary culture on children's brain development, set up by the neuroscientist Baroness Susan Greenfield. Awareness-raising is a very good start. If the findings of these enquiries can be communicated clearly enough, cultural change may soon begin to happen from the bottom up.

Parental love is the greatest force on the planet, and what all parents want—no matter what their social or educational background—is for their children to be happy, and to achieve their full potential. But in recent years parents have lacked solid information on what's really necessary to help their children grow up bright and balanced (i.e., emotionally resilient, socially competent, and well-equipped to learn). Instead, they've been bamboozled by marketers concerned with commercial gain or politicians motivated by their own short-term ambitions.

The information parents *really* need has to come from people whose only motivation is the well-being of children. And there are many of them around. The teachers who alerted me to the problems, the experts I interviewed, the signatories to the *Telegraph* open letter, the great-and-good who've organized the national enquiries cited above, and the contributors to this book are all such people. It seems to me that the good are now on the move, and all they have to do is recognize and support each other's efforts in sorting out different elements in the toxic mix. It's been an enormous privilege for me to meet so many of them, and I really do believe that their combined efforts will help parents detoxify childhood for the vast majority of children in the UK.

Notes and References

1. Sue Palmer, Richard House, & 110 others, Modern life leads to more depression among children. *Daily Telegraph*, 12 September, 2006; retrievable at: http://www.telegraph.co.uk/news/1528639/Modern-life-leads-to-more-depression-among-children.html
2. For a discussion of Sally Ward's research, see my *Toxic Childhood* (Orion, 2006), Chapter 4. Since Sally was very ill by the time the research was completed, it was not published in an academic journal; however, she explained her findings in her book *Babytalk* (Century, 2000).
3. I CAN report, *The Cost to the Nation of Children's Poor Communication*. I CAN, London, 2006.
4. Claire and David Mills, *Too Much Too Young*, Channel 4 Television, London, 1998.
5. The two British national strategies were established to raise standards in literacy and numeracy. The National Literacy Strategy, launched in 1997, and the National Numeracy Strategy, launched 1998, were

flagship projects of the new Labour government, directed from the then Department for Education and Skills by Professor Michael Barber.

6. Professor Dorothy Bishop & 6 others, Open Letter, Children need time to listen and learn. *The Times*, 12 December 2005.

7. Peter Hobson, *The Cradle of Thought*, MacMillan, Basingstoke, 2003.

8. Margaret Donaldson, *Children's Minds*, Fontana Press, London, 1978.

9. See, for example, Lev Vygotsky, *Thought and Language*, MIT Press, Baltimore, 1986.

10. 'The Blind Men and the Elephant', by John Godfrey Saxe.

It was six men of Indostan
To learning much inclined,
Who went to see the Elephant ~ (Though all
        of them were blind),
That each by observation ~ Might satisfy his mind.

The First approached the Elephant,
And happening to fall
Against his broad and sturdy side, ~ At once began to bawl:
'God bless me! but the Elephant ~ Is very like a wall!'

The Second, feeling of the tusk,
Cried, 'Ho! what have we here?
So very round and smooth and sharp? ~ To me
        'tis mighty clear
This wonder of an Elephant ~ Is very like a spear!'

The Third approached the animal,
And happening to take
The squirming trunk within his hands ~ Thus boldly
        up and spake:
'I see', quoth he, 'the Elephant ~ Is very like a snake!'

The Fourth reached out an eager hand,
And felt about the knee.
'What most this wondrous beast is like ~ Is mighty plain',
        quoth her;
'"Tis clear enough the Elephant ~ Is very like a tree!'

The Fifth who chanced to touch the ear,
Said: 'E'en the blindest man

Can tell what this resembles most; ~ Deny the fact who can,
This marvel of an Elephant ~ Is very like a fan!'

The Sixth no sooner had begun
About the beast to grope,
Than, seizing on the swinging tail ~ That fell within
    his scope,
'I see', quoth he, 'the Elephant ~ Is very like a rope!'

And so these men of Indostan
Disputed loud and long,
Each in his own opinion ~ Exceeding stiff and strong,
Though each was partly in the right ~ And all were
    in the wrong!

The moral of this poem is: Acknowledge the whole elephant and don't waste time on disputes!

11. ICEF report: UNICEF Innocenti Research Centre: *An overview of child well-being in rich countries: a comprehensive assessment of the lives and well-being of children and adolescents in the economically advanced nations* (UNICEF, 2007); retrievable at: http://www.unicef.org/media/files/ChildPovertyReport.pdf

12. The Good Childhood Enquiry (for an introduction, see Chapter 5, this volume); see also: http://www.childrenssociety.org.uk/all_about_us/how_we_do_it/the_good_childhood_inquiry/1818.html

13. See the Cambridge Primary Review website at http://www.primaryreview.org.uk/—where the Review's many research papers are freely downloadable.

Further reading

Palmer, S. (2006). *Toxic Childhood: How Modern Life Is Damaging Our Children ... and What We Can Do about It*. London: Orion Books.

Palmer, S. (2007). *Detoxing Childhood: What Parents Need to Know to Raise Happy, Successful Children*. London: Orion Books.

Palmer, S. (2009). *21st Century Boys: How Modern Life Is Driving Them off the Rails... and How We Can Get Them Back on Track*. London: Orion Books.

CHAPTER FOUR

The challenge of modern childhood

Christopher Clouder

Over the last few years there has been increased concern about the quality of childhood in the UK and in many other Western countries. This could also be construed as growing awareness about our contemporary complex life-styles as adults, and the effect such a life-style has on our children, in a similar way to Rachel Carson's ground-breaking insights in her book *Silent Spring* fifty years ago. The effects of pesticides on the environment were either unknown or wilfully ignored until she courageously focussed attention on the situation. Similarly, today various recent reports on the state of childhood have underlined the urgent necessity for a new approach to well-being in childhood, and the question is now how far teachers and carers should be playing a part in the social and cultural remedies to create an 'ecology of childhood'.

There has been a plethora of research-based concerns that have gripped the attention of the media, educators, and the public alike, such as the annual Innocenti reports, particularly *An Overview of Child Well-being in Rich Countries*[1] that placed the UK very low in its rankings in relationship to other comparative counties. At the time this attracted a lot of attention and led to a government report on the issue, *Children and Young People Today*,[2] which acknowledged there were severe problems with deprivation and mental health among children and teenagers, and that disorderly behaviour had increased substantially in the last 20 years. Its conclusions were not as bleak as the UNICEF report, but it also highlighted an increased level of anxiety among children, stating that younger children are worried about friendships and bullying, and older ones about examinations and their future. Commercial pressures were also cited as being of particular concern. Overall, parents felt that improvements in educational provision were a means that could keep young people out of trouble and help them on the path to success. Schools were seen as providing the best local service, and greater parental involvement in school life could bring more positive experiences of education for the children. It was also suggested that schools could give more emphasis to 'life-skills'.

Of late, public attention in the UK has been directed to many other childhood ailments that have negative social and emotional consequences. Although some symptoms of changing childhood may be unique to an Anglo-Saxon culture, there are countries throughout Europe and beyond where similar concerns are expressed, although not so vociferously. The school testing regimes that are being increasingly practised in schools are putting more pressure and stress on children and causing more anxiety, and even a worrying sense of unredeemable personal failure, at a vulnerable young age. The extensive use of video games and a taste for extremely violent video and films is leading to a tendency to an aggressive response when faced with a challenging situation, and younger and younger children are caught up in a culture of a bullying and violence. Permeable family structures, which are becoming the norm, can, if not handled with care, create deep insecurity in children and undermine their sense of self-worth. Children are losing opportunities to play physically, as some schools cut back on play time, designated play areas become building sites, and parents are under the impression that supervised outside play is dangerous. Instead, children are offered the temptation of bedrooms equipped with all the devices needed to live in a virtual world.

As well as the above, a plethora of concern has appeared in the media, for instance:

- An epidemic of childhood obesity with consequent effects on future health is clearly visible in the UK.

- There are signs of similar increase of depressive states at a younger age than hitherto, although more difficult to measure.[3]
- Children's mental-health figures are causing great concern. The proportion of 15-year olds with behavioural problems has doubled in Britain in the last 25 years.[4]
- The number of children disclosing self-harm has increased by 65 per cent in the last two years.[5]
- One in ten children between one and 10 suffer from psychological problems that are 'persistent, severe and affect functioning on a day-today basis'.[6]
- Consumption of alcohol among 11 to 15-year olds has doubled in 14 years.
- According to the UNICEF report, British children are among the unhappiest and unhealthiest in Europe. Although some of the findings of this report are contested, it cannot be easily dismissed, and exposes a situation that is increasingly found to a greater or lesser extent in other countries too.[7]

It is not without good reason that the media-catching concept of a *Toxic Childhood*[8] has gained general currency as an expression of concern, and is much debated.

We hear of an increased commercialization of childhood that nurtures cynicism.[9] The research report *Watching, Wanting and Wellbeing: A Study of 9 to 13 Year Olds*[10] has shown significant associations between media exposure (watching) and materialism (wanting), and between materialism and self-esteem (well-being): '... the relationship between materialism and self-esteem is bound up with family dynamics. This provides some support for the theory that materialism is associated with impaired social relationships, which in turn are associated with how children feel about themselves.' Consumer culture has its price, one of which is an increase in child–parent conflict, as children develop a lower opinion of their parents and argue with them more, leading consequently to a more divided society.[11] School is also affected in that television and computers are omnipresent. Children sit in front of them before they go to school and when they come back from school, a third of families accompany mealtimes with TV programmes and even the computer. In addition, excessive computer gaming has been shown to impair sleep and memory.[12] Pre- and post-computer cognitive tests show a decline in verbal memory—'... strong emotional experiences such as playing a computer game or watching a thrilling movie, could decisively impact the learning process ... because recently acquired knowledge is very sensitive in the subsequent consolidation period.'[13] A follow-up investigation into commercial activity on children's favourite websites, *Fair Game*,[14] found that although there were online rules for fair-trading and data protection, these are, in certain instances, flouted, and advertisements and commercial messages become difficult for children to identify, and are used dishonestly to manipulate children, potentially bringing additional emotional strain into the family context. It is not technophobic to suggest that we do not yet know the full impact of modern technology on children's lives and relationships, in spite of its other multiple benefits.

The present Children's Commissioner for England, Sir Al Aynsley-Green, who is also an eminent paediatrician, has sounded a warning note, that there is a loss of time for children to be children, with the incessant commercialization of childhood by the advertising industry, and the relentless sexualization of children at very young ages, with the media even demonizing children. The dramatically increasing use of behavioural control drugs such as the stimulants Ritalin and Concerta, at present prescribed to around 55,000 children for Attention Deficit Hyperactivity Disorder (ADHD), is being questioned, as they could stunt children's growth and, it has been claimed, tend to work no better than behavioural intervention therapy. It is accepted that 10 per cent of all 5 to 15-year olds have a clinically diagnosed disorder, ranging from anxiety to depression and autistic spectrum disorder, although the figure is sometimes contested as being a result of more accurate diagnostic criteria. Nevertheless the decline in social behaviours and an increase in aggressive tendencies are not similarly contested.

Robin Alexander, who is headed the current Primary Review 2007 and travelled around the country speaking to people inside and outside education, found unease about the present and pessimism about the future. His initial report also points to a way forward: 'where schools had started engaging children with global and local realities as aspects of their education they were noticeably more upbeat ... the sense of "we can do something about it" seemed to make a difference.'[15] Nell Noddings puts the challenge succinctly: 'The traditional organization of schooling is intellectually and morally inadequate for contemporary society. We live in an age troubled by social problems that force us to reconsider what we do in schools.'[16] She balances the common misperception that arises when assuming that social and emotional education is only about happiness, in that we must educate for unhappiness as well. Children learn that sharing the unhappiness of others paradoxically brings with it a form of happiness. 'This is the major conclusion reached by care theorists, who argue that things we do to improve the relationships of which we are part will work for our benefit as well as others.'[17] There is a sense of urgency for change in the air, and that something with the range of social and emotional education is needed, as summed up by the head of the children's charity National Children's Homes: 'We know from our own research the increasing importance of emotional well-being in childhood in determining life chances and later social mobility'.[18] So what can be done, and what could be the role of the school?

The changing role of the school

If schools are to play a part in remedying the situation and providing a new source for social cohesion, how can this be tackled? One approach that is coming to the fore comes under various variants of the term Social and Emotional Education (SEE), or Social and Emotional Aspects of Learning (SEAL). The Universal Declaration of Human Rights establishes the fundamental principles of human rights and freedoms, and that includes education: '... education shall be directed to the full development of the human personality and to the strengthening of respect for human rights and freedoms. It shall promote understanding, tolerance and friendship. ...' (Article 26.2). These competencies are in essence social and emotional. In 1996 UNESCO published a significant report, *Learning: The Treasure Within*, compiled by their Commission on Education for the 21st Century, which highlighted the value of diversity as an educational principle. 'Between the extremes of abstract and over-simplifying universalism and relativism which makes no higher demand beyond the horizon of each particular culture, one needs to assert both the right to be different and receptiveness to universal values'.[19] It outlines a new perspective on education constructed on four pillars:

- **LEARNING TO KNOW**, by combining a sufficiently broad general knowledge with the opportunity to work in depth on a small number of subjects. This also means learning to learn, so as to benefit from the opportunities education provides throughout life.

- **LEARNING TO DO**, in order to acquire not only an occupational skill but also, more broadly, the competence to deal with many situations and work in teams. It also means learning to do in the context of young peoples' various social and work experiences, which may be informal, as a result of the local or national context, or formal, involving courses, alternating study and work.

- **LEARNING TO LIVE TOGETHER**, by developing an understanding of other people and an appreciation of interdependence—carrying out joint projects and learning to manage conflicts—in a spirit of respect for the values of pluralism, mutual understanding, and peace.

- **LEARNING TO BE**, so as better to develop one's personality and be able to act with ever greater autonomy, judgement, and personal responsibility. In that connection, education must not disregard any aspect of a person's potential: memory, reasoning, aesthetic sense, physical capacities, and communication skills.

    [And the report adds: Formal education systems tend to emphasize the acquisition of knowledge to the detriment of other types of learning; but it is vital now to conceive education in a more encompassing fashion. Such a vision should inform and guide future educational reforms and policy, in relation both to contents and to methods.]

What previous generations had regarded as an educational system set, as it were, in stone and delivering traditional expertise and straightforward cultural transmission is now faced with new challenges that require quite radical reforms. To meet the needs of twenty-first century children and enable children to learn to learn, schools are being called upon to develop beyond being cloistered institutions that are removed from adult life. In this demanding undertaking, it becomes necessary to learn from each other beyond national boundaries and to share experiences internationally in search of life-long citizenship of our planet. As subsequently pointed out by Jacques Delors, 'Together the four pillars provide balance at a time when many policy makers still speak of education only in terms of the economy and labour market. We must not overlook the other aspect of education ... through which people are empowered to achieve self-mastery'.[20] Education is not a commodity, despite consumerist and financial jargon being imported into educational policy-making. Social and emotional learning processes can make an important contribution to enabling people to take hold of their own lives and finding their individual equilibrium:

> There is a contradiction ... between the utilitarian, that is to say economically useful, view of competencies on the one hand, and on the other, the view of competencies as being liberating forces, enabling individuals to take charge of their own lives.[21]

We are all conscious that the present is turbulent and uncertain, full of unforeseen and weighty questions, and that the answers to these will have a deep impact on the future world of our children—one of which is a perceived crisis in social cohesion. The identities and groups that held society together in the past are, like all human endeavours, evolving. This is not to deny the many catastrophic conflicts of the past, but recent advances in technology, new discoveries about the human impact on the natural environment, social upheaval and increased mobility, and our increasingly globalized world of interdependence bring new and complex dimensions. We are no longer so far removed from each other:

> Domination, oppression and human barbarities undeniably persist and aggravate our planet. These are fundamental anthro-historical problems which have no a priori solution: but they are subject to improvement and can only be treated by the multidimensional process that will strive to civilize all of us, our societies, the earth.[22]

This phenomenon cannot be without consequence for the upbringing and education of children. As Steve Biko pointed out, during his struggle against apartheid in South Africa, the route towards living together lies in the humanization of education. Martin Luther King likewise perceived that having brought ourselves closer through technological progress, our next task is to create global social cohesion. King said,

> We are challenged to rise above the narrow confines of our individualistic concerns to the broader concerns of humanity....

> Through our scientific genius we have made the world a
> neighbourhood; now through moral and spiritual genius we
> must make it a brotherhood'.[23]

So where else should one start but in the early years of life and school?

The task ahead

This sense of the need to change our contemporary educational culture has appeared repeatedly in recent publications produced by international organizations such as the OECD and UNESCO. In August 2007, UNESCO issued the *Kronberg Declaration on the Future of Knowledge Acquisition and Sharing*—a declaration that again calls for a radical change in perceptions. Among other things it promotes extensive, value-oriented education as a necessity:

> The educational institutions of the future need to dedicate
> themselves much more intensively to emotional and social
> capabilities and convey a more extensive, value-oriented edu-
> cation concept. The importance of acquiring factual knowledge
> will decline significantly, in favour of the ability to orientate
> yourself within complex systems and find, assess and creatively
> utilize relevant information. The learner will take on a much
> more active and self-responsible role in the learning process,
> including the creation of content.[24]

Whereas in the past, compulsion and regulation for the young were the norm, the last decades of the twentieth century have seen a change to negotiation and consensus-seeking in many areas of family and educational life. It has now been claimed that, over a dozen years, personal and social skills such as self-control and an ability to get on with others became 33 times more important in determining children's futures than they had been before.[25] In Western societies, the drift to greater individualism raises the question of the future social coherence and sustainability. The increase in family fragmentation can place new emotional strains on a child, faced with feelings of insecurity and risk over which they are powerless.

Working intensely with children challenges our humanity and our nature as beings of thinking, feeling, and volition, with our intricate involvement in the lives of others through social engagement. This is not a new discovery. As Dewey wrote in 1897,

> In sum I believe that the individual who is to be educated is a social individual and that society is an organic union of individuals. If we eliminate the social factor from the child we are only left with an abstraction; if we eliminate the individual factor from society, we are left only with an inert and lifeless mass. Education, therefore, must begin with a psychological insight into the child's capacities, interests, and habits.[26]

In conventional thinking, aspects of deep human significance such as love, companionship, happiness, and their contraries were regarded as appertaining to the private and family life of the children and, like disreputable or disorderly relatives, held at bay from the classroom. Now, as a result of methodological research into human nature through disciplines such as psychology, sociology, and human biology, alongside a greater understanding of learning skills, we can see that this was and is actually impossible. The children bring their culture, moods, attitudes, and inner life with them, even though they have often been expected to suppress these in a classroom situation.

The world of feelings can be explored and utilized to enhance how we work and influence our children's futures. Whoever is educating the child has to be aware that their feelings and relationships to what they are imparting are intrinsic to the process, and have an effect. We cannot really divorce our personalities from the process of teaching. Our character, as expressed for instance by our reactions, gestures, tone, underlying assumptions, expectations, creativity, and patience, is either implicitly or explicitly part of the process. The concept of social and emotional learning highlights the changing nature of being human for both the learner and the teacher. Pedagogical skill is the ability to use our attributes to serve the children. A lesson is a communal experience, and as such can be judged by all the participants in a variety of ways; but whatever the outcome it has wrought change. A social and emotional education approach has the potential to help children learn to learn by giving them a sense of self-mastery and an improved climate of learning in the classroom. School can be a happy and satisfying experience that provides a training or further development in awareness about our interactions with others. We can aim to create a more socially cohesive world, and it is when we are young that we are provided, either in the family or at school, with the optimum opportunity for developing such a world when in a secure and caring environment. The goal for social and emotional education is to give children the tools and understanding in order to enhance their resilience, and develop their ability to cope capably with the ups and downs of life.

Such potential changes are grounded in a growing evidence base in the area of social and emotional well-being which, in recent decades, has provided much theory and debate, and introduced a vocabulary through which to facilitate national and international discussion. Howard Gardner, in his theory of multiple intelligences, conceived of personal intelligences as based on an interpersonal and intrapersonal intelligence thereby linking the social and emotional dimensions. Daniel Goleman, in his book *Emotional Intelligence*,[27] highlighted the existence of the five domains of emotional intelligence—namely:

- the skills of understanding our own emotions;
- managing our feelings;
- self-motivation;
- recognizing emotions in others; and
- forming positive relationships.

Goleman went further, stating that emotional competencies are 'a learned capacity based on emotional intelligence that results in outstanding performance at work.'[28] According to this definition, we are going beyond a potentiality to develop and control certain emotional abilities, to a level of performance and effectiveness. This makes it different from what we usually see as general intelligence because this suggests that emotional intelligence is a capacity that can be developed. More recently Katherine Weare has described emotional literacy as:

> ...the ability to understand ourselves and other people, in particular to be aware of, understand, and use information about the emotional states of ourselves and others with competence.

It includes the ability to understand, express and manage our own emotions, and respond to the emotions of others, in ways that are helpful to ourselves and others.[29]

These statements go hand in hand with recent neurological discoveries. Scientists, like Damasio, have shown that, in our brains, emotion and thinking are not separable activities but constantly play on to one another:

Emotion appears to be the support system without which the rational building process cannot work. ... These results and their interpretation have questioned the idea of emotion as a luxury, as a disturbance or as a mere mark of previous biological evolution.[30]

Human beings do not think against their emotions or even in relation with them. We all think through our feelings. Such insights show that everything that an educator, whether teacher or parent, does has an influence, especially as the brain of a child is undergoing rapid growth and transformation:

There isn't an exclusive brain area that determines intelligence, nor is there one for emotions or social skills. Scientific knowledge on this issue is crystal clear—cognitive, emotional, and social competence evolve hand in hand. When a supportive environment is provided, the emerging structure is sound, and all parts work together.[31]

We know that decision making, problem solving, creativity, role play, repetition, rehearsal, the performing arts, and social relationships are essential for strong connections between limbic system (the seat of our emotions) and the cortex. A rich physical environment with movement and stimulation and a rich emotional environment are also necessary for the lobes in the cortex to develop well. Our decision-making circuit doesn't actually complete its development until we are well into our 20s. So social-emotional learning has deep relationship to our growth over time, and a certain age-appropriate awareness is required by adults who take on a responsibility for nurturing children.

Creating conditions for social and emotional education

'The need for change from narrow nationalism to universalism, from ethnic and cultural prejudice to tolerance, understanding and pluralism, from autocracy to democracy in its various manifestations ... places enormous responsibilities on teachers...'.[32] As argued in the Mckinsey report,[33] society expects much from its educators, and those countries, such as Finland and Korea, who give their teachers the status the vocation deserves are those which are most successful in certain educational terms. Much is spoken about the knowledge economy by governments and business, and in the media, but it is just as well to remember Rabelais's warning from the sixteenth century, that 'Knowledge without conscience is but the ruin of the soul.' Our knowledge has responsibilities attached to it, and the more accessible and wide-ranging it becomes, the more complex become our moral choices. Knowledge that works in a healthy conjunction with our emotions can become wisdom. Social and emotional education is value based in that it is perceived that in a given cultural or social context, some emotions are preferable to others. When dealing with other people, love is preferable to hatred. Aggressive self-assertion is not a passport to well-being for either the community or for oneself. Emotional literacy involves being able to work with, and even transform, emotions when relating to others. An attitude of understanding, tolerance, solidarity, empathy, and ultimately compassion can be practised and learnt. We can develop skills that enable us to reflect both in and on our actions, and find new ways of being. Teachers are the agents of change.

There is the possibility of significantly changing the educational landscape, as researchers consider how human beings interact with each other, that goes beyond purely cognitive theories of human nature. 'One way forward is to reinforce the socialization functions of schools and to recognize more explicitly their nature as communities in their own right. ...[I]t suggests acknowledgment of a comprehensive set of educational outcomes going beyond measurable standards.'[34] True leadership is service that involves personal emotional development too, and that sometimes requires an element of selflessness or even sacrifice. The great Polish educator Janusz Korczak, who perished voluntarily alongside the orphaned children in his care in Treblinka in 1942, wrote: 'Find your own way. Learn to know yourself before you know children. It is a mistake to believe that education is a science of children and not of man.'[35] In other words, to work with children positively and successfully we also have to know ourselves. Much depends upon the personality of the educator, whether parent or teacher, and all professional trainings and development through experience have consequences for who we are as individuals; and it is to this quality of developing personal integrity to which children are sensitive.

This may sound radical to some, but the narrative of social-emotional leaning is radical and transformative. The teacher as an agent of change is not only a reflective teacher, but one who will act according to the outcome of these reflections. Persuasion is the least effective mode of changing behaviour and attitudes; active attainment and modelling are far more powerful. Creating a caring environment in the school and being consistent are essential foundations, especially at a time when schools are being asked to play a greater semi-parental role in society, and with values being demanded that are conducive to the children acquiring good citizenship skills and constructive values.

This entails a transparency of purpose, well formulated and accountable forms of decision making, taking the views of all stake-holders seriously, and welcoming all who wish to be involved and carry responsibilities. In other words, making the school itself into a learning community in which all who wish have the opportunity to participate, thus creating shared values and understandings that enable individuals and groups to trust each other and work together. There is, of course, risk involved: what worked in one place might not work in another, and emotions have, by definition, the quality of constant movement. Nevertheless, 'Au fond de l'Inconnu pour trouver du nouveau' (Baudelaire: 'In the depths of the unknown, we will find the new') is true of all creative processes. Teaching and living happily in a changing social community is a creative art. To work in this area of endeavour, we have to look at and develop ourselves, and not regard the children as objects to whom we just deliver knowledge and precepts.

School as a learning community

Parenting has become an increasingly complex task, as traditional structures disappear, to be replaced by smaller and often more fluid family units, more mobile life-styles, a tendency for both partners to be in work, and the general pressures of modern life impinging on family relationships. Consequently, the welfare of the child in a rapidly changing society requires all agencies to co-operate in a meaningful and insightful manner. Families need to be to be appropriately involved in the schooling of their children by right, as they are the child's first and primary educators. Time and organizational energy need to be invested in finding ways for their positive participation. Schools following these routes have found that it pays dividends in many unforeseen and supportive ways. If all the adults caring and carrying responsibility for the education and upbringing of children could consider themselves as 'co-educators', then the barriers between those with professional skills and those within the family context can become more permeable, to the advantage of the child. Supportive families are vital in order for most children to do well at school, and in an age of many patchwork families, the school community can end up needing greater sensitivity and skills, compared to the previous times of comparative social stability. Emotional literacy is required from more than just the immediate circle of people around the child, and the healthy partnership between family and school can be determinative of a child's future. If social-emotional learning respects the education of the 'whole child', which seeks to integrate all facets of being fully human, then the whole social, moral, and natural environment plays a role.

Developing **emotional** competence—learning to regulate one's emotions, behaviours, and attention, and **social** competence—learning to relate well to other children and forming friendships—partly depends on two aspects of the child's upbringing. Success is influenced by a child's history of relationships with primary caregivers and other children, as well as the child's own physical and mental health. Learning to take another's perspective is formed by interplay with others at home, kindergarten, and school; 'They are important predictors of a child's ability to get along with peers and the adults in their lives, to learn effectively and ultimately to succeed in school.'[36] This begins in babyhood, when 'Wonder is the first of all the passions';[37] and the more this sense of wonder can be enlivened and not dissipated throughout schooling, the more chance there is of remaining open to new emotional experiences and, accordingly, developing empathetic understanding. A child needs to understand her own feelings in order to recognize those in others. Some emotions are more appropriate in certain situations than others, and a capacity for adjustment has to be learnt. Emotions are the inner equivalent of outer movements, and handling them is likewise a skill. By accepting that all learning has an emotional component and that we live in an increasingly fragmented and tense world, where the ability to co-operate becomes essential for our survival as a species, we are setting a new challenge to schools and placing a redefined responsibility on educators.

The Alliance for Childhood[38]

We are not only faced with new challenges in our social relationships with each other, but also with our relationship to the planet itself: 'Among the most important learning that schooling provides of relevance to sustainability are the attributes of critical thinking, self-reflection, media analysis, personal and group decision making and problem solving.'[39] We are witnessing an enormous growth of travel possibilities as well a great familiarity, at one level, with other cultures than our own. These tendencies are loosely termed 'globalization', which some see as creating new opportunities, and others as a threat to social coherence:

> Globalisation, because of the risk it brings of soulless standardi-
> sation, can lead to fragmentation and a reduced sense of belong-
> ing to a wider community. The excess of unbridled markets …
> [is] being met with an excess of nationalism, regionalism and
> parochialism. These threaten peace and raise the spectre of
> resurgent racism and intolerance.[40]

Our children face an age of hyper-complexity, and this has implications for how we assist them now in developing the competencies that will be demanded of them in the future. Unfortunately, there are also tendencies and social influences that work against this, and awareness of these multiple issues becomes the basis for any possibility of betterment. We cannot convince anybody to change their opinions, but we can help open the gates of perception and turn advocates into activists.

In April 2007, the European Commissioner for Freedom, Security, and Justice, Franco Frattini, announced that 'families and schools are in crisis' in Europe, not just the UK. Faced with all these symptoms, is it any wonder that people turn to early childhood centres and schools to help find the solutions? Yet dealing with these questions goes beyond the capacities of the State. It falls to the organs of civic society to develop awareness, disseminate research, activate change, and collaborate in bringing the urgency of the situation to the fore. A network of quality of childhood advocates that spans the globe, regardless of cultural or philosophical backgrounds, is attempting to do just that. Not by producing litanies of complaint that evoke a bygone golden age of childhood, because for many of the world's children that did not exist. But rather, by exploring the roots of our problems, and by sharing our common human sense of responsibility, those involved in such networks as the Alliance are looking for creative ways of improving the general well-being of children.

The nature of the questions on this subject will, of course, differ from country to country and from culture to culture, but our experience has shown that by concentrating our minds and hearts on this theme, we can cross all boundaries, whether ethnic, historical, national, or cultural. As colleagues, we can inspire each other and elicit new insights and remedies. The suffering of so many children in an age of such technological prowess is unconscionable, and it is not beyond our powers to make a positive difference. The plight of children who face impoverishment, abuse, inadequate healthcare, violence, and starvation has to occupy our conscience as much as the dilemmas and paradoxes of affluent societies, and the role of schooling and education. By networking, sharing, and taking an interest in each other's activities, we can find the strength and courage needed. Working for childhood enables people to find the buried roots of childhood optimism and hope in themselves, and draws the best out of us. By putting energy into free co-operation, and not into the complexities of the founding and funding of yet another organization, our personal resources can focus on the task in hand. A network is an ephemeral and a constantly changing phenomenon, but precisely in that condition it reflects our sense of wonder and imagination.

Paulo Freire puts this approach passionately in his seminal *Pedagogy of the Oppressed*:

> When a word is deprived of its dimension of action, reflection automatically suffers as well, and the word is changed into

idle chatter. ... It becomes an empty word, one which cannot denounce the world, for denunciation is impossible without a commitment to transform, and there is no transformation without action.[41]

By sharing our concerns and celebrating our successes in freedom, without the constrictions of self-justification or organizational ambition, we can find, in ourselves as adults, the resources that can contribute to childhood well-being. Although Freire was mainly concerned with the milieus of deprivation, disadvantage, and poverty in Sao Paulo, his words ring true because nearly 40 years later, we can see too many children facing new forms of disadvantage and lack in so-called prosperous societies too.

A global effort of civil society is called for to complement the activities of Inter-Governmental Organizations and national policies: 'The pursuit of full humanity, however, cannot be carried out in isolation or individualism, but only in fellowship and solidarity.'[42] Working on social and emotional education for our children means also working on ourselves.

Postscript

Some of the body of this text is extracted from Christopher Clouder's introduction to *Social and Emotional Education: An International Analysis* (2008) and is reproduced by the kind permission of the Fundación Marcelino Botin. This introduction and full report which describes the situation in six other countries, including the UK, and containing an evaluation of recent meta-analysis, can be found on: www.socialandemotionaleducation.com

Notes and References

1. Innocenti Report Card 7. Geneva: UNICEF, 2007.
2. Children and Young People Today: Evidence to Support the Development of the Children's Plan. London: Department of Children, Schools and Families, HMSO, January, 2007.
3. *The Depression Report—A New Deal for Depression and Anxiety Disorders*. London: London School of Economics, Centre for Economic Performance, 2006.
4. *Journal of Child Psychology and Psychiatry*, November 2004.

5. C. Richardson, *The Truth about Self-Harm*. London: Mental Health Foundation, 2006.
6. *Child and Adolescent Mental Health*. London: British Medical Association, 2006.
7. Innocenti Report Card 7. Geneva: UNICEF, 2007.
8. S. Palmer, *Toxic Childhood*. London: Orion Books, 2006.
9. B. Langer, Consuming anomie: children and global commercial culture. *Childhood*, 12 2005, p. 295.
10. A. Nairn & P. Ormrod, *Watching, Wanting and Wellbeing: Exploring the Links*. London: National Consumer Council, 2007.
11. Compass, *The Commercialisation of Childhood*. London, 2006.
12. H. Phillips, Mind-altering media. *New Scientist*, 21 April, 2007.
13. D. Christakis & F.J. Zimmerman, Violent television viewing is associated with antisocial behaviour during school age. *Pediatrics*, 120 (November), 2007, pp. 993–999.
14. A. Fielder, W. Gardener, A. Nairn, & F. Pitt, *Fair Game*. London: National Consumer Council & Childnet International, December 2007.
15. Robin Alexander, quoted in Polly Curtis, Study reveals stressed out 7–11 year-olds. The *Guardian*, 12 October 2007.
16. N. Noddings, *The Challenge of Care in Schools*. New York: Teachers College Press, 1992, p. 173.
17. N. Noddings, *Happiness and Education*. Cambridge: Cambridge University Press, 2003, p. 36.
18. Clare Tickell, quoted in John Carvel, Survey finds 1 in 4 teenagers depressed. The *Guardian*, Thursday 24 April 2008.
19. *Learning: The Treasure Within: Report to UNESCO of the International Commission on Education for the Twenty-first Century*. Paris: UNESCO, 1996, p. 59; see also *Learning Throughout Life: Challenges for the Twenty-first Century*. Paris: UNESCO, 2002.
20. J. Delors & A. Draxler, *Defining and Selecting Competencies*. Göttingen: Hogrefe & Huber, 2001, p. 214.
21. E. Morin, *Seven Complex Lessons in Education for the Future*. Paris: UNESCO, 2001, p. 94.
22. *What Schools for the Future*. Paris: OECD, 2001, p. 52.
23. Martin Luther King Jr., in his speech 'Facing the challenges of a new age', delivered in Montgomery, Alabama on 3 December 1956; see http://www.worldfamilyorganization.org/archive/editorial/news-editorial-06-05.html
24. *KronbergDeclaration*, http://www.futureknowledge.org/background/.Kronberg-declaration.pdf
25. *Freedom's Orphans*. London: IPPR, 2007.

26. John Dewey, My pedagogical creed. *School Journal*, 54 (January), 1897.
27. D. Goleman, *Emotional Intelligence*. London: Bloomsbury, 1995, p. 34.
28. D, Goleman, *Working with Emotional Intelligence*. London: Bloomsbury, 1998, p. 24.
29. K. Weare, *Developing the Emotionally Literate School*. London: Paul Chapman, 2004, p. 2.
30. A. Damásio, *O Sentimento de Si—O corpo, a emoção e a neurobiologia da consciência*. Lisboa: Publicações Europa-América, 2000, p. 62; cited by Maria do Céu Roldão in *How Useful is Imagination?* Vancouver: IERG Conference, 16–19 July 2000.
31. J.P. Schonkoff, *Science, Policy and the Young Developing Child*. Chicago, 2004; cited in Zigler & others, *A Vision for Universal Preschool Education*. Cambridge: Cambridge University Press, 2006, p. 134.
32. *Learning: the Treasure Within*. Paris: UNESCO, 1996, p. 141.
33. How the world's best performing schools systems come out on top. McKinsey & Co. (http://www.mckinsey.com/), 2007; cited in *The Economist*, 18 October 2007.
34. *What Schools for the Future*. Paris: OECD, 2001, p. 217.
35. J. Korczak, How to love a child. In: M. Wolins (Ed.), *Selected Works of Janusz Korczak*. Washington, D.C.: National Science Foundation, 1967, p. 248; originally published 1919.
36. E. Zigler, W.Gilliam, & S.M. Jones, *A Vision for Universal Preschool Education*. Cambridge: Cambridge University Press, 2006, p. 244.
37. R. Descartes, *The Passions of The Soul*. Article 53, 1645.
38. www.allianceforchildhood.org.uk
39. *Preparing Youth for the 21st Century*. Paris: OECD, 1999, p. 20.
40. Alain Michel, in *What Schools for the Future*. Paris: OECD, 2001, p. 217.
41. Paulo Freire, *Pedagogy of the Oppressed*. Harmondsworth: Penguin, 1996, p. 68.
42. Ibid., p. 66.

CHAPTER FIVE

The Good Childhood: An inquiry by the Children's Society

Bob Reitemeier

Introduction

The Children's Society launched The Good Childhood Inquiry in the autumn of 2006 and its findings were published in early 2009 (Layard & Dunn, 2009). It represents the United Kingdom's first independent inquiry into what makes for a good childhood.

The basic premise for establishing the Inquiry was that the way in which children today experience childhood has changed significantly, even from our own experiences, but certainly from our parents' and grandparents' experiences. These changes cover a broad spectrum, and include aspects such as technological advancements, family structure, and mental health.

New technology has led to vast changes in communications, where the mobile phone and the internet are now largely taken for granted by children, and continue to evolve at a pace with which few adults can keep up. From 1972 to 2004, the proportion of children in the UK living in single-parent families more than tripled to 24 per cent, the highest proportion in Europe.[1] Some 20 per cent of children have mental-health problems at some point,[2] and one in ten have a clinically recognizable mental-health disorder. Up to one in twelve British children deliberately hurt themselves on a regular basis, again the highest rate in Europe.[3]

The confusion surrounding childhood is a result of the contradictions and uncertainty that we demonstrate in our relations with children. On the one hand, we see children and young people as vulnerable and in need of protection, while on the other, we see them as a threat to society. To address this, we need to understand the context within which children experience their formative years.

At the same time we must also recognize the positive developments in the UK, such as increased life expectancy, and reduction in childhood diseases and mortality. However, the nature of change seems to indicate that just as old problems are tackled, new ones emerge. The Children's Society felt that it would be a dereliction of duty to ignore the calls for a national debate on childhood.

Why now?

Research points to dramatic differences in today's world. A significant number of academics and authors have written about how childhood is changing, and how difficult life can be for many children in the UK today. Examples include Richard Layard's work on happiness,[4] showing that although we are much wealthier than previous generations, we are no happier. The Nuffield Foundation's Seminars on Children and Families[5] describe significant levels of anxiety and depression amongst the teenage population. The Unicef Report[6] by Jonathan Bradshaw compares relative well-being for children across 21 OECD countries, with the UK coming in dead last.

The Children's Society has felt for some time that we need to stop and revisit what childhood means to all of us in society. Our organizational values lead us to put children and young people at the centre of society, and this will require a fundamental shift in the way in which we view, engage with, and value children and young people. The purpose of The Good Childhood Inquiry is, therefore, to help improve childhood in the UK today. It attempts to inspire all our relationships with children.

It is crucial for us to consider childhood in a holistic manner. The Good Childhood Inquiry covers the age group 0–18, and rather than concentrating on one specific area of children's lives, the Inquiry addresses six major themes: friends, family, learning, life-style, health, and values. These themes were designed to provide structure to the Inquiry's exploration of childhood.

Friends

We looked at how children and young people interact with their peers, and what activities and relationships give them pleasure and meaning. We explored how friends and peers influence their behaviour and aspirations in positive and negative ways, such as bullying.

Family

We looked at the family, its various forms and circumstances, and the primary relationships and attachments that shape children and young people's lives. We asked how families can be supported to provide a loving, supportive, and stable environment in which children and young people can grow.

Learning

We looked at the different ways in which children and young people learn, and develop a sense of wonder, alongside the quality and purpose of their education. We also explored how children develop and socialize, how they acquire skills and knowledge, and form attitudes and aspirations.

Health

We looked at children and young people as individuals, focussing on their health, mental health, personality, and behaviours. We considered their sense of self and worth, and how they feel about themselves. And we also asked how they could be supported to adopt behaviours that are good for their present and future well-being.

Life-style

We considered children and young people's place in the material world, their growing role as consumers, and the attitudes and values that shape the way they choose to live their lives. We also considered how new technologies have changed the things that children and young people do, the spaces that they inhabit, and the ways in which they communicate.

Values

We looked at how children and young people form values, beliefs, and faith, and find meaning and a sense of purpose in life. We asked how they view the world and those around them, and how the world views them. In looking at children's values, we also looked at values throughout society and how children learn from adults. We considered how children can be supported to develop a sense of wonder, and a sense of responsibility for others, and to participate in social, cultural, and political life.

The themes were identified through careful consultation with children, young people, and adults, through our knowledge of working with children and also by drawing on the expertise of our Inquiry panel.

The panel met some ten times over approximately 18 months during 2007 and 2008. Six of these meetings addressed each of the six chosen themes, and the remaining four meetings comprised the introductory session and three summary and concluding sessions. The panel meetings combined oral evidence and discussion and debate by the panel members. Oral evidence was provided by individuals and organizations requested by the panel. Each of the six themed meetings included oral evidence presented by children and young people from England, Scotland, Wales, and Northern Ireland. All four Children's Commissioners from Scotland, Northern Ireland, Wales, and England, as well as the Director of the Children's Research Centre, Trinity College Dublin, attended one of the summary sessions.

For each panel meeting, briefing papers were presented which covered:

- A summary of the views of children and young people for each theme from the call for evidence and from the BBC TV Programme, 'Newsround' (with whom The Children's Society has a partnership on the Inquiry);

- A summary of the views of adults and professionals for each theme from the call for evidence; and
- A set of papers highlighting key research findings for each theme.

All papers were available on The Children's Society's website at the time of publication of The Good Childhood Inquiry's Report.

Professor Judith Dunn, Professor of Developmental Psychology, Institute of Psychiatry, King's College London, chaired the panel. Panel members, in alphabetical order, included:

- **Professor Sir Albert Aynsley-Green**, Children's Commissioner for England
- **Dr Mohammed Abdul Bari**, General Secretary of the Muslim Council of Britain
- **Shami Chakrabarti**, Director, Liberty
- **Jim Davis**, Programme Manager, Children's Participation Project Wessex, The Children's Society
- **Professor Philip Graham**, Emeritus Professor of Child Psychiatry, Institute of Child Health
- **Professor Kathleen Kiernan**, Professor of Social Policy and Demography, University of York
- **Professor Lord Richard Layard**, Emeritus Professor of Economics, Institute of Economic Performance, London School of Economics
- **Professor Barbara Maughan**, Institute of Psychiatry, Kings College London
- **Dr Stephen Scott**, Department of Child and Adolescent Psychiatry, Institute of Psychiatry, King's College London
- **The Right Reverend Tim Stevens**, Bishop of Leicester
- **Professor Kathy Sylva**, Professor of Educational Psychology, Oxford Centre for Research into Parenting and Children, University of Oxford.

The patron of the Inquiry was The Right Reverend Dr Rowan Williams, Archbishop of Canterbury.

The involvement of children and young people in the inquiry

Over 125 years of The Children's Society's experience of working directly with children and young people significantly influenced the organizational thinking behind The Good Childhood Inquiry. One of the main reasons The Children's Society decided to undertake a challenge as extensive as The Good Childhood Inquiry was that we believed very strongly that the Inquiry needed to be conducted, and the findings written, from the perspective of children and young people. An organization like The Children's Society, which has a long and rich history in the field of children and young people's participation, was well placed to ensure that this was the approach taken.

In an adult-centred world such as ours, it is far too easy to fall back into the normal pattern of looking at children's issues as they affect adults, rather than through the eyes of the child. The reality is that society in the UK is far from attaining the 'child-centred' approach as promoted by policy documents such as the UK Government Department for Children, Schools and Families' *Every Child Matters* and *The Children's Plan*. The Good Childhood Inquiry was designed to provide tangible evidence and recommendations for action, which are truly child-centred.

In establishing the Inquiry, children and young people were involved in a national survey conducted by The Children's Society of 11,000 young people aged 14–16 in 16 different geographic areas of England in 2005, of which 8,000 responded to our questions concerning childhood. The survey was conducted in partnership with the University of York, and we also commissioned an NOP survey of 1,000 children and young people, and 1,000 adults in 2006. These findings were critical in informing how we framed the Inquiry's six themes. In both cases, the following questions were addressed:

- What do you think are the most important things that make for a good life for young people?
- What things do you think stop young people from having a good life?

In addition, over 700 children and young people responded directly to the call for evidence, and thousands more submitted their views through the two ongoing channels for soliciting their input: the BBC 'Newsround' surveys and The Children's Society's 'My Life' website and postcards.

What have children and young people told us?

Findings from the 8,000 young people who completed the national survey highlighted three cross cutting themes:

1. *Quality of Relationships*: Young people highly valued the love and care they receive by the people they want to love and care for them. They emphasized the support and advice they get from both family and friends. They appreciate the education and learn-ing they acquire about general life and a better understanding about people who are different from them.

   Young People also spoke of the importance of positive relation-ships in terms of being treated fairly. A very strong sense of fair-ness came out in much of what they said. They felt that people should respect other people in their community, and that people should respect other religions and promote the equality of all members of society.

2. *Safety*: Young people mentioned how their childhood was affected by crime, bullying, drugs, anti-social behaviour, racism, sexism, and having little or no money. They felt that they should not have to live in areas with high crime rates. They wanted to be treated 'right' by adults. They felt that it was wrong that they had to live in fear of druggies, drunks, gangs, and kiddie fiddlers (their words).

3. *Freedom*: The first two cross-cutting themes of relationships and safety are issues that adults would also raise. The third theme of freedom was more surprising, and demonstrated, in our view, the thoughtfulness of today's youth. Freedom was expressed as having freedom in what they think, say, and do; freedom to enjoy their lives and make their own decisions. This included making their own mistakes so they can learn from them. They were concerned about the age restrictions that are applied in childhood, and felt that adults were sometimes 'stopping' free will.

Family and friends

In addition to the three cross-cutting themes, the two most common topics mentioned were family and friends. In referring to family, many young people focused on the above issues—relationships, safety and freedom—and raised the potential for tension in providing these conditions. They also mentioned the importance of stability and security in the family.

Young people left no doubt as to the significance of friendships in their lives. They told us that spending time with their friends is very important to them, and that their friends are a valuable source of support. Not having friends, not being able to spend time with their friends, or falling out with them were all things that they felt inhibited a good childhood.

Interestingly, although young people cited friends as being a critical aspect of a good childhood, when adults were asked the same question, the importance of friendship was rarely mentioned.

Even further, when directly asked about one aspect of friendship—unsupervised play with friends—adults showed an extremely cautious side to their views. The Children's Society conducted a survey which asked the best age for children to be allowed out with friends unsupervised. Most respondents (43 per cent) said aged 14 or over, despite the fact that most of them had been allowed out without an adult at the much younger age of 10 or under. Respondents over the age of 60 went even further, with 22 per cent saying children should be over 16 before going out alone.[7]

As adults, we need to recognize this inconsistency, and look to ways in which we can not only allow, but encourage our children to play with their friends, unsupervised when appropriate, as it represents a valuable space for learning—something that most of us can remember benefiting from ourselves.

These differing responses also highlight the need for society to consider the world through the eyes of a child. Often, adults can become overly concerned with focussing on the skills needed to become a 'successful' adult, forgetting the importance of allowing children the time and space to enjoy simply being a child. If we are to successfully create a vision of childhood for the twenty-first century, we need to view childhood as an exercise in 'well-being' as well as 'well-becoming'.

Adults often underestimate the role friends play in childhood, yet research shows that early friendships are linked to the development of social and emotional understanding, and to moral sensibility. It must be acknowledged, however, that the importance of friendship was clearly recognized by many of the professionals who responded to The Good Childhood Inquiry's call for evidence.

Several of the submissions by professionals commented on the importance of friendships to children's development, including the value in having friends from diverse backgrounds.[8] The need for children to have space to play where they could set their own agendas was also frequently mentioned.

School and learning

Whilst family and friends were very important to the young people surveyed, so also was education. A good quality of education was cited by many as one of the key factors of a good childhood. Young people also recognized the importance of their own commitment to working hard and achieving for their future well-being. However, this generally positive picture was balanced by substantial comment about the negative impact of school pressure. Over half (58 per cent) of young people surveyed were worried about their exams at school, and almost half (47 per cent) said they often worried about schoolwork.[9]

There were both positive and negative comments about teachers. Positive comments emphasized support, help, and understanding; negative comments tended to refer to pressure at school. Finally, there was comment about the importance of wider learning about life and the need for positive role models. These findings throw up some interesting questions for education professionals, and the role they can play in creating good childhoods. For example, friendships play a key supportive role for children starting school, who adjust to the challenges more successfully if they start with a friend, and for those making transitions later in the school years. One submission drew on a survey of 2,527 primary and secondary school children in the north-west of England to illustrate how important friendship is to children. When the children were asked what makes them happy at school, 63 per cent stated that it was their friends, while 14 per cent said that what made them unhappy at school was falling out with their friends.[10]

The issue of bullying was raised in a number of submissions as a major and concerning issue. Several submissions drew attention to the fact that children who are perceived as being 'different' are more likely to be involved in bullying, either as victims or bullies.[11] Responses to bullying tend to focus on the role of schools and parents in promoting positive values.

The Children's Plan, cultural change, and the most disadvantaged

In the period between the launch and the publication of the findings of The Good Childhood Inquiry, 'The Children's Plan' was published by the British Government's Department for Children, Schools and Families (December 2007). In it, the Government set out its 10-year plan for making, '… this the best place in the world for our children and young people to grow up'.

This level of ambition should be acknowledged and applauded. And whilst we applaud, we should continuously remind ourselves of our role: to share in and support this ambition by providing evidence and insight into the world of children, and by holding the Government to account when they fail to grasp the opportunities presented, or allow the 'children's agenda' to be side-tracked.

The Children's Plan comes at a time when all sections of society are increasingly interested in childhood, fuelled by a mixture of real concern and a desire to rethink what childhood should be about. There are high expectations of the Children's Plan, not least because there is a growing acknowledgement that for all our carefully crafted policy and legislation, the experience of childhood has become impoverished for many children. Longer working hours, fears for safety, lack of freedom to roam, growing drug and alcohol problems, all contribute to this. While children themselves are more protected than before, the space of childhood is being eroded.

So what can the Government actually *do* about childhood? To what extent is the problem of childhood in modern-day Britain a cultural issue rather than a policy issue? Policy change is clearly within the Government's power—but underlying the Children's Plan is an idea that we want a different sort of childhood for our children, which means that a deeper cultural change is required. The question for the Government must be, how far can policy result in cultural change?

It is crucial that the Government keeps to its promise to eliminate child poverty. Everything we know about poverty tells us that children who could otherwise succeed in life will fail because of poverty. Children will do less well at school, suffer worse health, have worse jobs, get more depressed, and feel less in control of their lives because they live in poverty.

The plan's commitment to providing universal support for parents is welcomed. How parents became side-lined from the children's agenda is a mystery to many of us, but putting them at the heart of the plan demonstrates the importance of family in tackling children's well-being. But these commitments need to be matched with targeted support for some of the least popular children, and a move to start treating them as children first. This means, for example, ending the practice of locking up children in prison for minor offences or imprisoning children who have serious mental illnesses, or putting an end to the practice of keeping refugee children in custody for no other reason than they have fled their home country for their own safety.

These policy issues don't exist in a vacuum. They are part of a complex picture that includes our voting system, populist politics, and the culture of childhood we have created. The idea, as the Archbishop of Canterbury Rowan Williams put it, of childhood being a place where you are permitted to make mistakes—even very serious ones—is vanishing rapidly. Instead, we are too quick to condemn and judge. This is true of sections of the media, and is reflected in the hostility and fear that surrounds young people.

One of the positive sub texts of the Children's Plan is that it acknowledges that the space of childhood should be elevated. Hence there's a welcome commitment in the Children's Plan to restrict advertising to children, and to reduce the emphasis on testing. There's also an understanding that tackling poverty means opening up learning opportunities to all children. These initiatives tell us that we want childhood to be different to what it has become. We want childhood to be free from some of the stresses that the public world imposes on our children. A holistic approach requires a cultural change, not just in the way that the Government acts, but in the way it wants the public to act.

This cultural change is what we at The Children's Society warmly welcome. It's a change we ourselves are working towards through The Good Childhood Inquiry. But cultural change is complicated territory. In an age of high expectations and a desire for immediate results, this type of change is in many ways an unattractive proposition to politicians. Cultural change is difficult to measure, takes time, and can be costly. Cultural momentum is difficult to both maintain and control.

The optimist in me hopes that the more holistic view of children identified in the plan will open up a more sympathetic response to help children who are most in need—those in prison, or who are being detained in immigration centres, and those who are trapped in poverty.

By its very nature, The Good Childhood Inquiry looks at childhood for all children. However, another key reason that The Children's Society embarked on this initiative was to ensure that those children on the margins of society, those excluded from what we would deem normal activities and a normal experience, those whose childhood has been stolen from them, were also represented in the Inquiry. We mentioned at the time of the Inquiry's launch that only a quarter of the 60,000 children in care achieve any educational qualifications, and that half of all prisoners under 25 have been through the care system.[12] This reminds us of a depressing reality—that too many children living in care are subject to a double disadvantage. These vulnerable children have to deal not only with the traumatic events that lead to them being in care, but also with a system that then fails them.

This is equally a reminder that responsibility for childhood belongs to us all. If we are to really succeed in improving childhood for all children, including those living on the margins or in the care system, it is crucial that we listen to their views and expertise.

Shaping the future

As a leading children's charity, we believe that we have a duty to lead the way in questioning why so many children in the UK are still experiencing poor childhoods. They are neither able to enjoy their present childhood nor develop in order to reach their potential. At all times, a child is both a child in the hear-and-now, and a future adult. Both of these aspects of childhood need to be nurtured and celebrated.

Our ambition is that the Inquiry will have a far-reaching impact on children's lives in the twenty-first century. Through The Good

Childhood we have opened an inclusive public debate about the nature of childhood today. But creating discussion is only the first step, and rather than simply acting as a talk-shop, the Inquiry's findings are evidence-based, it includes the voices and views of children themselves, and it identifies existing obstacles which are preventing children from experiencing a good childhood and makes recommendations for change.

The inquiry's findings have been made available to the public and have been presented so that it is accessible and relevant to parents, teachers, community leaders, and, importantly, to children and young people themselves. For The Good Childhood to be successful, it must resonate with the public and provide a platform for action. It will only be through working together—with the public, the academics, the voluntary sector, the policy makers, the media, and importantly with the children and young people themselves—that we will succeed in creating a better world for all children.

Notes and References

1. The Health of Children and Young People. National Statistics, March 2004.
2. CAMHS Outcomes Research Consortium, National CAMHS dataset, Supporting information needs for child and adolescent mental health services. Dunstable: Durocobrivis Publications, 2004.
3. Mental Health Foundation, *Truth Hurts: Report of the National Inquiry into Self-harm among Young People.* London: Mental Health Foundation, 2006.
4. Richard Layard, *Happiness: Lessons from a New Science.* Penguin: Harmondsworth, 2005.
5. Ann Hagell, *Time Trends in Adolescent Well-being.* London: The Nuffield Foundation, 2004.
6. Report Card 7, Child Poverty in Perspective: An Overview of Child Well-being in Rich Countries. Innocenti Research Centre, Unicef, 2007.
7. Reflections on Childhood—friends poll conducted by GfK NOP in 2007. GfK NOP conducted a total of 1,148 interviews with a representative sample of UK representatives aged 18 or over.
8. The Children's Society, The Good Childhood Inquiry: Evidence Summary One—Friends. London, 2007.

9. Good Childhood? A question for our times. The Children's Society's National Survey of 8,000 14 to 16-year olds, conducted in 2005.
10. J. Whittaker, John Kenworthy, and Colin Crabtree, What Children Say About School, University of Bolton, 1998; available at: http://www.inclusion-boltondata.org.uk/FrontPage/data24.htm
11. The Children's Society, The Good Childhood Inquiry: Evidence Summary One—Friends. London, 2007.
12. Centre for Policy Studies, *Handle with Care: An Investigation into the Care System*. London, 2006.

Reference

Layard, R., & Dunn, J. (2009). *A Good Childhood: Searching for Values in a Competitive Age*. Harmondsworth: Penguin.

PART II

CHILDHOOD AND ITS DISCONTENTS: THE SPECIFIC CONCERNS

CHAPTER SIX

Childhood 'toxicity' and 'trauma': Asking the right questions

Ricky Emanuel

From the perspective I hold working as a psychoanalytic child and adolescent psychotherapist in the NHS and as Clinical Lead of CAMHS services in Central London, I have wondered whether it is true that children's childhoods are in fact more toxic than they have ever been before. It may be helpful in this context if I choose to define 'toxic' in relation to the notion of what supports development, and what impedes or perverts it. As I wrote this chapter, my perspective was influenced by the fact that I was involved with the police in investigating a sexual assault by a youth gang on one of my patients, which is so gross and in the police's view unprecedented in their experience, that it feels like we are in the midst of depravity and amorality which is reminiscent of the biblical Sodom and Gomorrah.

Some of the elements of the toxicity perhaps can be traced to a sense of chronic helplessness and loss of control that people feel in their lives. They feel they are being 'lived by' others, rather than living, controlled by outside forces like the media, peer, and other educational pressures and so on, which Sue Palmer describes in Chapter 3. Many people live in states characterized by reactivity rather than with a more proactive sense of making choices in their lives. This means that children cannot easily find meaning in things around them or in their experiences, and this itself does not pre-dispose them to a resilient facing of adversity. They become cynical and preoccupied with quick fixes to alleviate the incipient pain of living. These quick fixes are short-acting short circuits, and as such tend to lead on to quick repetition until habituation sets in, and more extreme fixes are needed.

We know that however toxic the experiences may be, the capac-ity to find meaning in them, to be able to reflect on them and think about them, is crucial for a resilient personality. This capacity derives from the internalization of multiple experiences of one's emotional experience being received, listened to, and thought about in an emo-tional relationship to a caregiver. In the educational sphere this can derive from what Richard North has called *authentic relational learning* (North, 1987). The internalization of an emotionally attuned relation-ship forms the basis of good mental health, and one can thus surmise that the rapid increase in mental-health problems in children may be partly attributable, in many instances, to the absence of good-enough experiences with an emotionally attuned, available caregiver. The rise in diagnoses in Attention Deficit Disorder, for example, often stems from serious deficits in attention in children's lives.

If it is true that children's lives are more toxic than ever before, it implies an inexorable increase in traumatization of our children. We know that often, traumatized children turn their own trauma into triumph, as they inflict on to others what has been done unto them with added vengeance. In trying to understand trauma and its consequences, it is vital to understand and appreciate that we can-not view toxicity and consequent traumatization only as an external event or manifestation. It is also important to try and foster experi-ences that promote development and resilience, rather than hinder it. I would want to caution, however, about a glib usage of the word 'trauma' in a similar manner to how we misuse the word 'unbear-able', and would not want to equate 'toxic childhood' with trauma-tization, although the word 'toxic' suggests this. Instead, I would like to reserve the use of the word 'trauma' for truly traumatic situa-tions, when childhood experience is truly toxic in the sense I defined it above, as seriously impeding or perverting development. To this end, it may be helpful in defining what I, as a psychoanalytically trained therapist, understand as the essence of trauma.

We all live in at least two different worlds, our own internal worlds of subjective psychic realty and a shared external world. In the course of development, we manage to differentiate them, although our perception of each of the worlds is influenced by the other. Traumatic experiences tend to conflate the two worlds, so that it becomes extremely difficult to maintain any differentiation between what goes on in our body/minds and what happens in the external world. This is one of the sequellae of trauma, so that if a child conflates the realities of screen life with real life, one may speculate on the presence of trauma.

There is a large body of literature on the subject of trauma and its consequences from many perspectives (Garland, 2002), so I am not going to try and summarize this here. However, there are several core elements present in any traumatic situation that I find helpful in defining it as such.

Sigmund Freud described the essence of trauma as an experience of *helplessness* of the ego, where the level of emotional arousal cannot be processed by the ordinary defence mechanisms usually deployed by the ego in managing anxiety (Freud, 1926). Trauma thus presupposes the body/mind being flooded or overwhelmed by the emotional and sensory aspects of the experience. Emotions need to be regulated by the mental apparatus responsible for processing them, but if this is overwhelmed or undeveloped, then trauma ensues, and a state of emotional dysregulation is the result. The mental representation of this dysregulated state becomes part of the encoded experience of the trauma. People will do anything they can to avoid re-experiencing states like these, which can feel life threatening, especially with trauma in infancy. Trauma thus causes acute and then sometimes chronic anxieties of varying sorts.

The capacity to make judgements in a given situation, and to use past experience, is a crucial ego function which can be disabled or damaged in traumatic situations and their sequellae. Psychotherapy attempts to repair this function so that the person does not seem so dominated by automatic ways of responding.

The capacity to cope with anxiety in a growth-enhancing manner depends, as we know, on whether the anxiety can be contained or regulated. This is true of all anxiety, from mild to severe. We particularly need others to help regulate anxiety in early childhood, as attachment theory or the psychoanalytic theory of container/contained implies (Bion, 1962; Emanuel, 1996). In a situation of stress, we turn to others to regulate this emotional state. The availability of a meaning-making container or attachment figure is thus crucial. In truly toxic childhoods, we are implying that it is precisely the absence of these attachment figures or containers in their lives that could be one of the sources of the toxicity, but containment within an emotional relationship to another is also desperately needed in order to help detoxify experiences.

In the absence of a containing experience, felt as emotional dysregulation, there is the danger of over-arousal which overwhelms the person. In this circumstance, people tend to act or react, and not to able to think or to make choices. The attachment system is the basis of this biophysical regulation. A state of dysregulation is itself an inducer of fear. The possibility of being in a dysregulated state can lead to avoidance behaviour or states of dissociation or freezing, as seen in post-traumatic stress disorder.

Confusion of external and internal reality

Normally in life experiences, one's worst violent, envious, or jealous phantasies are not confirmed or corroborated by external reality. Confusion arises if what one most fears (and sometimes wishes for) actually happens. It becomes much more difficult to differentiate the essential distinction between one's inner reality (what happens in the inner world of phantasy or dreams) and what actually occurs in external or outer reality. For example, the normal oedipal conflict, between the wish completely to possess one parent and rid yourself of the other, is counterbalanced by an equally strong desire for this not to happen, and for the parents to resist their being split apart; for the couple to be protected and allowed their freedom in privacy, especially behind the bedroom door. In intrafamilial sexual abuse, these issues come to the fore, which is often why reassurance of the 'it's not your fault' kind cuts no ice. Similarly, the violent phantasies associated with sibling rivalry and the birth of a new baby are counterbalanced by more loving or curious feelings towards the new arrival. However, in situations of traumatic bereavement, for example, of a parent or sibling, these more hateful or violent phantasies seem to find corroboration in the external world, and inner reality becomes confounded with external reality, and a trauma ensures.

With this in mind, it may be helpful to be circumspect in not using too over-emotive language and generalizing the notion of the toxicity when it is also evident that there still exists an abundance of healthy, creative, and emotionally literate children in our society. Instead, let us try and reserve the term for the truly toxic situations we know some children live in, and help them find resources for dealing with them. We can do so by offering them enough experiences with an emotionally attuned available person for them to internalize these qualities so that they can make sense of their experiences, and so develop more resilience.

Case example

I am going to give you a very brief example of a child who, from his point a view, suffered from a toxic beginning to his life. He cannot at this stage recognize that it was, in fact, life saving for him.

Mark

Mark was born at 25 weeks, and spent 4½ months in a special-care baby unit. His mother found it very difficult to cope with staying with him during this time, and would only be able to visit every two days or so. Mark had to have a whole range of intrusive medical procedures, where his body was invaded from every orifice and through his soft skin. His hands are scarred by all the cannulas he had in them. He also had to have heart surgery during that time to correct a congenital defect.

Mark is now 7, and very difficult to manage. He seems stuck in his own internal world where he cannot bear to not be in control. He is aggressive towards other children if they do not do what they are told, or if they happen to venture into his airspace, which is closely monitored and guarded.

He always carries some hard objects in his pockets which he clings on to, giving him the illusion of hardness and invulnerability. In the therapy sessions he hardly relates to me. He plays obsessive torture games in the sink, whereby a hard cruel object, usually the crocodile, suspends and tosses other animals into the sink which is filled with dirty water and poison, like a malignant sewer or toilet for them to drown in. They are shown no mercy. The hard-skinned elephant is singled out for the most vicious torture. Mark takes some string and ties it to the trunk, then hangs the elephant upside down over the filthy sink, making it swing like a pendulum. He then saws away slowly at the suspending string until the elephant plops like a giant piece of faeces into the toilet sink below, to drown or be poisoned. When I ask why this is happening to them, Mark replies 'don't know' or 'no reason'. I am often struck that much of his imagery seems to derive from computer games or TV programmes which, as has been stated (e.g. in Chapter 3), can blunt and strangle real imagination.

I usually take the position of the tortured animals, verbalizing what they may be feeling, their incomprehension, rage, helplessness, and terror. I am acutely aware that they represent the most vulnerable parts of him that felt cruelly tortured for 'no reason', not knowing what he had done, and at the hands of others who show no mercy. Usually it seems Mark ignores my comments, but he is very keen to come to the sessions, and become the hardened torturer and have me witness it. My position as a witness is crucial, I think, as Mark did not feel his experience was witnessed. He bore it alone, and is now determined to turn trauma into triumph, to do it to someone else. George Orwell describes this in his book *1984* in the rat torture, where the protagonist says, don't do it to me, do it to her (in the book, to Julia).

Mark does not seem to be suffering from any inner conflict, in that he is rock hard and will not budge from this position. I often fear he will become so hardened to emotional vulnerability that he could emerge as a psychopath. The tortured animals, by contrast, are left in a messy flood of incomprehensibility and rage. The only chink occurs if nightmares are mentioned, as I suspect all these injured and enraged tortured objects come home to roost to get their revenge in his nightmares. He vehemently denies having such nightmares, but by the manner in which he looks at me when I mention them, I suspect he knows what I mean.

However, in a recent session when I was talking about the experiences the tortured animals were having, it suddenly dawned on me that the elephant and the string torture may represent Mark's idea of birth with the cord being cut, landing him in an unbearable place. I decided to say this to him and link it to what happened to him as a baby, where he may have felt so soft and unprotected that anyone could do anything to him, whenever they liked, and there was nothing he could do. Now he is determined to do it the other way around, and be so hard and powerful like the Master of the Universe. Although I had said some of this before, the sight of the elephant having the cord cut seemed to have added resonance. Mark looked at me after I spoke and said very quietly, 'I wish it didn't happen to me'. He then returned to the torture. This was the first sign of a chink of recognition that these parts of himself belong to him and his experience. The first possibility of inner conflict. The conflict was to be externalized, though with me as the witness.

In the following session when I was quiet as the familiar torture was taking place, Mark spontaneously said, 'Talk what the animals are feeling'. It is as if he needs a wide perspective, with me as the witness, in order to begin to contemplate that all this may have happened to him. Conflict needs to be externalized at present until such time as he can believe that a container can exist for the mental pain contingent on recognizing the vulnerability in himself. He does not seem to realize that his relentless torturing will of itself create more persecution and fears of retaliation, which means he is engaged in a vicious circle of having to be even tougher or more ruthless and omnipotent.

Conclusion

Psychotherapy with traumatized children attempts to help them feel that their most unbearable anxieties stemming from traumatic dysregulated states can be received in the first instance, and then named. As Bion said, the 'What' has to proceed the 'Why' or the 'How' of any emotional experience (Bion, 1970). The name allows thought about why something happened, to enable a coherent narrative to be constructed so that the person is not compelled merely to repeat experiences, but to grow and develop from them. We know from both clinical experience and research that resilience stems from the capacity to make sense of emotional experiences, however toxic they are. This includes the capacity to have a coherent narrative of the experience so that it has meaning.

If thought-about emotional experience becomes possible whereby, in identification with the psychotherapist having internalized these functions in the context of an emotional relationship, the person is able to observe the relationships that exist between him and others or between parts of his mind, the judgements and choices can be made. We work on the basis of our conviction that psychotherapy brings about long-term changes in the various functions of the mind, and thus enable new brain pathways. Thus, traumatized children can move from a life of pure automatic reaction to traumatic situations, to more proactive choices on the side of life.

References

Bion, W.R. (1962). *Learning from Experience*. London: Heinemann.
Bion, W.R. (1970). *Attention and Interpretation*. London: Heinemann.
Emanuel, R. (1996). Psychotherapy with children traumatised in infancy. *Journal of Child Psychotherapy*, 22: 214–239.
Freud, S. (1926). Inhibitions, symptoms and anxiety. Standard Edition, Vol. 20 (pp. 77–125). London: Hogarth Press.
Garland, C. (2002). *Understanding Trauma, A Psychoanalytical Response*, Tavistock Clinic Series. London: Karnac.
North, R. (1987). *Schools of Tomorrow: Education as if People Matter*. Dartington, Totnes: Green Books.

CHAPTER SEVEN

The changing space of childhood and its relationship to narcissism

Sami Timimi

I first need to ask the reader to keep in mind my own scepticism about what I have written, as I fear it is often in danger of slipping into a romanticized, stereotyped view of childhood. This is an ever-present danger in most discourses on childhood, as children are so often receptacles for projections of our own unfulfilled wishes, and thus these discourses can easily become conflated with sentiments about the general state of society. In addition, my arguments necessarily suffer with the over-generalizations needed in order to give my narrative a sense of coherence. Real life is never as simplistic, and all cultures contain diversity at every level. Nonetheless, these genuine concerns about the difficulty of reaching beyond shifting social constructions should not deflect from pointing out that something is going on for children in rich, industrialized free-market based societies, and that this something is more than a little disturbing. What I shall limit myself to doing is to paint a bit of the background context into which children in such societies (like ours) are born, without attempting the more complex task of translating this into its effects at the 'micro' level of individual children and their families.

At the time of writing this chapter, I was reflecting on the case of bilingual support worker Aishah Azmi, who was notoriously suspended by a school in West Yorkshire after she insisted on wearing a veil in certain lessons, a decision supported by most senior politicians in this country. The decision to suspend Aishah was on the grounds that the veil impeded her communication with the children and therefore interfered with their education. Leaving aside whether this decision was right or wrong, I find it ironic that we attack the symbols of a belief system and culture from which we have much to learn with regards raising and educating our children, and instead paint them as detrimental to our children's well-being. After all, it is societies like that of the UK that are struggling with increasing problems of alienation, anti-social behaviour, alcohol and drug misuse, bullying, violence, eating disorders, self-harm, behaviour disorders, and neglect in the young, to mention but a few.

I do not wish to romanticize other cultures' concepts of childhood and child-rearing, nor do I wish to minimize the enormity of the task of improving children's lives across the world, particularly in the context of an aggressive market led neo-liberal globalization, destabilized communities, and regional conflicts, with all the devastation to family life this brings, and where some local cultural beliefs are clearly problematic (like female infanticide). However, I wish to state firmly and confidently that amongst those more stable and rooted cultures across the world, sophisticated discourses on childhood and child-rearing spanning millennia exist (including within Islam), with many anthropological and other studies confirming that such communities do not share the same magnitude of problems with anti-social behaviour, anxiety states and so on, amongst the young (see Timimi, 2005). I am not saying that we can import sets of beliefs and practices from other cultures and simply transplant them here in Britain, and expect them to work. However, some reflection on the nature of beliefs, values, and practices in our own and other societies may help inform us about things that we can do in our bid to develop these in a way that can be applied to the unique British context.

I also want to acknowledge that our ideas about what an ideal childhood should look like are themselves culturally constructed. Thus, whilst the immaturity of children is a biological fact, the ways in which this immaturity is understood and made meaningful is a fact of culture (Prout & James, 1997). Members of any culture hold a working definition of childhood, its nature, limitations, and duration, based on a network of ideas that link children with other members and with the social ecology (Harkness & Super, 1996). While they may not explicitly discuss this definition, write about it, or even consciously conceive of it as an issue, they act upon these assumptions in all of their dealings with, fears for, and expectations of their children (Calvert, 1992). This makes it difficult to pass a value or scientific judgement about whether children are better or worse off in any particular culture or society, as the idea that there are universal ideals or natural unfolding processes that all children should be able to 'have' is suspect. Nonetheless, children are socialized by belonging to a particular culture at a certain stage in that culture's history, so certain differences in children's behaviour can be seen as a result of different child-rearing philosophies and socialization processes. We can, therefore, make some comparisons, whilst keeping in mind the above caveats, and indeed using them to help us 'interrogate' any naïve or romanticized assumptions.

There are, however, some statements that we can make with reasonable certainty. We know that the space of childhood has changed. Contemporary Western culture has witnessed rapid changes that affect children. Well-documented changes include: children's diets (which have increased in sugar, saturated fats, salt, and chemical additives, and decreased in certain essential fatty acids, and fresh fruit and vegetables); family structure (which has seen the demise of the extended family, increase in separation and divorce, increase in working hours of parents, and a decrease in the amount of time parents spend with their children); family life-style (there has been an increase in mobility, decrease in 'rooted' communities, and an increasing pursuit of individual gratification); children's life-styles (which have witnessed a decrease in the amount of exercise, the 'domestication' of childhood due to fears about the risks for children resulting in more indoor pursuits such as computers and TV); the commercialization/commodification of childhood (increase in consumer goods targeted at children and the creation of new commercial opportunities in childhood, for example the 'parenting' industry and the pharmaceutical industry); and changes in the education system (modern teaching ideology is rooted in methods such as continuous assessment and socially orientated worksheets that favour the learning style of girls over boys). These changes are occurring at a time when our standards for what we consider to be acceptable behaviour in the young and acceptable child-rearing methods are both narrowing. It is now harder than ever to be a 'normal' child or parent (see Timimi, 2005).

In parallel with this, claims are being made that 'mental' disorders among the young (such as emotional, anxiety, eating, and behavioural disorders) have been steadily increasing in the past few decades (British Medical Association, 2006), despite the perception that recent generations have 'never had it so good'. Figures for prescriptions of psychotropic medication to children and adolescents both illustrate the depth of this problem, and our peculiar cultural style of responding to it. For example, researchers analysing prescribing trends in nine countries between 2000 and 2002 found that significant increases in the number of prescriptions for psychotropic drugs in children were evident in all countries—the lowest being in Germany, where the increase was 13 per cent, and the highest being in the UK where an increase of 68 per cent was recorded (Wong et al., 2004).

Of particular concern is the increase in rates of stimulant prescription to children. By 1996, over 6 per cent of school-aged boys in the USA were taking stimulant medication (Olfson et al., 2002), with children as young as two being prescribed stimulants in increasing numbers (Zito et al., 2000). Recent surveys show that in some schools in the United States, over 17 per cent of boys are taking stimulant medication (Le Fever et al., 1999), and it is now estimated that about 10 per cent of school boys in the United States take a stimulant (Sharav, 2006). In the UK, prescriptions for stimulants have increased from about 6,000 in 1994 to over 450,000 children by 2004—a staggering 7,000 + per cent increase in one decade (Department of Health, NHSE, 2005).

Is this the canary in the mine? These rapid changes in practice in the area of children's mental health have not come about as a result of any major scientific discovery (see Timimi, 2002; 2005; Timimi & Maitra, 2006). There are two other possibilities that could explain these dramatic increases. The first is that there has been a real increase in emotional and behavioural disorders in children, leading to greater public scrutiny and concern about such behaviours which, in turn, has resulted in a greater professional effort to understand and alleviate these behavioural and emotional problems. The second possibility is that there has not been a real increase in emotional and behavioural disorders in the young, but there *has* been a change in the way we think about, classify, and deal with children's behaviour—in other words, our perception of, and the meaning we ascribe to, children's emotions and behaviour.

Both possible causes for the rapid increase in our identification of and treatment for mental-health disorders in the young require an examination of contexts. Indeed the third, and in my opinion, most likely possibility that explains the increase is an interaction between the two aforementioned possibilities. In other words, it could be that changes in our cultural/environmental contexts are causing increases in certain emotional and behavioural problems, and that these, in turn, are changing our perception of, and the meaning we give to, childhood behaviour; and with this, in turn, changing the way we deal with childhood behaviour and our common cultural practices around children (such as child rearing and education), which in turn is further increasing the incidence of these behaviours—and so on.

The impact of 'narcissism'

In a short chapter such as this, I cannot possibly explore in any detail the impact of changes in the space of childhood in Western modernity that I listed earlier. Instead, I will confine the rest of this chapter to the impact of a particular aspect of our value system which has become embedded in our daily discourse due, at least in part, to our reliance on rather aggressive forms of neo-liberal free-market principles. This is the problem of 'narcissism'. Narcissism describes the character trait of 'self love', or in the more everyday sense, 'looking after number one'. The spread of narcissism has left many of our children in a psychological vacuum, pre-occupied with issues of psychological survival and lacking a sense of the emotional security that comes through feeling you are valued, and thus have an enduring sense of belonging.

One of the dominant themes used by advocates of neo-liberal free-market economy ideology is that of 'freedom'. At the economic level, this is a core requirement of free-market ideology. Companies must be as free from regulation as possible; to concentrate on competing with others, with the maximizing of profits being the most visible sign of success. There is little to gain from social responsibility (only if it increases your 'market share'). At the emotional level, the appeal to freedom can be understood as an appeal to rid us of the restrictions imposed by authority (such as parents, communities, and governments) (Richards, 1989). By implication, this value system is built around the idea of looking after the wants of the individual—narcissism.

Taking this a step further, once the individual is freed from the authority they are (in fantasy at least) free to pursue their own individual self-gratifying desires, free from the impingements, infringements, and limitations that other people represent. The effect of this on society is to atomize the individual and insulate their private spaces to the degree where obligations to others and harmony with the wider community become obstacles rather than objectives. In this 'look after number one' value system, other individuals are there to be competed against as they, too, chase after their personal desires. This post second world war shift to a more individualistic identity was recognized, as early as the mid-1950s, by commentators who first spoke about how the new 'fun-based morality' (Wolfenstein, 1955) was privileging fun over responsibility; having fun was becoming obligatory (the cultural message becoming that you should be ashamed if you weren't having fun). With the increase in new possibilities for excitement being presented, experiencing intense excitement was becoming more difficult, thus creating a constant pressure to push back the boundaries of acceptable and desirable experiences, and life-styles, opening the doors, amongst other things, to sub-cultures comfortable with drinking to excess, violence, sexual promiscuity, and drug taking.

In this value system, others become objects to be used and manipulated wherever possible for personal goals, and social exchanges become difficult to trust, as the better you are at manipulating others, the more financial (and other narcissistic) rewards you will get. Such a value system, which ultimately seeks to eradicate, or at least minimize, social conscience as a regulator of behaviour, cannot sustain itself without our moral conscience beginning to feel guilty (Richards, 1989). Thus, it is no coincidence that those who are the most vociferous advocates of free-market ideology tend also to advocate the most aggressive and punitive forms of social control. Whereas some of these guilt-induced policy proposals are aimed at putting some restraint on unfettered competitiveness, greed, and self seeking, amongst those more fanatical believers in the ability of market ideology to solve its own problems (and thus best to leave the market to get on with it), the most common defence used to try and deal with the anxiety produced by this guilt is through finding target scapegoats for this anxiety. In other words, instead of facing up to the suffering that the encouragement of narcissism brings to the world, our leaders need to convince us that our problems are due to other evils (like fundamentalist Islam, asylum seekers, homosexuals, single parents, bad genes, etc.). As a result, another hallmark of Western culture's increasing psychological reliance on developmentally immature impulses that encourage it to avoid taking responsibility for its beliefs and practices is the so called 'blame culture', which fills the media and contemporary discourse more generally. We are, to coin a well worn phrase, 'tough on crime/mental health', but getting nowhere with the 'causes of crime/poor mental health'. We build more prisons and employ more psychiatrists—a sure sign that despite best intentions, our approach to 'causes' is at best naïve, at worst a part of the problem.

In any culture, children and then adults come to acquire their subjective selves through incorporation of values, beliefs, and practices that sustain the desired social relationships of that culture (Althusser, 1969). People, Althusser argues, can only know themselves through the mediation of ideological institutions. So how do the ideologies of modern capitalism influence the way children and their parents see themselves, their roles, and subsequently the way they behave?

In this narcissistic value system, others can easily become objects to be used and manipulated for personal goals, thus social exchanges become more difficult to trust, as the better you are at manipulating others, the more narcissistic rewards you can get. Dependence, when it occurs, is more likely to happen with professionals, thereby reinforcing the idea and status of the expert. As Amin (1988) points out, Western capitalist ideology has necessarily led to the domination of market values, which penetrates all aspects of social life and subjects them to their logic. This philosophy pushes to the limit of absurdity an opposition between humankind and nature. The goal of finding an ecological harmony with nature disappears as nature comes to be viewed as a thing to be similarly manipulated for selfish ends.

With narcissistic goals of self-fulfilment, gratification, and competitive manipulation of relationships so prominent, together with the discouragement of the development of deep interpersonal attachments, it is not difficult to see why so-called narcissistic disorders (such as anti-social behaviour, substance misuse, and eating disorders) are on the increase (Lasch, 1980; Dwivedi, 1996). A heightened concern for the self can be both 'liberating' and, simultaneously, oppressive.

A system of winners and losers

The attention given to individual cases of child abusers whom society can disown as not belonging to, or being (at least in part) the product of, our culture masks Western governments' implementation of national and international policies that place children at great risk, and the extent to which we are an abusive culture. Monetarist policies of the 1980s and 1990s cut health, social, welfare, and education programmes as well as enforcing similar austerity measures on developing countries, policies that had a particularly adverse effect on children and families (Kincheloe, 1998; Scheper-Hughes & Stein, 1987). This also has a class-specific character, with the plight of poor children being viewed as self-inflicted, and the more insidious problem of neglect of their children by middle-class parents often passing unnoticed. With the increase in the number of divorces and two working parents, fathers and mothers are around their children for less of the day. A generation of 'home aloners' is growing up. The amount of time children have with their parents has dropped dramatically in recent decades, and the back-up systems that extended families presented are dwindling (Lipsky & Abrams, 1994). As families get smaller and spend less time with each other, children lose the learning opportunities that come in social systems more geared to social responsibility/duty—instead of having to negotiate several relationships within regular contacts with multiple kin, we increasingly live in more emotionally charged small units trying to psychologically survive within a fiercely competitive and individualistic culture.

Children are cultured into this value system by virtue of living within its institutions and being exposed daily to its discourse. Ultimately this is a system of winners and losers, a kind of 'survival of the fittest' where compassion and concern for social harmony contradicts the basic goal of the value system. As this system is showing itself to be bad for children's happiness, a similar process as above works to try and distance us from the anxiety arising from the guilt thus produced. Instead of asking ourselves painful questions about the role we may be playing in producing this unhappiness, we can view our children's difficulties as being the result of biological diseases that require medical treatment (we can blame their genes).

These social dynamics also get projected directly on to children. Children come to be viewed as both victims (through adults using and manipulating them for their own gratification) and potentially 'evil' scapegoats (as if it is these nasty children's bad behaviour that is causing so many of our social problems) (Stephens, 1995). This reflects a profound ambivalence that exists towards children in the West. With adults busily pursuing the goals of self-realization and self-expression (these being the polite middle-class versions of self-gratification), having absorbed the free-market ethic, children when they come along 'get in the way'. A human being, who is so utterly dependent on others, will inevitably cause a rupture in the Western value system goals of narcissism that individuals who have grown up in these societies will have been influenced by, to a greater or lesser degree. Children cannot be welcomed into the world in an ordinary and seamless way. They will make the dominant goals of modern life more difficult. They will to some degree be a burden.

More and more surveillance

Thus far I have suggested that a basic feature of modern Western free-market based culture is an increasingly narcissistic value system, which interrupts children's and families' lives in a number of adverse ways. The complex dynamics of our concepts of self increasingly shaped along narcissistic notions, interacting with the collective guilt and fear of retribution, becoming a loser in the competition, or fear of pilfering of one's accumulated resources, means that governments feel the need to police these potentially dangerous selves in an increasing variety of ways. Thus, one feature that has changed dramatically over the past century in Western society is the amount of surveillance to which parents and their children are subjected. The State has all sorts of mechanisms of surveillance, and an 'army' of professionals tasked with monitoring and regulating family life, as if they are aware that children are struggling in this culture, and deal with their guilt by individualizing and 'scapegoating'. This is not to say that we do not need surveillance, as the effects of child abuse are many and far reaching. But we must also ask the question of what the impact of this is on non-abusive families. The increase in levels of anxiety amongst parents who may fear the consequences of their action has reached the point where the fear is that any influence that is discernible may be likely to be viewed as undue influence, making it more likely that parents will leave essential socializing and guidance to the expertise of professionals (Maitra, 2006).

Life has thus become difficult for parents who are caught in a double pressure when it comes to raising their children. On the one hand, there are increased expectations for children to show restraint and self-control from an early age; on the other there is considerable social fear in parents generated by a culture of children's rights that often pathologizes normal, well-intentioned parents' attempts to discipline their children. Parents are left fearing a visit from Social Services, and the whole area of discipline becomes loaded with anxiety. This argument holds equally true for schools. Parents often criticize schools for lack of discipline. Schools often criticize parents for lack of discipline. This double-bind has resulted in more narcissistic power going to children. Parents are being given the message that their children are more like adults (cf. House's Chapter 10), and should always be talked to, reasoned with, allowed to make choices, to express themselves, and so on (Timimi, 2005).

The atomization of society also means that there is a lack of common ownership of rules and values with regards to the upbringing of children. Children may learn that only certain individuals have any right to make demands and have expectations regarding their behaviour, and with the task of parenting coming to be viewed in Western culture as one that needs childcare experts' advice in order to get it right, a form of 'cognitive parenting' has arisen whereby parents are encouraged to give explanation and avoid conflicts (Diller, 2002). This hands-off, particularly verbal model of parenting is both more taxing and less congruent with children's more action-based view of the world.

Into this anxiety-loaded, narcissistically pre-determined vision of childhood and practices of child rearing, new diagnoses (such as childhood depression, Attention Deficit Hyperactivity Disorder [ADHD], and Aspergers syndrome) appear to provide a temporary relief to the beleaguered, intensely monitored child carers.

By viewing children's poor behaviour and distressed emotional state as being caused by an 'illness', all are apparently spared from further scrutiny. The result, however, fits into another aspect of our 'fast culture'. With the widespread application of the techniques of medicine to manage our children's behaviour and emotional state, particularly through use of drugs, we have achieved what I call the 'McDonaldization' of children's mental health. Like fast food, recent medication-centred practice comes from the most aggressively consumerist society (USA), feeds on peoples desire for instant satisfaction and a 'quick fix', fits into a busy life-style, requires little engagement with the product, requires only the most superficial training, knowledge, and understanding to produce the product, and has the potential to produce immeasurable damage in the long term to both the individuals who consume these products as well as to public health more generally.

A final thought

How can the institutions of the state—such as government, legal, schools, and health services—play a part in shifting the values, beliefs, and, therefore, practices that provide the all-important backdrop into which children are born? Can we develop institutional responses that counteract some of the worst aspects of neo-liberalism and the narcissism that structures it? Not all cultures that have embraced the economic necessity of integration into the new world global free-market order have in the process eroded the values of social responsibility to achieve this. For example, in some Far Eastern economies, the traditional values of care and protection (social responsibility) have been taken up by some companies in exchange for loyalty to the company. There are likely to be a whole set of thoughtful institutional and legislative strategies that could make a real and positive difference to children's lives by helping to create a value system concerned more with care, nurture, and our responsibility to provide sustainable and stable community life, where children can feel they belong and are valued for just being, rather than having to achieve something to justify their worth. From making school curricula more 'boy friendly', through criminalizing wilfully absent parents, economically supporting and valuing the role of parents, right up to enforcing more family-friendly business practices. There are genuine opportunities to improve conditions if we have the imagination and the will to see it through. Indeed, it is our responsibility to do so.

References

Althusser, L. (1969). *For Marx*. Harmondsworth: Penguin.
Amin, S. (1988). *Eurocentrism*. New York: Monthly Review Press.
British Medical Association (2006). *Child and Adolescent Mental Health: A Guide for Professionals*. London: BMA.
Calvert, K. (1992). *Children in the House: The Material Culture of Early Childhood, 1600–1900*. Boston: Northeastern University Press.
Department of Health, NHSE (2005). Prescription Cost Analysis, England 2004. Available at: http://www.dh.gov.uk/PublicationsAndStatistics/Publications/PublicationsStatistics/PublicationsStatistics Article/fs/en?CONTENT_ID=4107504&chk=nsvFE0
Diller, L.H. (2002). ADHD: real or an American myth. Rome: paper presented at the 14th Annual Conference of the Associazone Cultural Pediatri. 10 October.
Dwivedi, K.N. (1996). Culture and personality. In: K.N. Dwivedi & V.P. Varma (Eds.), *Meeting the Needs of Ethnic Minority Children*. London: Jessica Kingsley.
Harkness, S., & Super, C. (Eds.) (1996). *Parents' Cultural Belief Systems: Their Origins, Expressions and Consequences*. London: Guilford Press.
Kincheloe, J. (1998). The new childhood: home alone as a way of life. In: H. Jenkins (Ed.), *Children's Culture Reader*. New York: New York University Press.
Lasch, C. (1980). *The Culture of Narcissism*. London: Norton (Abacus).
LeFever, G.B., Dawson, K.V., & Morrow, A.D. (1999). The extent of drug therapy for attention deficit hyperactivity disorder among children in public schools. *American Journal of Public Health*, 89: 1359–1364.
Lipsky, D., & Abrams, A. (1994). *Late Bloomers: Coming of Age in Today's America*. New York: Times Books.
Maitra, B. (2006). Culture and the mental health of children. The 'cutting edge' of expertise. In: S. Timimi & B. Maitra (Eds.), *Critical Voices in Child and Adolescent Mental Health*. London: Free Association Books.
Olfson, M., Marcus, S.C., Weissman, M.M., & Jensen, P.S. (2002). National trends in the use of psychotropic medications by children. *Journal of the American Academy of Child and Adolescent Psychiatry*, 41: 514–521.

Prout, A., & James, A. (1997). A new paradigm for the sociology of childhood? Provenance, promise and problems. In: A. James & A. Prout (Eds.), *Constructing and Re-constructing Childhood: Contemporary Issues in the Sociological Study of Childhood*. London: Falmer Press.

Richards, B. (1989). Visions of freedom. *Free Associations*, 16: 31–42.

Scheper-Hughes, N., & Stein, H.F. (1987). Child abuse and the unconscious in American popular culture. In: N. Scheper-Hughes (Ed.), *Child Survival*. New York: D. Reidel.

Sharav, V. (2006). ADHD drug risks: cardiovascular and cerebrovascular problems. Available at: http://www.ahrp.org/cms/content/view /76/28/

Stephens, S. (1995). Children and the politics of culture in 'Late Capitalism'. In: S. Stephens (Ed.), *Children and the Politics of Culture*. Princeton: Princeton University Press.

Timimi, S. (2002). *Pathological Child Psychiatry and the Medicalization of Childhood*. London: Brunner-Routledge.

Timimi, S. (2005). *Naughty Boys: Anti-Social Behaviour, ADHD, and the Role of Culture*. Basingstoke: Palgrave MacMillan.

Timimi, S., & Maitra, B. (Eds.) (2006). *Critical Voices in Child and Adolescent Mental Health*. London: Free Association Books.

Wolfenstein, M. (1955). Fun morality: an analysis of recent child-training literature. In: M. Mead & M. Wolfenstein (Eds.), *Childhood in Contemporary Cultures*. Chicago: University of Chicago Press.

Wong, I.C., Murray, M.L., Camilleri-Novak, D., & Stephens, P. (2004). Increased prescribing trends of paediatric psychotropic medications. *Archives of Disease in Childhood*, 89: 1131–1132.

Zito, J.M., Safer, D.J., Dosreis, S., Gardner, J.F., Boles, J., & Lynch, F. (2000). Trends in prescribing of psychotropic medication in pre-schoolers. *Journal of the American Medical Association*, 283: 1025–1030.

CHAPTER EIGHT

Why love matters in early childhood

Sue Gerhardt

... feeling of belonging as essential to mental health as vitamins were to physical health.

John Bowlby

Across the land, heated debates about 'toxic childhoods' periodically break out in pubs, the letters pages of newspapers, and on television—but I suspect that the participants rarely have toxic *babyhood* in mind. Instead, they conjure up a child at various ages who is the victim of poor social habits that corrupt good development, such as eating too much junk food, watching too much television, or playing too many computer games, along with not enough outdoor play. Fears are expressed that without appropriate stimulation and care, the child may not develop into a mentally healthy, well-socialized, and creative individual. However, this emphasis on the older child, which is often taken for granted, fails to recognize the possibility that babyhood can also be 'toxic'.

Perhaps babyhood is so rarely discussed because babies are more socially invisible. But perhaps it is also more challenging to acknowledge the existence of toxic babyhoods. When we consider what makes for a healthy and happy babyhood, it becomes clear that we are no longer just talking about social habits, but are asking real questions about the quality of babies' relationships with their parents. We are in danger of intruding into personal life. Just as with the sexual abuse scandals of the 1980s, which brought us face to face with the possibility that adult parents, teachers, relatives, or family friends could harm children, it is very hard for many people today to acknowledge that poor parenting at the earliest stage of life can cause significant long-term effects which may justify the need for professional intervention. As Mick Hume scoffed in *The Times* (15 January 2008):

> There is no right way to bring up baby. And whatever hotch potch method you use will have no long-term effect on your child. As one wise man said, if you can avoid locking them in a wardrobe or beating them on the head with a frying pan, they should be fine.

In fact, much of the behaviour that worries many of us in later childhood, such as aggression, hyperactivity, obesity, depression, and poor school performance, has already been significantly shaped by these children's experiences in infancy. We have increasing evidence that any old 'hotch potch' will not do, because a great deal of social and emotional learning takes place in babyhood, having a huge impact on a child's opportunity to be well-socialized, creative, and mentally healthy. In particular, infancy has a huge impact on each child's resilience in the face of stressful or traumatic circumstances, and on his ability to make use of positive social experience. Yet infancy is rarely the focus of concern, except to debate the merits or otherwise of nursery care. I believe there is a real lack of understanding of how crucial the experiences of babyhood are to our later lives.

When we come into the world, we are not just in need of physical support—food, clothing, and shelter—we are also born seeking an emotional connection, an attachment to a protective adult. The newborn eagerly seeks out familiar smells and voices, and looks for human faces. Babies are social animals right from the start, able to engage in a basic dialogue of whimpers and coos and grunts, to imitate a parent's facial expressions, and to cry when distressed by separation from the protector. If a baby doesn't feel connected to others and valued, he or she may even die, despite having food and shelter.

Brain development

All sorts of systems are shaped by early social experience, but particularly the systems that regulate emotion. The brain's emotion tools are needed urgently to navigate the social world, and so it is no surprise that these are among the first systems to develop, after the basic systems for breathing, temperature regulation, and so on, that ensure bodily survival. The most essential systems develop first, followed by developmental refinements. For example, at birth the amygdala—in the more primitive core of the brain—is one of the first basic emotion systems to come 'on-line' in order to alert us to danger and immediate threats, triggering a basic 'fight or flight' response. The amygdala reads social situations using its own unconscious memory system which is conditioned by early experiences, picking up on who and what are dangerous in a particular social context. If a baby has consistently unpleasant experiences with a purple-haired babysitter, he may well grow up with an unconscious aversion to people with purple hair, which might get triggered unexpectedly when, as an adult, he meets his future mother-in-law who happens to have purple hair.

Biochemical pathways are being laid down early on, too, and some of these, like the serotonin and dopamine pathways, may be skewed by negative early experiences, such as too much isolation or separation (Jezierski et al., 2007), or neglect and poor attachment (Gerra et al., 2007), in particular. When this happens, the individual is left more vulnerable as an adult to dysfunctions involving these biochemical responses—such as a vulnerability to drug and other addictions in the case of dopamine. The dopamine pathway may also be adversely affected by nutritional experiences such as being offered sugar, or being deprived of iron, or of sufficient omega 3 fatty acids which are present in breast milk (Zimmer et al., 2001). Recent research is showing that obesity may be linked with the way the dopamine system in the prefrontal cortex functions (Campbell & Eisenberg, 2007), raising new questions about the role of infancy in the current obesity epidemic.

Clearly, nutrition plays an important part in these biochemical pathways But longer-term research projects are beginning to suggest that both early nutrition and early social experience in the early stages of development may programme the structure or the function of an organism across a wide range of mental and physical health issues, affecting adult size, metabolism, blood lipids, diabetes, blood pressure, obesity, atherosclerosis, learning, behaviour, and life span (Lucas, 1998).

The stress response is a crucial aspect of our emotional equipment, enabling each of us to cope with whatever life throws at us and recover our balance quickly. Yet the stress response itself is another biochemical system which may be 'set' by early experience. This may even start in the womb, since some research has found that poorly nourished low-birth-weight babies have higher stress hormone (plasma cortisol) levels throughout adult life, suggesting that their HPA or stress response has already been programmed in the perinatal period (Seckl & Meaney, 2004). But it is not just nutrition which affects the stress response; early social experience can also leave its mark. If parents consistently allow a baby to become over-aroused (or under-aroused), the baby may feel overwhelmed by stress. And a baby who repeatedly experiences more stress than he or she can manage is in danger of becoming over-reactive to future stressors. Most of these very early processes are shared with other mammals, and are to do with basic needs for safety, protection, and physiological regulation.

It is important to recognize that babies cannot regulate themselves very effectively. They have very limited tools to manage their own states, such as turning their heads away from too much stimulation or comforting themselves by sucking their own fingers. Both of these basic strategies for self-management came very clearly into play with a 5 month old baby I saw in my clinical practice at the Oxford Parent Infant Project (OXPIP), an Oxford-based charity which provides parent–infant psychotherapy. The baby, Nina, attended the clinic with her father, who did not at the time live with her, although he had done so previously. She immediately made searching eye contact with me, in a way that left me feeling that she was asking me for a protective response. Her father, on the other hand, was a very tense, emotionally cut off sort of man who could not manage eye contact for more than a few seconds, did not know how to play with his daughter, and was emotionally very rigid and easily angered. I dreaded having to spend an hour with him myself, and so apparently did his baby (who was only seeing him a few hours a week, as she was in foster care).

Nina and her father sat on the comfortable padded mat in the room, with Nina lying on her back in front of her kneeling father. He didn't offer her any toys, nor did he manage to engage her attention with his face or voice. He just sat back on his heels, looked at her from a distance, and murmured to her 'what are you doing?', over and over again. The baby was not actively exploring her body or looking at the room. Instead, what she was doing was using all her concentrated attention to get away from his gaze. She deliberately turned her head away from him, staring at the wall, and she maintained this for most of each session for many weeks. As each session wore on, she would start to fret and whimper with the effort. On one such occasion, her father did try to comfort her by picking her up and rather woodenly patting her on the back, but once again she demonstrated her aversion to him, avoiding a real cuddle, not sinking into his body in a relaxed way, and again turning to her own defences to manage her distress. First she sucked her thumb with an anxious expression on her face, staring into the distance, and then after a while, she fell asleep—to her foster mother's utter astonishment, when she came to collect her—as it turned out, she had slept well the previous night and had already had a long unscheduled sleep that morning just before the session.

I think that what happens as babies like Nina grow up and become more autonomous is that some of these early basic defences get elaborated into more complex ways of switching off from stressful experience and self-comforting. This can take many forms, like various addictions and habits, including the practice of dissociating when unpleasantly aroused—the kind of behaviour Nina was already showing at five months.

As well as learning healthy or dysfunctional forms of regulation, we also begin to learn more complex forms of self-management in infancy. Unlike other animals, we have uniquely human higher-brain potentials which are only activated through social interaction with other humans. This starts to happen with amazing rapidity from birth. In fact, it is during the first couple of years that a baby's brain is developing at the most rapid rate it will ever develop, making neural connections and establishing pathways that the mature individual will come to rely upon. In particular, the area of the brain called the pre-frontal cortex, which is adjacent to many of the core primitive systems, starts to develop in babyhood. This is the beginning of a brain structure that has the capacity to manage and direct the more basic biochemical and behaviourally instinctive reactions.

One key area of the pre-frontal region is the orbitofrontal cortex (situated behind the eyes), which achieves its basic maturation between about 6–18 months. This area of the brain plays a central role in our social lives, along with the anterior cingulate and the medial prefrontal area in general. The orbitofrontal cortex in particular is involved in our ability to judge social cues, to adapt to changing situations, to hold back our tendency to react impulsively, and to be able to take the perspective of other people and have empathy for others (Ohnishi, 2000; Rankin 2004, 2006). It is central to what has been called 'mentalization' and 'mind-mindedness'—that is, the ability to pay close attention to others, to notice their intentions, and realize that they have an inner world that motivates their behaviour. This helps us to predict what others might do next. However, this too depends on parental input; when parents name feelings, and explain how others might feel, they are promoting the development of these capacities. Parents who are 'mind-minded' also convey that this process of interpreting other people is an imprecise activity, and can be wrong—they are mentally flexible and help the child to develop the same capacity.

Like so much else in emotional development, both the emotional learning, and the brain development that goes with it, do not happen automatically, but only in response to the experiences a baby has with other people—they are what is known as 'experience dependent'. In other words, they depend on what the more mature people in a child's life do or don't do. And like most forms of learning, emotional development is best achieved within the context of a positive relationship. According to Allan Schore, the development of the orbitofrontal cortex is facilitated by the release of the biochemicals of well-being, the opioids (Schore, 1994). All the social experiences of being cuddled, stroked, kissed, and held, as well as having fun and games, being accepted, and being understood and responded to, may play a part in promoting connections in the orbitofrontal cortex. When these are in short supply, it is likely that the orbitofrontal cortex does not develop as well—which is just what was found in the case of some extremely deprived Romanian orphans (Chugani et al., 2001).

However, some forms of learning do involve negative emotion. As the baby becomes a toddler, he will start to have new experiences of being inhibited by his parent-figures; for his own safety, he is told not to touch the plug, not to pull the dog's tail, and so on. Within an established, largely positive relationship, the toddler has the motivation to pay attention to what the parent says, to maintain the good feelings he has come to rely upon. The parent in a good relationship will also be more likely to use techniques such as distraction rather than coercion. If this process goes well enough, the toddler will gradually learn to internalize parental prohibitions and inhibit himself, to hold back his impulses. According to Schore, this is when his orbitofrontal cortex completes its basic development by connecting up with the amygdala, enabling some control over the more impulsive self, which enables concern for other people and their needs to emerge. The whole process depends on the baby's social motivation and sense of connection to others.

Toxic parents

But babies are highly vulnerable creatures, and the development of these human, emotional capacities can easily be derailed. Since so much of early emotional development is organized socially, through the quality of the baby's interaction with others, inevitably we must turn the spotlight on to the parents or other caregivers who provide that interaction. This can be an uncomfortable, guilt-inducing exercise.

The problem is that if the parental figures in a baby's life can't manage their own feelings well, they will have great difficulty in passing on these capacities. Their sensitivity and willingness to meet the baby's needs depends very much on their own inner state. Their own level of self-control and ability to defer gratification will affect the baby's learning of such qualities. We tend to think of learning as a conscious process of transferring information, but emotional learning is about passing on information about how to manage feelings and relate to others, and is achieved mostly unconsciously, through the right brain, through imitation and experience, not through words. Nina's father, for example, wanted to relate to his daughter, but he simply had no idea how to do it; something had been missing from his own experience.

When parents are depressed or unhappy, this can also affect their ability to pay close attention to their baby. Post-natal depression is a common experience, thought to be suffered by at least 10 per cent of new mothers. This may have its roots in the mother's own early experiences, or it may be influenced by cultural factors such as the sudden isolation experienced by many new mothers, deprived of their former working identities and alone in their homes for much of the day. But no matter how her state of mind arose, a depressed mother will often find it very difficult to respond to her baby. Her own distress can be so draining that she can't find the energy to tolerate the baby's distress and soothe him. Often, she is in need of care herself, and is not able to provide care for others. When this state of mind persists, it can have a big impact on the baby's development. We know that babies of depressed mothers show signs of having slightly different brain development: their left brains are less active and their stress response is hypersensitive. (Living with a depressed mother later in childhood doesn't have the same effect on the stress response, presumably because it has already been 'set' by early experience—Essex et al., 2002.) These babies grow up at increased risk of depression themselves.

Parents who are substance abusers of any kind have a similar difficulty in focusing on the needs of their children. Even when the parent is fond of her child and doesn't believe there is any problem with her parenting, there may well be serious neglect going on. One charming, dreamy young mother I worked with had been addicted to heroin whilst her babies were small, and was managing her addiction with methadone when I saw the family. She couldn't understand why she was being referred to me by her health visitor. But it was apparent to me from the first session: she tended to passively ignore her two children no matter what they did. The older one hit and scratched the baby and she didn't react—nor did the baby. She didn't talk to them or put their feelings into words. Although she loved her children, she had little awareness of their emotional needs. Her life had long been organized around her own needs, in particular her drug addiction, which meant that her habit was to get up in the late morning and take the children to bed with her at 10 p.m. But in fact her own emotional needs had been neglected during her infancy and childhood. I discovered through our work together that her own parents had not talked about feelings at all, and had never hugged or touched her as a child. She had found that using heroin helped to soothe her painful longing for contact.

Other forms of neglect may arise from ignorance of children's needs, particularly for interaction or supervision. The parent may expect too much too soon from their child. Such parents often describe their babies as 'difficult' or 'irritating', describing their own difficulty in responding, as much as the nature of the baby himself. This can shade into emotionally abusive parenting, where parents are critical, belittling, rejecting, and ridiculing of their child. As psychologist Robin Balbirnie once memorably put it, these are families which look fine 'with the sound turned off'. But turn up the volume and you feel the hostility and negativity.

Many parents find it hard to tolerate their child's emotions, and dismiss feelings, tending to minimize them or laugh them off. Sometimes this leads to parenting which uses coercion, bullying, and punishment to manage the child, and this in turn has been linked with the development of child anti-social disorders. Some research has found that a parent's coercive attitude to her baby is already predictive of anti-social behaviour (Tremblay, 2004), whilst other research has linked it with a lack of affection for a two-year old (Pettit & Bates, 1989; Belsky et al., 1998). I believe that many parents find it particularly hard to tolerate negative feelings in their children because they have never learnt how to manage their own. But then this gets passed on: their children in turn learn to suppress feelings that they can't regulate without parental help. Anti-social children often have a peculiar stress response: it is flattened, with a low heart rate and low baseline cortisol. It has been speculated that these are children who have learnt to switch off their reactions altogether, to manage chronic stress or distress. However, they will at times find this defence breaking down and rage breaking through.

Parents who are extremely impulsive and unregulated can affect their children in a different way. When parents are particularly unpredictable and confusing in their responses to the baby, a 'disorganized' form of attachment may result, which has been linked to the later development of a borderline personality disorder. Although such families are often found to be neglectful or abusive, one piece of research suggests that what is really disturbing to the child's sense of identity is the parents' failure to repair breaches in the relationship, and failure to soothe anxieties and upsets (Patrick et al., 1994). For example, every parent has had the experience of a toddler disobeying, playing up, and running around when he has been asked to sit still. When the toddler falls over and badly hurts his knee and starts to cry, a poorly regulated parent can become overwhelmed by her own anxiety and helplessness. At this point, instead of calming the child, she might manage her own intense feelings by yelling at him 'You stupid child, you'll be the death of me!'. But since this is likely to escalate the child's distress rather than soothing it, it fails to achieve the regulation and safety which are the main purposes of an attachment relationship. If the parent then doesn't make it up with her son, she will leave the toddler feeling bad, with no way to disperse his own stress hormones.

Although an occasional incident like this is unlikely to leave a lasting impression, when such events are a regular occurrence, levels of the stress hormone cortisol can continue to circulate, and may eventually have a toxic effect on a number of developing brain systems—such as the stress response itself, but also the amygdala and the pre-frontal cortex (De Bellis, 2005; Lyons et al., 2000)—the end result being the passing on of poor brain development, as well as poor self-management, to the next generation.

Government responses

It has been difficult in the past to look with a clear and objective eye at parenting behaviour. When parents were seen as authority figures, it was hard to question anything they did. Then during the era of feminism, there was huge hostility to anything that smacked of 'mother blaming'. We are now just beginning to emerge into a new era that can recognize that parents are only grown-up children; they learnt how to regulate themselves emotionally through the care they received as children. When that care is inadequate, developmental disorders can arise. Since this is not their fault, and is largely unconscious, it is not helpful to blame them. Equally, it is not helpful to deny that it is happening, because then the cycle of inadequate regulation will simply continue.

As Western societies have got richer, they seem to have become more psychologically sophisticated, and more concerned about the quality of their relationships and their happiness or emotional fulfil-ment. Governments are no longer simply concerned to ensure the physical safety and material well-being of their citizens, but have begun to intervene in matters once regarded as private. For example, there are now government documents that talk about improving attachment security, and that have set the goal of 'strong, capable, confident and self-assured' children based on loving and secure early relationships (Department for Children, Schools and Families, 2005). This is a very positive step towards ensuring that all children are well cared for. However, whilst materialistic values remain dom-inant, the commitment to realizing such goals has to compete with other goals. Balancing the financial books of the NHS has recently been more important than providing the health visitors that are needed to support early parenting. Getting advertising revenues appears to be more important than protecting very young children from junk culture. Perhaps we are in a transitional phase between an exhausted materialism and a renewed valuing of human relation-ship—but we aren't there yet.

There remains a credibility gap about how to achieve secure, confident children, and to promote loving and secure early relation-ships. The current trend is for mothers to return to work earlier and earlier, leaving their babies with other caregivers whose emotional regulation may not be as sensitive. Governments wanting a pro-ductive workforce tend to focus on the provision of child-care. In Britain, very little of Sure Start or Children's Centres' expenditure goes on providing psychological help for parents and their babies. Most CAMHS teams have not until now focused on infant mental health, but tend to wait for problems to be diagnosed in pre-school and school aged children. When the authorities are faced with poor behaviour in children, they tend to respond with programmes that offer conscious 'Parenting skills'. But the in-depth psychological sup-port and interventions that might break the unconscious cycles of poor regulation, and stop them being passed on, are more expensive and difficult to establish. There are few health visitors who special-ize in infant mental health. Specialist parent–infant psychotherapy is not universally available, as it should be. On the other hand, the positive news is that government has set up a pilot programme, based on specially trained health visitors supporting and working psychologically in the home with high-risk families. This is the sort of programme which could have a big impact if the finance was found to make it available for all parents who need it.

The image of children stuck in front of TV or computers, eating junk food, never having conversation with adults is one of emotional neglect in the midst of material plenty. This is part of the picture. But the quality of relationships in childhood also builds on the foundations established much earlier on, in infancy. When adults fail to appreciate the unique unfolding of their baby's personality, and his or her need for consistent, attentive parenting, the scene is set for careless parenting practices, of the 'any old thing will do' variety endorsed by Mick Hume, quoted earlier. Parents may then under-rate how much they influence and shape their baby's development, and may end up believing that a baby can be equally well cared for by a teenager or an untrained nursery worker, or that relying on television programmes or computer games as substitute parents is not a problem.

On the other hand, parents who are interested in their babies' minds and feelings from the start are likely to go on being interested throughout childhood. Babyhood establishes the connection between parent and child, on which a lifelong relationship is built. Without being overly precious about parental devotion, we cannot ignore the evidence that positive early experience confers huge advantages on a child, whilst inadequate early care has a disproportionately negative effect on a child's life. Babyhood really is the foundation for emotional health and physical well-being. But as long as we continue to fail to understand this, and to ensure that good care starts in babyhood, toxic childhoods will go on happening.

References

Balbirnie, R. (n.d.). Unpublished personal communication.

Belsky, J., Hsieh, K.-H., & Crnic, K. (1998). Mothering, fathering, and infant negativity as antecedents of boys' externalizing problems and inhibition at age 3 years: differential susceptibility to rearing experience? *Development and Psychopathology*, 10: 301–319.

Campbell, B.C., & Eisenberg, D. (2007). Obesity, Attention Deficit-Hyperactivity Disorder and the dopaminergic reward system. *Collegium Antropologicum*, 31: 1: 33–38.

Chugani, H.T., Behen, M.E., Muzik, O., Juha, C., Nagy, F., & Chugani, D.C. (2001). Local brain functional activity following early deprivation: a study of postinstitutionalized Romanian orphans. *NeuroImage*, 14: 1290–1301.

De Bellis, M.D. (2005). The psychobiology of neglect. *Child Maltreatment*, 10: 150–172.

Department for Children, Schools and Families (2005). *Every Child Matters* (see www.everychildmatters.gov.uk).

Essex, M. (2002). Maternal stress beginning in infancy may sensitize children to later stress exposure: effects on cortisol and behavior. *Biological Psychiatry*, 52: 776–784.

Gerra, G., Leonardi, C., Cortese, E., Zaimovic, A., Dell'Agnello, G., Manfredini, M., Somaini, L., Petracca, F., Caretti, V., Saracino, M.A., Raggi, M.A., & Donnini, C. (2007). Homovanillic acid (HVA) plasma levels inversely correlate with attention deficit-hyperactivity and childhood neglect measures in addicted patients. *Journal of Neural Transmission*, 114: 1637–1647.

Jezierski, G., Zehle, S., Bock, J., Braun, K., & Gruss, M. (2007). Early stress and chronic methylphenidate cross-sensitize dopaminergic responses in the adolescent medial prefrontal cortex and nucleus accumbens. *Journal of Neurochemistry*, 103: 2234–2244.

Lucas, A. (1998). Programming by early nutrition: an experimental approach. *Journal of Nutrition*, 128: 401S–406S.

Lyons, D.M., Lopez, J.M., Yang, C., & Schatzberg, A.F. (2000). Stress-level cortisol treatment impairs inhibitory control of behavior in monkeys. *Journal of Neuroscience*, 20: 7816–7821.

Ohnishi1, T., Matsuda1, H., Hashimoto, T., Kunihiro1, T., Nishikawa1, M., Uema, T., & Sasaki, M. (2000). Abnormal regional cerebral blood flow in childhood autism. *Brain*, 123: 1838–1844.

Patrick, M., Hobson, R.P., Castle, D., Howard, R., & many others. (1994). Personality disorder and the mental representation of early social experience. *Development and Psychopathology*, 6: 375–388.

Pettit, G.S., & Bates, J.E. (1989). Family interaction patterns and children's behavior problems from infancy to 4 years. *Developmental Psychology*, 25: 413–420.

Rankin, K.P., Rosen, H.J., Kramer, J.H., Schauer, G.F., Weiner, M.W., Schuff, N., & Miller, B.L. (2004). Right and left medial orbitofrontal volumes show an opposite relationship to agreeableness in FTD. *Dementia and Geriatric Cognitive Disorder*, 17: 328–332.

Rankin, K.P., Gorno-Tempini, M.L., Allison, S.C., Stanley, C.M., Glenn, S., Weiner, M.W., & Miller, B.L. (2006). Structural anatomy of empathy in neurodegenerative disease. *Brain*, 129: 2945–2956.

Schore, A.B. (1994) *Affect Regulation and the Origin of the Self*. Philadelphia: Lawrence Erlbaum.

Seckl, J., & Meaney, M.J. (2004). Glucocorticoid programming. *Annals of the New York Academy of Sciences*, 1032: 63–84.

Tremblay, R.E., Nagin, D.S., Séguin, J.R., Zoccolillo, M., Zelazo, P.D., Boivin, M., Pérusse, D., & Japel, C. (2004). Physical aggression during early childhood: trajectories and predictors. *Pediatrics*, 114: e43–e50.

Zimmer, L., Vancassel, S., Cantagrel, S., Breton, P., Delamanche, S., Guilloteau, D., Durand, G., & Chalon, S. (2002). The dopamine meso-corticolimbic pathway is affected by deficiency in n-3 polyunsaturated fatty acids. *American Journal of Clinical Nutrition*, 75: 662–667.

PART III

TOWARDS A THERAPEUTIC ETHOS
FOR CHILDHOOD

Resisting images of the 'diminished self' in education policy and practice for emotional well-being

Kathryn Ecclestone

Introduction

Children, young people, and adults are increasingly receiving assessments of their emotional vulnerability. A further education college in the Midlands has recently instructed teaching staff on Entry to Employment and adult literacy and numeracy programmes not to ask challenging questions in class, or write critical comments on students' work, in case these damage their self-esteem. In a presentation to new staff in a pre-1992 university, the vice-chancellor attributed low self-esteem and 'emotional baggage' to 'our widening participation students', asserting that these problems were a challenge for universities used to 'traditional' students. Teachers and researchers refer increasingly to 'vulnerable learners', 'at-risk learners', learners with 'fragile identities', and 'low self-esteemers'. A university counselling service offers 'support' for students who feel threatened by challenges to well-being caused by new ideas in subjects like philosophy, history, and politics, suggesting that knowledge itself makes us vulnerable or emotionally unwell!

Although labelling of pupils and students as 'thick', 'stupid', 'bright', and 'clever' (rooted in discredited measures of intelligence) are commonplace in the British education system, labels that associate achievement, attitude, or behaviour with emotional vulnerability and emotional well-being are new. Sometimes, whole groups, such as asylum seekers learning English or 14-year olds disaffected with school education, are deemed to 'suffer from low self-esteem'. Sometimes, students on particular courses or programmes are singled out for concern. End-of-year reports for primary-school children routinely refer to 'low self-esteem' as the cause of social and educational difficulties. Children as young as 8 talk about 'anxiety', 'being stressed out', and feeling 'got at'.

These random examples reflect a rising tide of concern about people's emotional well-being in education policy, research, and practice (for detailed analysis and further examples, see Ecclestone & Hayes, 2008). This chapter explores the relationship between cultural and educational accounts of emotion and the language, assumptions, and labels of popular therapy that Dennis Hayes and I have evaluated in relation to educational goals and practices in our recent book, *The Dangerous Rise of Therapeutic Education* (ibid.). First, it offers examples of these populist assumptions. Secondly, it explores how they permeate emotional interventions, sponsored as part of the British New Labour Government's particular view of social justice. Thirdly, it summarizes the main strands of influence on policy in this area. Fourthly, it argues that a diminished sense of subjectivity lies behind these educational and cultural accounts. Finally, it concludes with my concerns about the implications for education based on the arguments in the chapter.

Cultural accounts of emotional vulnerability

The popular rise of emotional vulnerability and dysfunction

Popular culture is saturated with the vocabulary, mindset, and assumptions of therapy. Lifestyle, confessional and reality television, the huge literary genre of biographies and autobiographies titled in bookshops as 'tragic life stories', women and men's life-style magazines, and the ever-expanding self-help industry—all offer an endless stream of stories about emotional vulnerability and the life-lasting psychological legacy of childhood experiences, with accompanying 'explanations' and 'solutions'. There are growing numbers of books to help you diagnose mental illness or to understand the emotional effects of your life's events, and a corresponding number on 'happiness', either finding and developing it or understanding why you don't have it (see, for example, Connelly-Stephenson, 2007; James, 2007).

An up-market monthly magazine, *Psychologies*, carries detailed features and 'diagnostic' quizzes on a huge array of psychological problems: between March and September 2007, these included 'approval addiction disorder', 'responsibility aversion', 'fear of rejection', 'low self-esteem', 'sex addiction', and 'fear of intimacy'. The magazine popularizes an eclectic mix of explanations and insights drawn from psychoanalysis, relationship counselling, and cognitive and social psychology. The overall effect of reading consecutive monthly editions is to see no part of life as immune from emotional problems, and to be both confused about one's problems and even more confused by the 'plausible' explanations offered for their roots and solutions. If you diagnosed yourself with normal levels of self-esteem in the March edition, you found out that this might mask unhealthy 'self-love' in September!

One section of the local bookshop in the small town where I live is depicted as 'Tragic life stories': it carries 69 titles. Next to it, the sub-titles of some of the autobiographies of minor and major celebrities suggest they could easily cross into the other section: tales of 'love and fame' are illuminated through 'battles with addiction', 'low self-esteem', 'childhood abuse', and 'personal demons'. From chat shows to the autobiographies of famous and successful people such as ex-American president Bill Clinton and Hollywood actress and political activist, Jane Fonda, to British Olympic athlete Kelly Holmes, insecurity, emotional 'pain', and vulnerability have created a flourishing genre, depicted by BBC presenter Jonathan Ross as 'cry-ographies', and by some American commentators as 'pathographies' (Furedi, 2003).

Television programmes have also turned insecurity into a new genre, with a plethora of life-style 'experts', from cosmetic and fashion pundits to family therapists, focusing on the emotional vulnerability caused by life events, being middle-aged, lazy, having a poor diet, or lacking good dress sense. These draw out the emotions of their subjects to painful levels on television, and then supposedly build them back up again. And the more vulnerable and fragile the account, the better the cameras like it. In March 2007, TV presenter Ulrika Johnsson, ostensibly researching and presenting a programme on sex addiction, ended up with her own therapeutic assessment of the 'disorder', and its partner, 'emotional intimacy disorder'. Prolonged scenes of her very personal disclosures and her emotional accounts of realization and salvation, drawn out by a therapist, were accompanied by populist therapeutic explanations of their causes: 'wanting to please my father', 'wanting my mother's affection', 'always pleasing other people'.

Deeper problems of emotional fragility or outright mental illness are also mainstream media fare. British ex-footballer Paul Gascoigne's outpourings, with transcripts of his therapy sessions and his body map of ailments and their mental causes, were serialized in *The Times* in July 2006. In April 2007, psychotherapist Pamela Connelly presented a series of therapeutic sessions with famous people, with the ensuing revealing and emotional accounts widely reviewed in the press.

Celebrities who promote their emotional difficulties are widely praised for doing so, especially if they are men, because it supposedly frees others to talk openly about their mental-health problems. Writing in the British newspaper, the *Guardian*, journalist Catherine Bennett argued that the rise of public disclosures of depression and self-harm by celebrities were a positive sign, because they provide relief to others who suffer, so that rather than being a sign of 'a debased deal between victims and voyeurs, [it is] the first step towards a mentally healthy society in which everyone feels at liberty to admit mental illness' (Bennett, 2005, p. 9).

It is not only celebrities who are praised for their willingness to disclose feelings of vulnerability. At the annual conference of the British National Union of Teachers in 2006, a school teacher who broke down during his account of stress at school was praised for enabling others to come forward and admit difficulties. The popularity of the British film *The Queen* is also evidence of interest in the emotional vulnerability of a figure who epitomizes old-fashioned English stoicism and emotional repression.

Preoccupation with emotional vulnerability parallels a more judgmental trend that dwells on difficulties in dealing with strong emotion, thereby threatening one's own well-being and that of others. The debacle over the alleged 'racist bullying' by Jade Goody of

Shilpa Shetty in the British 'reality TV' programme 'Celebrity Big Brother' in February 2007 revealed the emotional fragility of both sides in being unable to deal with confrontation without breaking down into extreme anger and distress. In programmes such as 'Wife Swap', the working-class participants are invariably shown as unable to express emotions calmly or reasonably, or 'appropriately and constructively', as advocates of emotional literacy would have it. In everyday life and work conversations, it is becoming commonplace to judge crass, rude, or aggressive treatment, especially if from men, as a sign of being 'emotionally illiterate' or as a threat to others' well-being.

Toxic childhood

Popular manifestations of emotional vulnerability and 'dysfunction' promise redemption and transformation through self-awareness and emotional survival in an endless quest for the authentic self. Yet they also encourage unchallenged assumptions that we all suffer, to a greater or lesser extent, from the negative emotional effects of diverse life experiences and events: merely getting through the trials and tribulations of life becomes the ultimate goal, sold as 'emotional survival'.

These ideas are reinforced by media and political attention to a plethora of fears about the impact of modern life on how people feel about themselves and their lives, emanating from a wide range of sources (see Furedi, 2003). Like popular interest in emotional vulnerability, attention to these fears has intensified over the past five years. According to research, there is a crisis of unprecedented proportions in the mental health and emotional problems of children and young people. These findings have been widely taken up by the British media. The *Daily Mail* reported on 20 July 2007 that a recent study for the Nuffield Foundation found that more than a million children have mental-health problems, doubling the numbers of a generation ago. Another study of mental health amongst young people in Britain claims that 10 per cent of children aged 5–16 had a clinically diagnosed mental disorder, 4 per cent had an emotional disorder, and 2 per cent a hyperkinetic disorder, with such problems more prevalent in lone-parent or reconstituted families, jobless families, those on low incomes, and those where parents had low qualifications (Spratt et al., 2007).

In a book on emotional literacy, Peter Sharp cites figures that show 14 per cent of children with mental disorders come from social class V, compared to 5 per cent from social class 1. Other factors were also correlated to the likelihood of childhood mental illness: 20 per cent of children from unemployed parents compared to 8 per cent from employed families; 15 per cent from families with no qualifications compared to 6 per cent where parents had been to university. He infers that '... it is more likely that emotionally literate parents will have emotionally literate children who will go on to be emotionally literate parents themselves', and that

> ... if a child is given insufficient emotional nurturance, this can lead to poor mental health and ultimately can be life-threatening: approximately 1 in 4 of us will have a mental health problem at some time in our life, requiring treatment or support from the caring professions.
>
> (Sharp, 2001, p. 5)

A widely reported survey for UNICEF (2007) showed that feelings amongst young people in Britain about their lives make them the unhappiest in Europe: worldwide, only teenagers in the United States reported higher levels of unhappiness. Another survey, funded by the Nuffield Foundation and overseen by the Children's Society, was reported in the *Guardian* on 5 June 2007. It showed that today's 16-year olds are less likely than their counterparts 20 years ago to have a best friend they can trust. Psychiatrists quoted in the article raised concerns about the effects of problems with friendship on children's well-being and mental health, and therefore on the quality of childhood. On 6 August 2007, *The Times* carried a report from a survey of 1,000 children by Charity4Children, that showed 70 per cent 'not looking forward' to the summer holidays because they feared for their safety, through bullying and accidents. The most recent report by the Children's Society, published in February 2009, presents the same wide array of concerns, with calls for, amongst other things, formal monitoring of children's emotional well-being (Layard & Dunn, 2009).

The book *Toxic Childhood* by literacy specialist and childhood campaigner, Sue Palmer (see Chapter 3, this volume), was promoted in 2006 through a letter to the *Daily Telegraph* signed by some 110 experts on childhood, including academics (including this book's co-editors), psychologists, and heads of mental-health and children's organizations. It warned that children's lives 'are being poisoned' by an overwhelming range of concerns: materialism; depravity; spiritual breakdown; testing and an arid school curriculum; too much emphasis on rational, cognitive learning; too much freedom; not enough freedom; too much risk adverse parenting; technology, advertising, and the media.

An ever-widening spectrum of emotional and mental-health problems is reflected in these reports. Expansion of meanings about poor well-being and mental ill-health encourages a view that emotional vulnerability besets growing numbers of people. The intuitive appeal of the idea that how we feel about ourselves affects our capacity and competence for life, together with the vagueness that surrounds the notion of well-being, has allowed policy makers and professionals in welfare, guidance, education, and counselling to elide a plethora of ideas around it. In educational settings, the idea that we must address the emotional needs of students and pupils before they can learn effectively is widespread and unchallenged (see, for example, Claxton, 2002; DfES, 2005).

The popularization of therapeutic orthodoxies

Far from being trivial, irrelevant anecdotes, these examples reflect the growing influence of everyday interest in emotional problems, in the way we think about ourselves and others, whether in educational settings or in life generally. This interest also popularizes simplistic therapeutic explanations of life's events and responses to them: whether rooted in cognitive behaviour therapy, Freudian or Jungian analysis, transactional analysis, or Rogerian counselling, therapeutic insights and justifications have become part of the way we explain our own reactions to life, and those of others, at the levels of popular culture and everyday discussion. Simplified explanations of behaviours and feelings draw on an eclectic mix of ideas: for example, articles in *Psychologies* draw on the magazine's staple array of insights from biological programming, neuroscience, Freudian psychology, transactional analysis, and couples' counselling.

One effect is that reductionist therapeutic orthodoxies take hold of our imaginations. For example, the recent autobiographies of Jane Fonda, Bill Clinton, and Paul Gascoigne all legitimize ideas that we all suffer, in varying degrees, lasting emotional damage from life events, particularly childhood ones. Repression of either serious emotional 'pain' or more mundane feelings of low self-esteem, and the effects of childhood on adult behaviours and feelings, is a staple of popular therapeutic orthodoxy. In a televised interview with comedian Stephen Fry in April 2007, Pamela Connelly pressed him to admit that sex with an older boy at school had caused him to create a comedian's façade. His repeated protestations that he had far more serious things to trouble him met with stony disapproval of his 'repressed pain' and his 'typical' comedian's tendency to hide behind humour.

The tendency to talk about behaviours and causes in terms of emotional states, syndromes, addictions, and dysfunctional categories is assisted by proliferating categories: the latest list from the American Psychological Society, for example, identifies over 800 psychological syndromes and disorders that create physical symptoms and behaviours (Nolan, 1998). Taken together, slippery terms, expansion in definitions of disorders and difficulties, invocations of cycles of deprivation, and permanent damage wreaked by 'emotionally illiterate parents'—all reinforce the popular cultural explanation that behind our apparently confident façades lurk low self-esteem and unresolved emotional 'issues' that lead to a growing array of emotional problems.

Institutionalizing emotional vulnerability in educational settings

Emotional well-being and New Labour's view of 'social justice'

It is easy to ridicule the reductionism, contradictions, and clichés of popular therapy, and to see them as irrelevant in political responses to concerns about the public's emotional problems. Yet it is precisely the incoherent, ubiquitous nature of therapeutic orthodoxies, and their symbiotic relationship with cultural explanations about emotional vulnerability and dysfunction, that enable policy makers to show themselves as responsive to such concerns, and uniquely placed to develop people's emotional resources. Texts written to help teachers develop emotional literacy and well-being, for example, and of the evidence upon which government draws to promote emotionally based interventions, show the extent to which popular images of emotion and its lasting psychological effects permeate policy and practice (see Ecclestone & Hayes, 2008).

Understanding the effects of this interplay between cultural accounts and political responses is crucial because culture and education create and reproduce particular subjectivities: 'people's perception of their ability to cope with the problems of life is shaped by the particular account that their culture offers about the nature of human potential' (Furedi, 2003, p. 113). Policy connects cultural perspectives to practice and

> ...increasingly shapes the way individuals construct themselves as subjects. Through policy, [individuals are] categorized and given statuses and roles as 'subject', 'citizen', 'professional', 'national', 'criminal' and deviant... but they may have little consciousness of or control over the processes at work.
>
> (Shore & Wright, 2005, p. 4)

The unchallenged assumption that we face an unprecedented epidemic of mental ill-health is now central to social and welfare policy in the UK: the chief executive of the charity NCH was quoted in the *Daily Mail* on 20 July 2007, saying:

> ...the lack of emotional well-being amongst our children and young people is undermining the foundation of any social policy to combat social exclusion, deprivation or lack of social mobility. We urge Gordon Brown and his new Cabinet to commit to tackling this hidden and fast-growing problem.

The Conservative Party has commissioned a review of children's unhappiness, as has the national Children's Society (see Chapter 5, this volume). In this context, the renaming of the Department for Education and Skills (DfES) as the Department of Children, Families and Schools reflects these concerns about unhappiness and well-being, and prepares government to intensify its responses.

Significantly, the renaming of the DfES removes 'education' as a social aspiration from the history of education policy for the first time since 1899, and embeds much broader notions of well-being and welfare into the remit of schools. Under the requirements of *Every Child Matters* (DfES, 2004), this reflects a fundamental shift in what government regards as key roles for educational institutions. A crucial theme in this shift is the way in which the British government has responded to popular concerns about emotional vulnerability and unhappiness by incorporating them in educational policy and practice.

Emotional well-being is integral to New Labour's belief in what ex-Prime Minister Tony Blair regarded as the 'equal worth of all', and a corresponding shift from equality of opportunity or outcomes to 'equality of esteem' (Blair, quoted by Furedi, 2004, p. 169). Making those who are deemed to be 'excluded' from society and work feel 'included' in public services has become a central strand in public policy, where building self-esteem and responding to expressions of emotional vulnerability enable the State to confer recognition and affirmation (see, for example, Furedi, 2004; Giddens, 1998).

A fundamental principle that has informed all social policy since 1997 is widespread agreement that social exclusion is inextricably linked to destructive influences that damage self-esteem and emotional well-being. In political and professional accounts of the damage being done to self-esteem by poverty, unemployment, and social exclusion, political and professional claims mirror many of the therapeutic orthodoxies summarized above.

Concern about emotional well-being and the role of welfare and education agencies in its development constitute a central theme in policy makers' view of the effects of low educational achievement and participation on particular groups, such as young people and single mothers, where low self-esteem, feelings of vulnerability, and risk to particular groups are depicted as part of a cycle of deprivation. Breaking out of this cycle depends upon educational and welfare initiatives that address the emotional impact of deprivation, as well as practical strategies for leading people back into work and education (see, for example, SEU, 1999, 2005).

In their presentation of a complex and powerful cycle of social and psychological deprivation, politicians are careful not to elide environmental and structural causes, such as unemployment and communal breakdown, with individual 'traits' or attributes of low self-esteem and emotional vulnerability. Nevertheless, arguments that emotional dysfunction both arises from, and contributes to, inequality enable policy makers to focus on its emotional, individual, and social outcomes instead of material causes and effects. In this scenario, emotional or mental ill-health, feelings of low self-esteem, and exclusion are not only part of a cycle of deprivation passed on to subsequent generations, but they are medicalized and therefore treatable.

At a seminar on 'Childhood, well-being and a therapeutic ethos', hosted by the Research Centre for Therapeutic Education at Roehampton University in December 2006, and on which this book is based, some 70 representatives from mental-health organizations, children's charities, education psychologists, psychiatrists, and therapists could not agree how many people needed therapeutic interventions, but they all agreed that the scale of emotional problems was huge and growing. Education was seen as a key site of influence: in his introduction, the director of the research centre, Del Loewenthal, argued that

> If we are to stand a chance of our children and ourselves leading good lives, it may be vital for psychotherapists, amongst others, to examine how we can influence education in general. ... Perhaps, therefore, those of us who are psychotherapists need to look at psychotherapy as an educational practice, not only in the consulting room but to see the wisdom for both children and adults to learn from each other and for our society to continue to attempt to ensure that scientific and technical learning, whilst important, is secondary to the resources of the human soul. ... Thus, education and therapy might be seen not so much about knowledge but rather about awakening ... by imparting and acquiring through the relational. [cf. his Chapter 2, this volume]

In an emotional state

Ideas about elevating relational and emotional aspects of life as a focus for education over more traditional scientific and technical learning find a ready audience. Four broad strands of thinking have influenced policy makers and think-tanks such as DEMOS and the Institute of Public Policy Research.

Emotional intelligence

Ideas about emotional literacy derive from work on emotional intelligence originated by John Mayer and Peter Salovey, who defined it as 'the capacity to reason with emotion in four areas: to perceive emotion, to integrate it into thought, to understand it and to manage it'; and, in developing measures of EI, they present it as 'the co-operative combination of intelligence and emotion' (Craig, 2007, p. 7).

Daniel Goleman's best-selling book (1996) is widely credited for bringing the idea that there are measurable psychological constructs that comprise emotional intelligence into popular and political thinking in America and Britain and, crucially, that it is more important to life and work success than traditional academic intelligence. Goleman developed this construct from a range of personal and intra-personal intelligences, arguing that it comprises 'abilities such as being able to motivate oneself and persist in the face of frustrations; to control impulse and delay gratification; to regulate one's moods and keep distress from swamping the ability to think; to empathise and to hope' (Goleman, 1996, p. 43).

According to Gordon Stobart, Goleman's book was influential as a journalistic blast and a rallying call about the lack of recognition that emotional skills are given in a culture influenced heavily by a history of 'IQ' (Stobart, 2007). As Stobart points out, Goleman has managed to persuade millions of readers, including policy makers and the advocates of emotional literacy for schools, 'that emotional intelligence is more important than traditional measures of intelligence': this 'is a message of comfort because emotional skills can be learned'. This resonates with the popular idea, promoted by psychologist Howard Gardner, that we have 'multiple intelligences', although Gardner has distanced himself from Goleman's ideas (see Craig, 2007). A bleak view that intelligence is innate and therefore limited to a small pool of people has given way to a more inclusive idea that everyone is a unique combination of separate abilities. This appears to offer a more holistic, humane, liberal view of how children learn and also, what they should learn.

Emotional literacy

The influential pressure group Antidote defines emotional literacy as: 'the practice of interacting with others in ways that build understanding of our own and others' emotions, then using this understanding to inform our actions' by enabling people to:

- Find ways to feel connected to each other and of using their relationships to deal with emotions that might otherwise cause them to lash out in rage or withdraw in despair;
- Deal with the emotions that can render them unable to take in new information, access emotional states such as curiosity, resilience, and joy that lead to a rich experience of learning;
- Engage in activities that promote physical and emotional well-being and broaden the range of what they can talk about with each other in ways that make it less likely that they will abuse drugs and alcohol, bully their peers, or engage in other forms of self-destructive activity.

Antidote offers a vision where:

> the facility to handle the complexities of emotional life is as widespread as the capacity to read, write and do arithmetic. [In an] ... emotionally literate society ...:
> **families and friends** provide us with emotional security;
> **communities** create opportunities for neighbours to connect with each other;
> **government** engages us in its deliberations and is responsive to ideas that emerge;
> **work-places** cultivate creativity and draw upon our potential to contribute;
> **economic policy** promotes social and emotional well-being alongside prosperity;
> **our environment** becomes more sustainable as we embrace change in life-styles and attitudes;
> **schools and colleges** stimulate curiosity, creativity, and the desire to learn;
> **our criminal justice system** addresses the emotions that drive some of us to crime;
> **our health providers** attend to the emotional aspects of physical illness.
>
> (www.antidote.org.uk)

In her critique of current developments for emotional intelligence and emotional literacy in the British education system, Carol Craig argues that 'those favouring more focus on social and emotional education in schools are aware that to make real progress, they have to show that emotional intelligence/literacy is important for children's success in life' (2007, p. 21).

Emotional well-being and emotional health

Practitioners and researchers from the field of mental health provide another influential spur to arguments that educational institutions need to pay much more explicit attention to emotional dimensions of young people's lives than they have in the past. Notions of mental well-being, and the prevention of mental ill-health, expand notions of emotional intelligence and emotional literacy into 'emotional health' and 'well-being'. For example, Gloucester County Council has adopted a definition offered by Young Minds, a charity committed to the improvement of the mental health of all children. This defines good mental health in children and adolescents as a number of abilities, including the ability to develop emotionally, intellectually, and spiritually, and to initiate, develop, and sustain 'mutually satisfying' personal relationships. Notions of emotional literacy are also evident in the goal of developing an ability to become aware of others and to empathize with them, as is a more sophisticated therapeutic goal of using psychological distress as a form of development rather than allowing it to get in the way of further development (Gloucester County Council, 2006).

More recently, ideas about emotional health, mental health, emotional intelligence and emotional literacy have been encompassed by the emergence of 'emotional well-being'. Its rise as an educational concern reflects a significant shift from mental-health work as a marginal activity and concern, to its re-presentation as an important consideration for mainstream education and welfare services. Organizations such as MIND have long campaigned to promote the voice of people with mental-health problems who want to feel less marginalized and stigmatized. As Spratt et al. argue, the importance of 'supporting mental well-being' is a significant change from a sickness model of mental health, where mental health is 'no longer seen simply as the absence of mental illness, but as encompassing emotional health and well-being' (2007, p. 415). In the requirements of the DfES's *Every Child Matters*, schools working with voluntary organizations and health and welfare agencies 'have a crucial role in promoting positive mental health, and in identifying and remediating difficulties' (ibid.).

Policy initiatives therefore encourage schools to destigmatize mental-health problems and enable more people to admit to problems, whilst also preventing their emergence amongst children. A project funded by the former Department for Education and Skills to develop Emotional Health and Well-being for All in Secondary Schools involved psychiatrists, psychologists, counsellors, and researchers in finding ways to combat increasing rates of mental-health difficulties amongst children and young people. Authors of a book for schools from this project define mental and emotional health problems as:

> A 'disturbance in functioning' in one area of relationships, mood, behaviour or development. When a problem is particularly severe or persistent over time, or when a number of difficulties are experienced at the same time, a child is said to have a mental health disorder.
>
> (Cowie et al., 2004, p. 1)

Reflexive modernization and identity 'narratives'

Academic credibility for the idea that an emotionally self-aware and emotionally literate public is a progressive political goal comes from growing interest in what influential sociologists Anthony Giddens and Ulrich Beck call 'reflexive modernization'. Reflexivity is, according to Giddens, a self-defining process that enables individuals to monitor psychological and social information about possible life trajectories, choices, and relationships (Giddens, 1991). He sees this as a positive trend, arguing that psychoanalysis and therapy flowing from a quest for self-awareness provide a setting and a

> rich fund of theoretical and conceptual resources for the creation of a reflexively ordered narrative of self. In a therapeutic situation, whether of the classical psychoanalytical type or not,

individuals are able (in principle) to bring their past into line with the exigencies of the present, consolidating a story-line with which they feel relatively content.

(Giddens, 1995, p. 31)

The breakdown of collective ties, the rise of individual isolation and increase in fears of risk, and the future, lead Beck to argue that increased individualization offers opportunities for people to construct more aspects of their 'life explanations' and 'biographies' than ever before (Beck, 1992). For both Giddens and Beck, this is a key factor in creating progressive forms of democracy because they encourage 'reflexive self-awareness' on the part of the public and policy makers alike.

Theories of the 'risk society' and 'reflexive modernization' have had a strong influence on think-tanks as well as researchers in diverse social science disciplines, including education. In the context of a cultural turn towards popular therapy, exploring and engaging with the inner self has become an important constituent of contemporary identity. One effect is that eliciting life histories and biographies has moved from the realms of specialist therapeutic interventions and research methods into everyday pedagogy (for discussion, see Ecclestone, 2007, 2009 [Chapter 8]; Gordon, 2003).

The 'soft' outcomes of learning

A functional view of emotion is not confined to its importance as a commodity in work roles and the economy. Indeed, as a counter to an overly instrumental focus on the needs of employers, researchers, practitioners, and development and lobbying organizations, the National Institute for Adult and Continuing Education, for example, offers a different focus for an instrumental view of education by arguing that public funding for adult education should be maintained because of the emotional benefits of education through raised self-esteem and confidence as part of 'identity capital'.

There is growing research interest in the idea that soft outcomes of learning, particularly for adults disaffected from formal education, are either as important as other outcomes such as qualifications, or more important (see, for example, Ecclestone and McGiveney, 2005;

Parrott, 2005). Government-funded research regards these 'soft outcomes' and personal dimensions of participating in education as a measurable component of human capital (see www.widerbenefit soflearning.org).

Emotional interventions

There is an overwhelming consensus that the State and its educational and welfare institutions must address emotional problems and foster emotional well-being and happiness (see, for example, Layard, 2005; Toynbee, 2005). The goals and institutional arrangements of *Every Child Matters* (*ECM*) require welfare and education agencies to ensure that, as part of being 'safe' and able to achieve educationally and socially, children's well-being is paramount. *ECM* institutionalizes concerns about the state of children and young people's emotional lives, and rationalizes the diverse initiatives that have emerged to address them over the past ten years.

Such initiatives include circle time, nuture groups, anti-bullying and mentoring schemes, drama workshops to deal with the trauma of transitions and bullying, activities to develop learning power, learning to learn and philosophy for children, emotional audits and whole-school strategies for emotional literacy (see, for example, Antidote, 2006; Bailey, 2007; Cowie et al., 2004; Sharp, 2001; Weare, 2004). The Qualifications and Curriculum Authority requires schools to assess young children's emotional competence in a Foundation Stage Profile, while the National Institute for Clinical Excellence is drawing up guidelines for primary schools to diagnose emotional well-being. A recent report for the former DfES shows that there are 28 instruments currently in use for assessing different aspects of emotional competence (Stewart-Brown and Edmunds, 2003).

Emotional interventions attract large amounts of public funding. The government's Social, Emotional and Affective Learning strategy for schools cost £10 m in 2007–8, with a further £31.2 million ear-marked over the next three years. Anti-bullying schemes cost £1.7 million a year, while peer mentoring currently receives £1.75 million. Another £60 million was added in July 2007 to educational expenditure for schools to improve emotional well-being, phased over the next three years to be £30 million in 2010–11.

A thriving commercial and educational industry, then, flourishes around policy and practice, encompassing a range of slippery constructs, such as emotional well-being, 'emotional literacy', 'emotional intelligence', 'self-esteem', 'mental health and well-being', and 'emotional competence'. Personal, social, and health education and citizenship are also increasingly incorporated in initiatives for emotional literacy and well-being (see, for example, Antidote, 2006). The former Department for Education and Skills (DfES) listed over 70 organizations working in this area, ranging from specialist consultancies for circle time and emotional literacy, mental health and children's organizations, to lobbying organizations and pressure groups. Universities such as Cambridge and Glasgow have research centres focussing on emotional well-being. A rapidly growing consultancy business, comprising academic researchers, educational psychologists, psychotherapists, psychiatrists, and an array of therapeutic charities, such as the Oxford Parent Infant Project (see Chapter 8, this volume) that provides psychotherapeutic help to parents and babies, runs courses, carries out emotional audits and training for senior managers, and produces guidance and materials for teachers and parents.

Children and young people are being co-opted as key workers in emotionally based interventions. For example, the role of peer mentors now extends far beyond support for study skills: buddy schemes in secondary schools train 14-year olds in counselling techniques, so that teenagers can be empathetic mentors to 11-year olds moving to secondary school: one scheme in the South-West of England is called 'Angels'—'a nice guy every time life sucks'. Pupils designated as Angels can take a GCSE in Peer Mentoring. Children moving from primary to secondary school can take part in 'drama workshops' with their parents, in which theatre educators and peer 'bully counsellors' help them 'explore and deal with' the trauma of transition. In some schools, ten-year olds are allocated e-buddies to support transition. The government is currently evaluating a scheme to bring school leavers into schools as mentors. In universities, peer mentoring roles can be assessed for credits as part of a degree.

Universities and further-education colleges run certificated courses in emotional well-being for teachers, parents, nursery nurses, and support workers, including cleaners and canteen staff. Local authorities and their newly formed 'integrated children's services' run evening classes in emotional literacy and well-being. Trainee teachers on teacher training courses around the UK produce displays and reports about circle time and personal and health education that uncritically reproduce claims from advocates of emotional literacy about the links between self-esteem, emotional well-being, and personal education as the fundamental basis of citizenship and social harmony.

Day-to-day teaching activities, reflective diaries, and personal-development portfolios in colleges and universities, and on professional development courses, also reveal an emotional, introspective focus. There has been a large expansion of counselling and support services for stress, anxiety, and distress in schools, universities, and colleges. In one university, of 2,800 students diagnosed with a 'disability', over 1,000 have what the disability liaison officer called 'low-level' mental disorders. Self-reporting and the loosening of what a 'clinically well-recognized' diagnosis means have led to a huge rise in students presenting themselves as in need of special help to get through their university course.

The rise of the diminished self

Despite the rhetoric of empowerment that accompanies the emotional initiatives summarized above and which is also evident in the examples of popular therapy summarized in the first section, discourses of emotional well-being and engagement mask a pessimistic tone that privileges damage, vulnerability, and fragility. Despite optimistic promises made for emotional intelligence and emotional literacy, a pessimistic emotional determinism underlies them in a thinly veiled concern about social disorder. For example, Goleman warns that societies 'face a growing calamity in our shared emotional life' (Goleman, 1996, p. 56), whilst Antidote made the argument that the unhappy state of affairs results from a reluctance to acknowledge that feelings influence almost everything we do.

One effect of presenting emotional intelligence and literacy, and self-esteem, as solutions to a huge array of social, personal, and educational problems is that contradictory beliefs about learning, determinism, and socially induced characteristics permeate support for them. Text books on emotional literacy and well-being offer an eclectic, simplistic array of 'theories' made up from relevant insights from: Maslow's hierarchy of motivation; self-concept theory; positive psychology; multiple intelligences; Rogerian counselling; emotional intelligence; brain science; and learning styles (see, for example, Cowie et al., 2004; Sharp, 2001; Weare, 2004).

Other orthodoxies are also evident. It is commonplace to offer accounts of emotional literacy that present the different 'emotional styles' that men and women 'typically' display, leading to assertions that women are more emotionally literate (see, for example, Sharp, 2001; Weare, 2004). This resonates with the popular idea that boys and men are emotionally inarticulate, and that traditional attributes of masculinity are pathologically damaging to their educational and social success, an idea evident in the government's advocacy of emotional literacy for boys (see Francis & Skelton, 2005).

Diminished images of human potential that lie behind contemporary preoccupation with emotional vulnerability are illuminated by work in cultural and political studies, and in sociology that explores a deep cultural shift from belief in human potential and collective and individual striving for agency, towards demoralization about humanity and people's capacity for agency (see Fevre, 2001; Furedi, 1999, 2003; Heartfield 2002; Lasch, 1979; Malik, 2001; Nolan, 1998; Rieff, 1966; Rose, 1990; Sennett, 2003). This body of work illuminates the concept of the 'diminished self', and charts its emergence through public and political preoccupation with risk, danger, and vulnerability in the face of life events, and the parallel erosion of belief in agency, resilience, and collective support to overcome problems. Taken together, this work argues that the idea of humans as conscious agents who realize their potential for individual and social change through projects to transform themselves and their world has given way to beliefs about a narrow, introspective view of what it means to be human, embedded in evolutionary psychology, determinism, and postmodern 'deconstructions' of the human subject.

Citing myriad examples of initiatives and interventions based on beliefs that life events cause emotional difficulties and must be exposed and managed in therapeutic ways, Furedi presents a strong case that there is a growing 'cultural perspective that regards most forms of human experience as the source of emotional distress' (2003, p. 110). Interventions based on such beliefs create a popular view that, to a greater or lesser extent, we are all vulnerable and emotionally damaged by life events, but that some groups and individuals are especially damaged. In this depiction, social and educational success is increasingly attributed to emotional factors.

Diminished images offer a further elision by singling out, simultaneously, the emotional vulnerability of particular groups, whilst normalizing similar feelings in the general population. The idea that our confident public façades belie our fragile self-esteem and emotional vulnerability promotes feelings of inclusion based on the shared belief that we are all damaged, to a greater or lesser extent, by life events. Studies of therapeutic interventions by State and other agencies show a fundamental shift from a liberal-humanist belief that fragility and damage are the exception and innate capacity for potential and agency are the norm, to one where fragility is universal (see Nolan, 1998; Pupavac, 2001, 2003). A therapeutic ethos extends therapy-based activities into an everyday mindset or sensibility that both accepts and expects emotional fragility, and which sees therapeutic support as both normal and necessary. Magazines such as *Psychologies* popularize this ethos overtly, and so do other examples of popular preoccupation with vulnerability, cited in the first part of this chapter.

Following this argument, cultural images of the diminished self are inscribed within and fuelled by a therapeutic ethos embedded in popular and political preoccupation with emotional well-being, and associated constructs of emotional intelligence, emotional literacy, and self-esteem. A therapeutic ethos is reflected in the extension of activities such as counselling, psychoanalysis, and psychology into more areas of social activity, policy, and professional practice, and the exponential rise in such activities is relatively easy to chart. Yet the real significance of a therapeutic ethos is that it offers a new popular and political sensibility, a form of cultural script, a set of explanations, underlying assumptions about appropriate feelings and responses to events, and a set of associated practices and rituals through which people make sense of themselves and others.

Arguments that such views reduce the complexities and specialisms of therapy and psychology to a populist caricature miss the significance of the rise of the diminished self. Instead, the diminished self is both a product and a cause of a broader therapeutic turn in popular culture, and the professionalization of more areas of private life. These shifts produce a sense of self which Furedi argues 'characteristically suffers from an emotional deficit and possesses a permanent consciousness of vulnerability' (2004, p. 414). Reductionist, populist images of therapy respond to this subjectivity: so too does education policy.

Conclusions

So far, little attention has been paid to the iteration between cultural accounts of the diminished self, policy, and educational practices in a British context. In our provocative and challenging critique of this state of affairs, Dennis Hayes and I acknowledge that our arguments, some of which have been presented in this chapter, need exploring empirically in future studies (Ecclestone & Hayes, 2008; Ecclestone et al., 2008).

The implications of these arguments for current developments in education policy, and the ways in which these developments are typically presented, can be summarized here. First, images of, and beliefs about, people's vulnerability and fragility lie behind the rhetoric of 'empowerment', 'authenticity', and 'positive identity' that permeate therapeutic interventions for emotional well-being in education. Secondly, preoccupation with emotional well-being encourages activities and assumptions that help people live with their supposedly flawed and vulnerable selves, and to see others as similarly flawed and vulnerable. Thirdly, emotional interventions based on a diminished subjectivity formalize and encourage dependence on external emotional support offered by State agencies and a growing work-force of mentors, life coaches, counsellors, psychologists, and therapists. Fourthly, beliefs that education can transform lives through an optimistic vision of the potential for humans to change themselves and their world are giving way rapidly to a deeply instrumental view of education where curriculum subjects and relationships between teachers and students, and between students, become mechanistic opportunities to turn everyday life, and how we feel about it, into the processes and content of education.

Yet, the diverse concerns, and claims that drive emotionally based interventions, and their underlying assumptions of a 'diminished self', remain largely immune from critique. Nor are there any rigorous independent research studies of the validity and reliability of psychological inventories that claim to measure emotional domains, and no independent evaluation of interventions that have been introduced. Similarly, the inexorable rise of self-esteem in popular, political, and professional thinking has not been inhibited by a systematic review of research studies about the psychological construct and its links to a range of life problems, which casts serious doubt on the validity and reliability of both the construct itself and interventions to develop it (Emler, 2001). Despite these problems, the industry that is fuelling interest in emotional well-being, and its affirmation in *Every Child Matters*, appears to be influencing political and professional ideas to an unprecedented degree.

In 2002, Dennis Hayes and I began, separately, to analyse the rise of a 'therapeutic ethos' and its effects on different sectors of the education system. Our critique is, so far, the only challenge by educational researchers to current developments. Our arguments attract much interest, and occasional support, but more often, strong hostility and incomprehension, sometimes personal criticism. Arguments, such as those offered in this chapter and developed in our own book, are complex because they draw on events and practices across diverse areas of social policy and contemporary culture. They show that the origins of concerns, and responses to them from a large number of organizations, including policy makers, are not only diverse but contradictory. Challenge is also controversial because it confronts an overwhelming tide of support for emotional interventions amongst policy makers and educators from liberal and Left traditions.

It is important to discount old labels such as 'left', 'radical', and 'liberal', and to question how associated notions of 'social justice' and 'empowerment' are being used, because these have become mantras with very little meaning in relation to educational or political ideals. This problem is particularly evident in the rise of a therapeutic ethos based on a diminished subjectivity. Our challenge to such ideas routinely attracts accusations that we are 'right wing', 'uncaring', and, shifting the argument to an emotional, personal terrain, that we clearly have our own 'emotional issues'!

Such anti-rational, simplistic, and inaccurate criticisms make the task of articulating a clear educational position both novel and difficult. Nevertheless, this chapter has aimed to show that the institutionalizing of emotional well-being reinforces the diminished therapeutic focus of New Labour's approach to social justice. This suggests a dangerous prognosis for social justice based on optimism about human potential.

References

Antidote (2006). *Philosophy for Children* (a video for schools and parents). London: Antidote (see also www.antidote.org.uk).

Bailey, S. (2007). Nurture groups and children with Attention Deficit and Hyperactivity Disorder. University of Nottingham: unpublished Ph.D. thesis.

Beck, U. (1992). *Risk Society: Towards a New Modernity*. London & New York: Sage.

Bennett, C. (2005). The benefits of headline therapy. The *Guardian, G2 Supplement*, 31 May: 9.

Claxton, G. (2002). *Building Learning Power: Helping Young People Become Better Learners*. Bristol: TLO.

Connelly-Stephenson, P. (2007). *Head Case: Treat Yourself to Better Mental Health*. London: Headline Publishing.

Cowie, H., Boardman, C., Barnsley, J., & Jennifer, D. (2004). *Emotional Health and Well-being: A Practical Guide for Schools*. London: Paul Chapman.

Craig, C. (2007). *The Potential Dangers of a Systematic, Explicit Approach to Teaching Social and Emotional Skills (SEAL)*. Glasgow: Centre for Confidence and Well-Being.

Department for Children, Schools and Families (DCSF) (2008). *Childhood Well-Being: Qualitative Research Study*. London: DCSF Research Report.

Department for Education and Skills (DfES) (2004). *Every Child Matters*. London; see DfES website, www.dfesf.gsi.gov.uk

Department for Education and Skills (DfES) (2005). *Emotional, Behavioural and Social Skills—Guidance*. See www.dfes.gsi.gov.uk

Ecclestone, K. (2007). Resisting images of the 'diminished self': the implications of emotional well-being and emotional engagement in educational policy. *Journal of Education Policy*, 22: 455–470.

Ecclestone, K. (2009). Managing and supporting the vulnerable self. In: K. Ecclestone, G.J. Biesta, & M. Hughes (Eds.), *Transitions and Learning through the Lifecourse*. London: Routledge.

Ecclestone, K., & Hayes, D. (2008). *The Dangerous Rise of Therapeutic Education*. London: RoutledgeFalmer.

Ecclestone, K., & McGiveney, V. (2005). Are adult educators obsessed with developing self-esteem? *Adults Learning*, January: 8–12.

Ecclestone, K., de Abreu, G., & Quinn, J. (2008). Exploring the impact of interventions for emotional well-being on constructions of the self in educational settings. A research bid to the Economic and Social Science Research Council, October.

Emler, N. (2001). *Self-esteem: The Costs and Causes of Low Self-worth.* York: Joseph Rowntree Foundation.

Fevre, R. (2001). *The Demoralisation of Western Culture: Social Theory and the Dilemmas of Modern Living.* London, Continuum.

Francis, B., & Skelton, C. (2005). *Reassessing Gender and Achievement.* London: Routledge.

Furedi, F. (1999). *The Culture of Fear: Risk Taking and the Morality of Low Expectations,* 2nd edition. London: Cassell.

Furedi, F. (2003). *Therapy Culture: Creating Vulnerability in an Uncertain Age.* London: Routledge.

Furedi, F. (2004). Reflections on the medicalisation of social experience. *British Journal of Guidance and Counselling,* 32: 413–417.

Giddens, A. (1991). *Modernity and Self-Identity: Self and Society in Late Modern Age.* Oxford: Polity Press.

Giddens, A. (1995). *The Transformation of Intimacy: Sexuality, Eroticism and Love in Modern Societies.* Oxford: Polity Press.

Giddens, A. (1998). *The Third Way: The Renewal of Social Democracy.* Oxford: Polity Press.

Gloucester County Council (2006). Children and Young People's Plan. See www.gloucester.gov.uk

Goleman, D. (1996). *Emotional Intelligence: Why It Can Matter More than IQ.* London: Bloomsbury.

Gordon, J. (2003). *Beyond the Classroom Walls: Ethnographic Inquiry as Pedagogy.* London: Routledge.

Heartfield, J. (2002). *The 'Death of the Subject' Explained.* Sheffield: Sheffield Hallam University Press.

James, O. (2007) *Affluenza: How to be Successful and Stay Sane.* London: Vermillion.

Lasch, C. (1979). *The Culture of Narcissism: American Life in an age of Diminishing Expectations.* New York: W.W. Norton, 1991.

Layard, R. (2005). *Happiness.* London: Allen Lane.

Layard, R., & Dunn, J. (2009). *A Good Childhood: Searching for Values in a Competitive Age.* Harmondsworth: Penguin.

Malik, K. (2001). *Man, Beast or Zombie?* London: Weidenfield.

Nolan, J. (1998). *The Therapeutic State: Justifying Government at Century's End.* New York: New York University Press.

Palmer, S. (2006). *Toxic Childhood.* London: Orion.

Parrott, A. (2005). Education *for* Health. *Adults Learning,* January: 14–15.

Pupavac, V. (2001). Therapeutic governance: psycho-social intervention and trauma risk management. *Disasters*, 25: 358–372.

Pupavac, V. (2003). War and conflict: the internationalisation of therapy culture. London: paper presented to Institute of Ideas Conference, Therapy Culture, 22 November.

Rieff, P. (1966). *The Triumph of the Therapeutic.* New York: John Wiley.

Rose, N. (1990). *Governing the Soul: The Shaping of the Private Self.* London: Routledge.

Sennett, R. (2003). *Respect: The Formation of Character in an Age of Inequality.* London: Allen Lane/Penguin.

Sharp, P. (2001). *Emotional Literacy: A Practical Guide for Teachers, Parents and Those in the Caring Professions.* London: Kogan Page.

Shore, C., & Wright, S. (Eds.) (2005). *Anthropology of Policy: Critical Perspectives on Governance and Power*. Routledge: London.

Social Exclusion Unit (SEU) (1999). *Bridging the Gap: New Opportunities for 16–19 Year Olds not in Education or Training*. London: SEU.

Social Exclusion Unit (SEU) (2005). *Transitions for Young People with Complex Needs.* London: SEU.

Spratt, J., Shucklesmith, J., Philip, K., & Wilson, C. (2007). Embedded yet separate: tensions in voluntary sector working to support mental health in state-run schools. *Journal of Education Policy,* 22: 411–429.

Stewart-Brown, S., & Edmunds, L. (2003). Assessing emotional competence. London: Department for Education and Skills.

Stobart, G. (2007). *Testing Times: Uses and Abuses of Assessment.* London: RoutledgeFalmer.

Toynbee, P. (2005). They must be having a laugh—the battle for the heart of government. The *Guardian,* 19 April: 40–41.

UNICEF (2007). Report Card 7, Child Poverty in Perspective: An Overview of Child Well-being in Rich Countries. Innocenti Research Centre, Unicef.

Weare, K. (2004). *Developing the Emotionally-Literate School.* London: Paul Chapman.

CHAPTER TEN

The 'mind object' and 'dream consciousness': A Winnicottian and a Steinerean rationale for avoiding the premature 'adultifying' of children

Richard House

> The reliance on mind and the intellectual function at the expense of action and bodily experience can be a serious pathological factor in early development.

> (Corrigan and Gordon, 1995, p. 4)

Many early-years authorities and commentators on child-hood believe that immense damage is being wrought in our modern technological and overly permissive culture through children being inappropriately 'dragged into' adult aware-ness and consciousness at far too early an age. Britain's very high teenage pregnancy rate is arguably just one of the many unfortu-nate symptoms of this damaging process. The current UK govern-ment's preoccupation with learning 'outcome targets' and cognitive learning biases for England's pre-school-age children via the Early Years Foundation Stage seems to many to be a particularly damag-ing aspect of this alarming cultural trend (e.g. Ellyatt, 2009; House, 2007a), which is robbing children more and more of their right to a childhood relatively free of adult anxieties, preoccupations, and intrusions.

Given the widely acknowledged existence of this 'toxic' cultural trend, and the appalling behavioural and social consequences arising from it which we can see unfolding all around us, it should arguably be government's central task to do all it can to reverse, or at least halt, this pernicious trend—and certainly not to exacerbate it in its policy-making interventions and prescriptions. It is in the early-years sphere where policy makers and politicians can have by far the most direct impact in influencing, and even reversing, these cultural forces, to which (as I write in July 2009) the current British government seems alarmingly oblivious. And paradoxically and counter-intuitively, it will often be by consciously choosing to do *less rather than more* that government will have the most favourable influence in education in general, and in the early-years sphere in particular.

In this chapter I will draw on the inspiringly insightful writings of D.W. Winnicott to show how modern culture's uncritical treating of children as if they are 'mini-adults' may well be perpetrating untold harm on children's development. I argue that Winnicott's more narrow clinical concerns can be generalized to a cultural level, in that the kind of *premature awakening of the mind* in children that Winnicott put down to a failure in the individual child's facilitating environment can actually be observed as a rapidly sedimenting cultural norm in the way that very young children are treated and related to in modern technological culture—and not least in terms of the educational regimes to which they are increasingly being subjected. I also draw some revealing comparisons between Winnicott's view, and the spiritually informed insights on child development derived from Rudolf Steiner, the founder of Steiner/Waldorf education.

My thesis is not a research paper in the conventional academic sense. Rather, the kind of 'research' upon which it is based is derived from my own direct personal experience and observation working as a Steiner early-childhood group leader (parent and child groups and Kindergarten) over many years; from speaking to many other early-years practitioners; and from the perennial wisdom about child development built up over many decades, both with the global Waldorf community and in holistic educational approaches more generally.

For some years now, a number of childhood campaigners (including myself) have been predicting a major increase in child mental-health and behavioural problems if both current approaches to early education and learning, and cultural trends towards 'adultifying' young children, continue unchanged; and these predictions seem now to be coming true in a way, and with a ferocity, that hardly anyone foresaw. On 20 June 2007, the NCH charity reported a research project, the results of which were headlined in the *Daily Mail* as 'a million children now suffer from mental health problems' (Anon, 2007; see also BBC News, 2007). It is necessary to raise immediately one misleading but persistent challenge to data like this—that is, the view that there hasn't actually been any significant increase in child mental-health problems, but rather, our *sensibility* to such problems is far more developed than it used to be, so we're simply now reporting problems that, in the past, just weren't labelled as such, but did nonetheless exist. There might, of course, be *some* limited degree of truth in this argument; but my own experience and perception, added to the many discussions I've had with people working with children, seem to confirm that the incidence of children's emotional difficulties is indeed discernibly increasing—and quite possibly dramatically (cf. Palmer, 2006; Chapter 3, this volume). And as the *Daily Mail* reported, this Nuffield-sponsored research 'found evidence that escalating mental health problems were the result of real changes in behaviour and *not* increased reporting of problematic behaviour' (op. cit.). There is surely a need for detailed and concerted further research to reinforce this finding—or else the apologists for 'modernity' and 'technocracy' will likely continue to sew seeds of doubt about childhood's toxicity with their studied scepticism.

The theme of children's 'growing up too soon' is one that is threaded through all of the debates about toxic childhood (e.g. Elkind, 2007; Postman, 1996; Winn, 1984). In general terms, the argument is that human development is a complex holistic process—one that simply cannot be mechanistically broken down into controllable, plan-able, measurable 'outcomes' (Ellyatt, 2009). The arguable arrogance and the unacknowledged anxiety that underpin the 'managerialist' desire to control child-developmental outcomes in this way is, I maintain, the greatest existing danger to and intrusion upon our children's well-being. We can look at this premature 'waking-up' of children in modern culture in a number of ways, but here I want to refer to the work of the great British paediatrician and psychoanalyst Donald Winnicott (1896–1971). Winnicott was a genius of a man who worked with literally thousands of children and

158 CHILDHOOD, WELL-BEING AND A THERAPEUTIC ETHOS

families in his career, and by all accounts had remarkable success as a clinician, both psychoanalyst and paediatrician. Winnicott brought a delightfully flexible, playfully 'postmodern' sensitivity to his clinical work many years before the term 'postmodern' was even coined (e.g. House, 2005a).

The argument linking Winnicott's clinical work and children growing up too soon is relatively straightforward to articulate. Winnicott wrote about what he called the 'mind-psyche' (Winnicott, 1949), subsequently developed into the notion of the 'mind object' by Corrigan and Gordon (1995), referring to a pathological psychological phenomenon in his patients which he put down to *precocious intellectual development* in very young children. Put simply—and for current purposes there is no need to go into complex psychoanalytic theoretical detail here (see ibid.)—some children are exposed to such noxious environments in early life that they have to find some way (or psychological mechanism) of defending themselves against the resulting overwhelming environmental impingements. Faced with a situation, then, in which there is no reliable and consistent attachment figure in their early life, some, and possible many children respond by developing their own minds (or the 'intellectual function', as Winnicott termed it) to rely upon, in a way that is developmentally out of balance and highly inappropriate, as intellectual/cognitive capacities are then developed out of harmony with the 'going on being' of 'psyche-somatic' development that Winnicott rightly saw as an indissolubly holistic experience.

Rudolf Steiner's model of child development has many similarities to a Winnicottian view. Thus, in the first seven years, Steiner argued, the child is predominantly developing *the physical body* and *the (crucially unconscious) will forces* (cf. Eugene Schwartz's Chapter 14, this volume), and is learning predominantly through movement and imitation. There are also interesting parallels here with the work of Guy Claxton, who graphically shows how children (and sometimes adults) learn most effectively in a non-self-conscious way through their whole psycho-somatic organism; and when learning is made reflectively and cognitively conscious, then the learning process and experience is often compromised and substantially disrupted (Claxton, 1997; see also Atkinson and Claxton, 2000).

On this view, then, to 'wake children up' into self-conscious cognitive awareness of their learning experience is developmentally inappropriate and potentially very harmful. Moreover and relatedly, Claxton's approach privileges space for 'just' being, reverie, authentic play, and environments conducive to unhurried imaginative elaboration (cf. Isaacs, 1930)—or what he calls 'slow learning'. Young children, it is argued, need to be left space and freedom, unimpinged upon by the world of adults, to engage with the world at their own pace, and not to be exposed to anxious adults (because the latter are themselves being monitored and assessed on their children's 'outcomes') guiding children towards what *the adults* think they *should* be learning. Claxton also refers to the importance of practitioners working with children being 'intuitive' (Atkinson and Claxton, 2000)—which quality is intrinsically paradoxical, and necessarily very difficult to define in procedural, 'modernist' terms. And the very act of trying to measure and control these subtle early-learning experiences or practitioner qualities almost necessarily compromises, and at worst destroys them—and yet they are absolutely central to effective early learning and practitionership.

In his archetypal developmental cosmology, and similarly to Winnicott, Steiner argued that if the feeling realm or the mind are unduly emphasized in this first 7-year period for any reason, then the child's development is interfered with, and becomes unbalanced—and this in turn commonly leads to life-long health problems, both emotional and 'psycho-somatic' (the various chapters in Corrigan and Gordon [1995] give ample clinical case examples of such phenomena). Tellingly, then, this is exactly the kind of argument developed by Winnicott, based on the latter's many thousands of clinical observations from working therapeutically with both children and adults.

Winnicott describes at length the kinds of pathological symptoms that such patients display in later life—patients whose minds have developed in a precious way far earlier than their natural time. To illustrate this phenomenon, I will quote briefly from *The Mind Object* by Corrigan and Gordon (1995). The authors acknowledge that while such patients often have gifted minds and unusual intellectual ability, they display a range of chronic symptoms:

> ...some are narcissistic, some depressed, some boringly obsessive, while others are wonderfully quick and humerous. None of these patients are on particularly good terms with their instincts or their bodies in general. ... Somatically, all ... suffer

from a variety of serious [medical] conditions. ... They cannot relax into just being, but must be constantly stimulated and enlivened by something or someone outside themselves. Yet, essentially fearful and negativistic, they do not surrender to any relationship. ... We have come to view each of these patients as fiercely attached to their mind as an object, an object whose use is overvalued and exploited, whose existence is vigilantly protected, whose loss is constantly dreaded. Striving to disavow reliance on others, they have empowered the mind as the locus of self-holding and self-care. ... (p. 3)

Do we recognize any of these relatively non-specific symptoms?— so-called 'ADHD' immediately comes to mind (House, 2002–3; Timimi & Leo, 2009, and Timimi's Chapter 7, this volume). To the extent that we are, as already argued, living in a culturally ubiquitous and politically sanctioned (and colluded with) *waking up* of young children into their intellects and thinking minds in a way that is unbalanced and lacking in a broadly based developmental foundation of 'body–soul–spirit–mind', then it seems at the very least plausible, if not highly likely that **the explosion of children's mental-health problems is directly attributable, at least in part, to this premature and unbalanced waking-up of our young children**. And if childhood campaigners are anything like right about this, then the implications are grave indeed: State-imposed and compulsory synthetic phonics at 3–4 years of age, and a 'curriculum' for babies and toddlers being just two of the 'toxic' examples that the Open EYE Campaign, which I co-founded in December 2007 (www.savechildhood.org), is assiduously campaigning against. The damage that these policies may be having on a generation of children may well be sufficient to keep an army of psychotherapists and counsellors in work for literally decades to come (and I really do wish I were exaggerating—but I fear I'm not).

As with the physician's solemn Hippocratic Oath, I argue that it should be every professional's and practitioner's moral calling to refuse to impose anything on the young children in their charge that they deem, based on their informed professional judgement, to be harmful to those children. It would certainly be fascinating indeed to see an early-years practitioner in court being charged with invoking their professionalism to protect their children from State diktat that they deem to be harmful to children! Will the courts and the judicial system dare to say that pre-school workers must treat their children in a way that those professionals believe will harm them?

What we urgently need, then, is a 'cultural stand' to be taken, through which the benefits that *all* children will derive from the protection of their childhood experience will massively outweigh the benefits that any ephemeral, short-termist interventions might give, whether it be synthetic phonics for 3–4 years olds or cervical cancer vaccines for 12-year old girls (the latter being just one of the latest 'brain-waves' of the apologists for technocracy).

Another important aspect of this question is to look at the phenomenon of the young child's consciousness, and *just how* it is decisively different from adult consciousness. For this difference has enormous implications for how we parent and educate our young children—for both the type of home environments we create for them, and the kinds of care and 'educational' experiences to which we expose them.

In Steiner education, for example, we often speak of the importance of not 'waking children up' prematurely and inappropriately into adult-like consciousness. Bintein (2005, mimeo) puts it thus:

> The young child is not an unfinished adult; the child has a different state of consciousness, which allows her to be nearer to spiritual reality than an adult. ... It is difficult today for adults not to relate with children as little adults.

Signs are certainly present all around us of adult-driven intellectual agendas and a hyper-active, materialistic culture impinging ever more relentlessly on the lives of children at ever younger ages (cf. Palmer's Chapter 3, this volume). Anyone working attentively with young children will be all too aware that already in the first months of life, the 'cultural attack' on the very young child is very considerable, especially in terms of the young child's delicate emerging senses (cf. Sardello & Sanders, 1999; House, 2005b).

Rudolf Steiner was alluding to such dangers some 85 years ago. In a lecture given shortly before his death, in Torquay in 1924, he said,

> If something takes place in the child's environment ..., the whole child will have an internalized picture of [it] ... The results of [such an] implanted tendency in the early years will

> then remain throughout the rest of the child's life ... (E)*verything*
> *that you do yourself passes over into the children* and makes its way
> into them.
>
> (Steiner, 1995, p. 17, emphasis added)

It follows from this that, as Winnicott also forcefully argued, the environments and experiences to which we expose our young children will have a major impact on their whole being—physically, emotionally, and spiritually. So with modern culture's assaults upon young children becoming ever-more strident and difficult to avoid, key questions must be faced about just how we might protect our young children from these toxic forces.

Against this disquieting cultural backdrop, it is little wonder that mental-health problems and children's so-called 'behavioural disorders' seem to be ever-escalating, and that the anxiety-driven hot-housing atmosphere of mainstream educational settings and hyper-parenting practices are now demonstrably leading to severe psychological and emotional difficulties for many children. Although it is very difficult to verify empirically, it is a strong contention of 'toxic childhood' campaigners that modern society's intrusion into, and violent attacks upon, young children's naturally occurring 'dream consciousness' constitutes a major causative factor in these mounting symptoms of disturbance and malaise.

The nature of 'dream' or 'participative consciousness'

> The clumsy adult must be careful not to destroy this web of
> magic by stupid and tactless intervention. ... It is a world we
> adults have lost, and we can only regain understanding of it ...
> by sympathetic intuitive insight and *faithful non-interference.*
>
> (Eva Frommer, 1969, emphasis added)

The perspective offered by Rudolf Steiner and other holistic educationalists is, of course, founded in an explicitly spiritual (and therefore controversial and unverifiable) cosmology, with the 'dream consciousness' of the young child referring to a state of openness and an awareness of the invisible world around the child and in nature. Such a metaphysical worldview maintains that the child still has a very strong connection with the spiritual world from which she has come. The young child's natural state is not to be self-conscious, and not to be aware of being separate from the world around him; rather, he is fully and unselfconsciously immersed in what is sometimes called 'participative consciousness'. As stated earlier, the child also lives primarily in his unconscious 'will' activities during the first 7 years, and for this reason, it goes against the natural grain of the child's being, and is therefore developmentally inappropriate, to make the child self-conscious and self-aware of her own learning, as is commonly done in mainstream educational and some child-care settings.

The incarnating process is seen as a continuous experience of gradually awakening consciousness in the earthly realm. It is very important that this process of developing consciousness occurs gradually, as everything on the earth is very different compared to the spiritual world. We therefore want to keep this connection to the spiritual world open for as long as the child needs it, as the transition from one world to the other is assumed to be at best challenging, and at worst traumatic. Thus, the young child is not separated from the physical world around him: rather, he experiences himself united with both the spiritual and physical worlds. The young child also needs to negotiate experientially, through recapitulation, the previous stages of humankind's evolving consciousness before he is able and ready to develop his own self-consciousness.

If we accept such a worldview, which of course requires a level of faith and commitment, then it should be clear that to relate to, and think about, the young child in a non-spiritual, materialistic way is to do a particularly cruel violence to the soul and very being of the child. As just referred to, in Steiner and others' so-called 'recapitulationist' cosmology, this state of dream consciousness is a reflection of a stage of consciousness through which humankind has also had to develop. The more self-conscious is young children's state of being, the more difficult it is for them to incarnate healthily into their physical bodies—which view, again, is entirely consistent with Winnicott's views about the psycho-somatic mal-consequences of premature intellectualization through the 'mind-psyche'.

In Steiner early-childhood settings (with which I am familiar as an until-recently practising Steiner early-years teacher), delicate qualities like subtlety, presence, and ways of being are seen as being far more important at this age than are didactic instruction and the imposition of adult-centric learning agendas which, it is argued, so easily interfere with and subvert the child's own natural developmental needs and dream-like consciousness. Through conventional mainstream teaching approaches to instruction and direction, children are therefore seen to be prematurely and inappropriately awakened into self-consciousness. In contrast, Steiner argued how crucial it is that young children do not divert their vital life forces into premature, adult-imposed intellectual activity and awareness, when those forces should be being used in early childhood to develop a healthy physical body.

Children therefore *learn by 'doing'*, and through freely chosen *imitation*, with the construction of their experience being left to their own free imaginations, unintruded-upon as far as possible by an adult perceptual world which is qualitatively very different from their own. In this approach, *free play* is also essential—that is, play which is freely chosen and autonomous, rather than the fashionable, adult-led 'structured' or 'directed' play of the mainstream—which, of course, is not *truly authentic* play at all, in any meaningful sense (House, 2008).

So what are the implications of these views for the way in which we create environments for our young children? First, the provision of *space* and *unhurried opportunity* is crucial (cf. Elkind, 1982; House, 2007b), with opportunities for free imaginative play to the forefront, and with adults intruding only to the absolutely minimal extent that is required by the specific situation. In terms of our own personal development (which having one's own children most definitely calls forth), adults need to know their own 'inner child' and her/his needs very well, in order that they do not unconsciously 'act out' their own issues with their children. I believe that this is in fact what is often happening when adults *do* routinely and unawarely over-intrude with adult-centric demands (and with policy-makers often actually advocating it!) into the worlds of the young children in their charge.

Another key issue is the *over-intellectualization* that has tragically become routine practice in mainstream pre-school settings—as to take children into reflective intellectual thinking is by definition the very antithesis of the kind of dream consciousness I discuss in this chapter. In England's compulsory Early Years Foundation Stage (EYFS), for example, there is the very strong injunction to practitioners to ask young children questions in order to (I joke not) *extend* their thinking'. This is an extraordinary example of the way in which a waking-up, adult-awareness ideology has infiltrated early-years settings, certainly in England (and, I suspect, further afield, too).

Looking briefly at a recently published academic paper, co-written by one of the chief movers behind England's EYFS and the famous EPPE research programme, Professor Iram Siraj-Blatchford (Siraj-Blatchford & Manni, 2008), interesting things emerge. First, the whole paper is based on the tacit, unargued assumption that it is more appropriate to ask young children 'open' rather than 'closed' questions. From the perspective adopted in this chapter, the *very act* of asking young children any kind of question is itself thrown into severe question. 'Open' questions are, of course, widely viewed in *adult* circles (note) as being preferable to 'closed ones'—for example, within my own professional field of counselling and psychotherapy. Yet why uncritically assume that what is seen as being appropriate to adults is equally appropriate to young pre-school children?—unless, of course, one is assuming that the consciousness of both age groups (i.e. adults and pre-school children) is comparable and legitimately subject to the same treatment, which, I am arguing here, they most decidedly are not. And to add to the irony, on the basis of the arguments developed in this chapter, if we accept for a moment that questions must be asked, then a very strong case could actually be made for 'closed' questions being more appropriate for young children than 'open' ones!—an interesting counter-intuitive possibility that these researchers don't even begin to consider.

We also encounter another uncritically embraced ideology in this academic paper—this time regarding something called 'sustained shared thinking' (SST), which is, incidentally, also legally enshrined in England's EYFS framework. According to Siraj-Blatchford and Manni, SST refers to '... practitioners supporting *and challenging* children's thinking *by getting involved in the thinking process with them* ...; [and with adults] clarify[ing] ideas and ask[ing] open questions which ... *extends children's thinking and helps them to make connections to learning*' (ibid., p. 15, my emphases). Again, we can see in this the advocacy of early-years practices which are *guaranteed* to wrench young children out of the kind of dream consciousness discussed in this chapter. It's not so much that the authors are arguing this case that is objectionable, but rather, that they show no awareness of the implications of their position, and make no attempt to engage in the kind of complex arguing-through that would be needed to support it. This in turn illustrates all too graphically the extent to which the 'ideology of modernity' and materialistic thinking more generally have come to dominate mainstream practice in the early-childhood realm, where they are singularly inappropriate.

Before concluding this chapter, I just wish to 'pre-but' the most obvious objection to the arguments presented—that is, that if it is simply wrong that children are in any sense 'spiritual' beings, then all of the practices and considerations discussed here are irrelevant and wrong-headed. There is a fundamental logical problem with such a critique, and it is this. In terms of the 'truth criteria' beloved of people making this kind of a-spiritual argument, it is simply impossible to say who is right about children's alleged innate spirituality and developmentally natural 'dream consciousness'. And given this unavoidable uncertainty, the key question then becomes, **Which position is likely to generate more net damage to children and their development: assuming that children live in a spiritual 'dream consciousness' when in reality they don't; or assuming that they don't, when they really are?**

I believe that any dispassionate commentator would agree that, all other things being equal, it is potentially far more harmful to treat a spiritual being in a thorough-going non-spiritual way, than it is to assume children's innate spirituality, when in reality such assumed spirituality is a fiction. In his important book *The Secret Spiritual World of Children*, Tobin Hart (2004) argues that children's spiritual experiences have often been misunderstood: dismissed as fantasy, labelled as pathology, or feared by a parent, teacher, or therapist who has no map for understanding them. Ultimately this attitude can easily lead to repressing rather than refining the child's spiritual nature.

Most decisively, assuming the veracity of children's spirituality leads to all kinds of decisions about how we treat and relate with children that pretty much everyone would agree are nourishing and empowering, whether we be 'militant atheists' or not! So when taking on the objectors on their own kind of rational ground, that ultimately we can't prove in an empirical, scientific sense whether children possess innate spiritual dream consciousness or not, in my view the case for assuming children's innately spiritual-like consciousness becomes quite overwhelming.

Conclusions and implications

> ...the time of awakening is also beautiful – unless we are called awake too soon.
>
> Friedrich Holderlin's 'Hyperion'
> (transl. by Anna Meuss)

It seems that the majority of influences acting on the child today attempt prematurely to 'awaken' children into the adult Cartesian conceptions of time, space, and cognitive thought. This is why many holistic educators are actively campaigning against the kind of mainstream educational and care environments that are being foisted on to young children today in many developed countries, from England to New Zealand. Although no doubt well intentioned, such approaches fundamentally misunderstand young children's need for space, time, reverie, and, above all, their need for protection from the crass materialistic, commercialized world, and the assaults it routinely makes on young children's delicate and developing senses and wider experience.

As the great scientist and sage Albert Einstein variously said:

> The true sign of intelligence is not knowledge but *imagination* ... Imagination is more important than knowledge. ... The gift of fantasy has meant more to me than any talent for abstract, positive thinking. He who can no longer pause to wonder and stand rapt in awe, is as good as dead; his eyes are closed. ... Never lose a holy curiosity. ... The most beautiful thing we can experience is the mysterious. ... The pursuit of truth and beauty is a sphere of activity in which we are permitted to remain children all our lives.

Amen to that.

References

Anon. (2007). A million children now suffer from mental health problems. *Daily Mail*, 20 June; retrievable at: http://www.dailymail.co.uk/news/article-463194/A-million-children-suffer-mental-health-problems.html

Atkinson, T., & Claxton, G. (2000). *The Intuitive Practitioner: On the Value of Not always Knowing what One Is Doing*, Buckingham: Open University Press.

BBC News (2007). Child mental health ills 'rife'. 20 June; retrievable at: http://news.bbc.co.uk/1/hi/health/6221240.stm

Claxton, G. (1997). *Hare Brain, Tortoise Mind: Why Intelligence Increases when You Think Less*. London: Fourth Estate.

Corrigan, E.G., & Gordon, P.-E. (Eds.) (1995). *The Mind Object: Precocity and Pathology of Self-Sufficiency*. Northvale, NJ: Jason Aronson.

Elkind, D. (1982) *The Hurried Child: Growing up Too Fast Too Soon*. New York: Perseus Books (25th Anniversary edition, 2007).

Ellyatt, W. (2009). Learning and Development: Outcomes – own goals. *Nursery World*, 15 July; retrievable at: http://www.nurseryworld.
  co.uk/inDepth/920092/Learning---Development-Outcomes---Own-goals/

Frommer, E.A. (1969). *Voyage through Childhood into the Adult World: A Description of Child Development*. Oxford: Pergamon.

Hart, T. (2004). *The Secret Spiritual World of Children*. Makawao, HI: Inner Ocean Publishing.

House, R. (2002–3) Beyond the medicalisation of 'challenging behaviour'; or protecting our children from 'Pervasive Labelling Disorder' (in 3 parts), *The Mother* magazine, issues 4–6 (Issue 4, 2002: 25–26, 43; Issue 5, 2003: 44–46; and Issue 6, 2003: 44–46).

House, R. (2005a). Review of André Green, *Play and Reflection in Donald Winnicott's Writings*. *Ipnosis* magazine, 19 (Autumn): 25.

House, R. (2005b). The highly sensitive child. *The Mother* magazine, 14 (Summer): 34–36.

House, R. (2007a). Schooling, the state and children's psychological well-being: a psychosocial critique. *Journal of Psychosocial Research*, 2 (July–Dec): 49–62.

House, R. (2007b). Arresting children's premature growing up: a crucial imperative of our time. *The Mother* magazine, 24 (Sept–Oct), 2007: 24–25.

House, R. (2008). Guest Editorial Introduction: Play and playfulness in therapeutic and educational perspectives. *European Journal of Psychotherapy and Counselling*, 10: 101–109.

Isaacs, S. (1930). *Intellectual Growth in Young Children*. London: George Routledge.

Palmer, S. (2006). *Toxic Childhood*. London: Orion.

Postman, N. (1996). *The Disappearance of Childhood*. New York: Vintage.

Sardello, R., & Sanders, C. (1999). Care of the senses: a neglected dimension of education. In: Jeffery Kane (Ed.), *Education, Information, and Imagination: Essays on Learning and Thinking.* Columbus, OH: Prentice-Hall/Merril.

Siraj-Blatchford, I., with Manni, L. (2008). 'Would you like to tidy up now?' An analysis of adult questioning in the English Foundation Stage. *Early Years*, 28: 5–22.

Steiner, R. (1995). *The Kingdom of Childhood.* Herndon, VA: Steiner Books.

Timimi, S., & Leo, J. (Eds.) (2009). *Rethinking ADHD: From Brain to Culture.* Basingstoke: Palgrave Macmillan.

Winn, M. (1984). *Children without Childhood.* New York: Penguin.

Winnicott, D.W. (1949). Mind and its relation to the psyche-soma. In: his *Collected Papers: From Paediatrics to Psychoanalysis.* London: Tavistock (1958).

CHAPTER ELEVEN

First catch your child

Andrew Samuels

(With apologies to Mrs Beeton, who began her recipe for jugged hare with the exhortation 'First, catch your hare'.)

Introduction

In this chapter, I'm addressing three issues: first, who or what is the child that we have in mind when bemoaning the advent of toxic childhood? Secondly, can therapy really make a difference to whatever educational malaise Britain is currently suffering from? Thirdly, is it possible that our educational debates and discussions have become too 'heady' and abstract, and could this imbalance be managed better by more of a focus on the body?

In search of the child

The child in question is, of course, a real person, and childhood is a genuine phase of life with real ups and downs, joys and sufferings. But there has always been something beyond the literal child that awakens when the image of the child arises in an individual or within a group. This imaginal child is something more than a recognition that there is a child in every adult. This child is the best known and most potent symbol of renewal, renaissance, and repair. It is nothing short of the divine (or very special) child, and we see this phenomenon in all cultures and at all historical times—the Christ child is merely the majoritarian version in the West. If a culture loses contact with this collective image of the child, as ours may have, then it is in the deepest possible crisis.

Clients in therapy dream of babies and children at moments of change and at turning points in their lives. But the child of renewal is very vulnerable, and those same clients will perhaps also dream of the child being gobbled up by a monster or mistreated by abusive adults. I suggest that it is the paradox of divine power coupled with appalling vulnerability that is the essence of the child image. This is the mix that makes all our discussions about the literal, fleshy, actual child so hot, so divisive, and so emotionally draining. It is not just the sense of responsibility for the weak that drains, but also the sense that we are really on to something fulfilling needs that are as deep and complex as is imaginable.

So the image of the child makes our discussions of childhood harder than they might otherwise be. There's more to think of in the same vein. When we speak or write of childhood, we tend to project our adult worries and anxieties on to the image or icon of the child. So the child becomes the carrier of, the projection screen for, our adult angst. Please note: this is not the same as saying that adults are responsible for the problems faced by children. I am saying that the child in the adult mind is not only objectively a child, nor the adult's child bit—it is put into the adult's mind by the adult to do a job for an adult. Hence, all the evils that constitute toxic childhoods—the time problem, the lack of imaginative play, the obstacles to finding long-standing good-enough relationships—are contemporary adult problems writ large upon the personification we call the child. Is this abusive? Some might think so. What can be said confidently is that the child we think about today may be akin to the canary the miners used to take down the pit to check for gas. At the moment, the child is the diagnostic problem. In the 1980s and 1990s it was men who were the problem. Before that, in the 1950s, 1960s, and 1970s, women were the problem.

This observation leads me to pose the question often posed in therapy circles: do adults really love children? The official answer is that we are ambivalent towards them, meaning that we both love and hate them. The hating bit is worth considering, for it brings up the question of whether or not adults can ever get over their envy of children. Envy is a very complex emotion because, though markedly negative, it usually conceals grudging, secret admiration. But envy often leads to profoundly destructive behaviour and so we have to face the possibility that we have created a crappy world for children because at some level we wanted to do it.

Envy has another element to it, which is even more relevant for debates on childhood that have an educational focus. Envy is the fuel of conformism. When we envy someone, we are often trying to cut them down to size, to our size, in what the Australians call the 'tall-poppy syndrome' where the outstanding one has to be dealt with and forcibly reintegrated into the normal, the mass, the conventional.

A final point about this child we are trying to catch concerns our anxiety about ways we believe childhood to be a decisive era of personal development, controlling and causing all that we perceive in the adult personality. Here, therapists seem to divide into two camps. One group sees the events of early childhood as absolutely decisive for the individual's future, whether this is expressed in the language of attachment or in the terminology of the new 'science' of affective neuroscience. So we had better worry a lot about childhood because what happens then is going to be so important for the future. And as parents are the ones who have to do the job of bringing up the children, it is parents who need to be educated, cajoled, bribed into good practices.

The problem with this is that no-one really knows what good practices are. Most of the contributors to this book will feel completely out of sympathy with all the stern 'nanny' books that have become the current parenting bestsellers. They will have other, equally certitudinous views of their own, and they will put them into their own books (likely to be read by the better-educated and more affluent readers). The trouble is, fashions in parenting change. In the 1970s, a wonderful book entitled *For Her Own Good: 150 Years of the Experts' Advice to Women* (Ehrenreich & English, 1978) made this point with effortless impact. Over time, the experts of the day will contradict the experts of yesterday. Maybe it is a special example of the use of the child as a projection screen that I mentioned earlier.

Other therapists are less sure that the early years are as decisive as their colleagues say they are. This second group believes in the possibility of recovery from childhood difficulties (with or without therapy), and at any time in life. Some therapists believe that adversity and trauma can stimulate growth and development, that suffering brings its own gifts with it. This second group of therapists tends to welcome the idea that babies and children are individuals from conception onwards. Though marked by life, they are who they are, and we should be careful not to jump to conclusions about someone's life prospects based on recovery of facts that are, as often as not, very far from one single truth about a life.

Therapy thinking and educational practice

Contrary to what our critics splutter, therapists with an interest in public policy are not trying to put everyone on a couch. Rather, they want to use their knowledge base in a public way in the same manner that other professions—sociology economics, medicine—seek to. To illustrate what I have in mind, I'm going to take a few ideas from each of the three main schools of therapy and show how these inform what we might hope for from a teacher today. It seems to me important to take the ideas from all schools of therapy because, at the time of writing, there is a serious risk that the British Government will privilege one of them over the others in terms of public funding. I hope to show that it is not necessary to be an expert in the therapy field to understand how its ideas might turn out to be useful within education.

Psychoanalysis

Psychoanalysis is the oldest of the three schools of therapy, and its current focus is on the role of 'relationality' in most aspects of life, including in learning. But for psychoanalysis, relationships are not only between persons: we also relate to a version of another person inside ourselves. So there is an anticipation of all kinds of distortions, and this is not something confined to the person who seeks therapeutic help—the practitioner is also in the same boat, full of her or his own subjective distortions with respect to the client and to much else. Teachers, too, bring their inner worlds to their relationships with their pupils. So a teacher might learn to ask her or himself: 'Do I really like this child?' 'If not, why not? Is it something to do with me?' 'Do I care?' 'What in my own childhood has been awakened by this particular child or class of children?' In this way, to use a further term from psychoanalysis, education becomes a 'third', something co-created between teacher and pupil or class.

Psychoanalysis also makes use of a definition of 'thinking' that is far wider than the one most people use. What goes on behind our conscious knowledge is not only crazy or out of control, but is also quite sensible and 'intelligent'. That's why we sleep on problems, or, to be a little more positive, how creative ideas arise. They just do! The famous analyst C.G. Jung said there were two types of thinking—directed thinking, which is the kind most people are referring to when they use the word, and undirected thinking. Undirected thinking is sometimes called fantasy thinking or intuitive thinking, and in many ways it involves thinking in images or thinking through the body and its sensations.

The point is that learning does not only take place at the cognitive level but also at this other level of undirected, fantasy, intuitive thinking. The difficulty is that most educational practice does not explicitly recognize that this other level exists at all. The conditions for realizing the potential of this second type of thinking are not, in principle, difficult to achieve. There needs to be a safe place, a relationship of trust, and the active encouragement of a passive approach to learning with great respect paid to the dreamy, fantastical, imaginative, and generally 'pointless' sides of being. I think many readers will recognize what I am saying about the immensely creative power of undirected thinking but, for the most part, will not have seen this as a social and educational good.

Humanistic psychology

Humanistic psychology began as a reaction against psychoanalysis (and also against behaviourism, of which more in a moment). Generally speaking, humanistic approaches to therapy refer to the potential for growth and self-realization that exists in everyone, no matter what their apparent circumstances. In its positive and optimistic outlook, humanistic psychology sometimes resembles a secular religion, though, as the name suggests, it is certainly not a religion. But sometimes, humanistic ideas do excite the derision that we have come to expect when religious ideas are introduced to public debates: too idealistic, out of touch with reality, won't work in practice, if only people were really as nice as that... .

For educationalists, the tenets of humanistic therapy are extremely relevant. If one recalls the questions I imagined a teacher asking her- or himself on the basis of psychoanalytic ideas, the equivalent ones stemming from the humanistic field would be: 'Can I find something good in this child?' 'What is this child good at?' 'What could this child teach me?' 'Am I in fact expecting this child to fail (or misbehave or go crazy)?' There is a wealth of empirical evidence concerning the efficacy of optimism, and many people can track back in their lives to a time when someone in authority, not necessarily a parent but often a teacher, seemed to 'believe' in them.

Cognitive behaviour therapy

Cognitive behaviour therapy is the third and last of the three main schools of contemporary psychotherapy. This is a structured approach to problems that rests on the idea that much mental and emotional distress, and many disturbing symptoms such as obsessions, compulsions, and phobias, are due to the acquisition of bad habits by faulty learning. Once these bad habits have been dissected and understood, the individual will be free of them.

In the educational context, the uses of therapy thinking derived from cognitive behaviour therapy are almost endless. I would like to single out the idea that much anxiety—which is generally agreed to interfere with learning—is the result of the acquisition of what seemed to be coping strategies that have, so to speak, gone sour. For example, a child who cannot concentrate may be understood as having stopped thinking about anything at all, lest she or he have to think about something horrid. Drifting off was a coping strategy that is, after some time, manifestly destructive and useless to the individual. Teachers could begin to make notes on this particular phenomenon, trying to ascertain what the mis-learned coping strategy is, and helping the child to address the problems in a different and more productive way.

Let me reprise what I have tried to achieve in this section of the chapter. I wanted to show how therapy thinking, not therapy itself, could contribute to how we understand the learning process in an educational setting. I took some ideas from each of the three main schools of therapy, and tried to demonstrate their utility to teachers. From psychoanalysis, I took the ideas that learning takes place within a two-way highly subjective and emotionally charged relationship and that there is more to thinking than meets the eye; from humanistic therapy, the idea that optimism works; from cognitive behaviour therapy, the idea that what was learned as yesterday's coping solution becomes today's diversionary problem.

Learning the body

This section makes use of work I did with the Personal, Social, and Health Education (PSHE) team at a small North London Independent School covering the age range 2–8. Its roots are therefore highly practical, and actually involve attempts to align innovative practices with what the National Curriculum requires for its Foundation Stage.

This school opted to teach PSHE on a markedly bodily basis. So, for example, reproductive and sex education did not omit questions of desire and pleasure. Touch, mutual grooming of a simple kind, and the management of aggression were highlighted. Hygiene and self-care were, similarly, looked at in a more psychological way than is often the case. For example, it was proposed that children discuss the words they might use to express the nature, intensity, and duration of pain. This would include the more emotional side of pain as well as the obviously needed informational aspect.

One specific example of the use of an approach to PSHE derived from therapy thinking was to approach the senses through the imaginative conceit of being deprived of them. Not what we see, but what it is like not to see. Look at something—then cover your eyes—what do you see and feel now?—and so on and so forth, through the senses. In this way, the darker and more complex aspects of having a body are introduced at an early stage. This is a culturally congruent way of freeing children from the restrictions imposed on them in an age of anxiety and panic over every aspect of our corporeal existence.

Everything starts in psychology and ends in politics

In this short chapter, I have tried to show what a therapeutic ethos can bring to our discussions about children, teaching, and personal, social, and health education. But these are matters that are 'bigger' than education, aren't they? They are also profoundly political issues—and so I want to end with some thoughts about the relationship between therapy and politics and, at the last, introduce a spiritual grain or two.

Many therapists now feel that their ideas could contribute to a general improvement in the political world. After all, the official politicians and the academic disciplines on which they traditionally draw have not created as happy and productive a world as had been hoped. Therapists are starting to consider how they might transform self-concern and personal growth into social and political concern, thereby helping to revitalize politics.

Our inner worlds and our private lives reel from the impact of policy decisions and the existing culture. Why, then, do our policy committees and commissions not have a therapist sitting on them, as part of a spectrum of experts? This is not a call for a committee of therapists, by the way! But, just as a committee will often have a statistician present, whose role might not always be fully appreciated by the other members, so, too, there should be a therapist at the conference table.

Phrases like 'emotional literacy' and 'emotional intelligence' encapsulate calls for an increase in self-knowledge. But such phrases can be taken as addressing more than the private side of life. Modern society plunges us into a condition of uncertainty in which we often lose track of what we feel, and slip into states of depression and helplessness. The idea of emotional literacy can be extended into the public sphere, so that we can envision a citizenry wanting to engage with politics in a feeling-based way, secure in the awareness that they will still be coherent.

One poignant contribution that a psychotherapy viewpoint might make to political life is to help people face up to the inevitability of disappointment and failure. It is one of the more valuable outcomes of therapy, derived from the struggles experienced in the process itself: people realize that it is possible to gather the strength to push through the despair barrier and move on.

Regarding spirituality—what I call the 'S' word—we have to accept that this term and what it stands for are very problematic. I try not to get bogged down in definitions in the many attempts I have made to show how full engagement in society is, inevitably, a kind of spiritual happening. Really caring about one's work, to the degree that this is possible under current conditions—that, too, is potentially a spiritual dimension of experience. Democracy and equality are values that have profoundly spiritual roots—equality in the eyes of the Lord being but one. It may be that the religions have exercised a retrogressive as much as a progressive influence on political process. But contemporary spirituality is too powerful and fertile a phenomenon to leave to reactionary and elitist politicians to exploit for their own purposes. I will conclude by giving the quotation from Charles Peguy upon which the title of this section was based: 'Everything starts in mysticism and ends in politics'.

Reference

Ehrenreich, B., with English, D. (1978). *For Her Own Good: 150 years of the Experts' Advice to Women*. New York: Bantam.

PART IV

PLAY, PLAYFULNESS,
AND CHILDREN'S WELL-BEING

CHAPTER TWELVE

The importance of play and playfulness*

Biddy Youell

This chapter focuses on the roots of play and playfulness in children's early experience of relationships. It seeks to argue that the current debate about the loss of safe outdoor play spaces, and the dangers of over-reliance on digital entertainments, sometimes neglects the fact that play and playfulness are developmental achievements, and that there are huge variations in children's capacity to make use of the opportunities they have.

The open letter 'Let our children play', published in the *Daily Telegraph* in September 2007 and signed by some 270 experts, focused on the risks to play from changes in the social environment and educational system. The letter appealed for more 'unstructured, loosely supervised play outdoors', and listed the benefits in terms of healthy physical, psychological, and emotional development. The enemies of play are seen as the proliferation of sedentary, 'screen-based' activities and the aggressive marketing of toys. The emphasis on formal learning at pre-school levels and the influence

---

* An earlier version of this chapter appeared in the *European Journal of Psychotherapy & Counselling*, 10, 2008: 121–130; reproduced here by kind permission of Routledge publishers.

of 'stranger danger' on the movement of children beyond the home are cited as further causes of the demise of play. It would be difficult to take issue with any of these important points, but I have a slightly different area of interest. I am concerned to locate the origins of play and playfulness as being in a child's early experience, and to illustrate the ways in which children's development can be compromised if play and playfulness are not established in those early stages.

Judith Edwards (1999) draws our attention to Freud's answer to the question as to what a normal person ought to be able to do well. Freud's reply was 'lieben und arbeiten'—'to love and to work'. Several psychoanalysts and psychoanalytic therapists since Freud, particularly those working with children, have sought to add 'the capacity to play' as the third essential ingredient in adult functioning. Indeed, Edwards quotes Erik H. Erikson (1950) in identifying play as the vital precursor of the capacity for work and love. What, then, is the difference between play and playfulness? In ordinary parlance, the word 'playful' carries an assumption of enjoyment, fun, or amusement. In the context of this chapter, I am using it in a very specific way to describe a state of mind in which an individual can think flexibly, take risks with ideas (or interactions), and allow creative thoughts to emerge.

The aim of this chapter is to argue the following points:

- Playfulness happens in a relationship; it is a two-person phenomenon. We can be playful alone but only if we have first had the experience of being playful with another.
- Playfulness is an essential part of play. Much of what passes for play in our current society is devoid of playfulness.
- Play and work are not opposites, nor are they mutually exclusive.
- Playfulness is an important factor in effective teaching and learning, both formal and informal.
- Inhibitions in play are an important diagnostic factor when thinking about children's emotional, psychological, and cognitive development.

Twenty-first century European society maintains a clear distinction between what is described as work and what is described as play.

Although it is acknowledged that some people are fortunate enough to enjoy their work, work is most often represented as an unavoidable necessity. Play is seen as compensation, a reward. Schools promote this view from the earliest years, when children are encouraged to earn 'golden time' (play) by hard work and good behaviour. Bad behaviour or poor work is punished by the loss of playtime and the imposition of extra work. At the same time, playing is often equated with 'wasting time'. It is a confusing picture for the average five-year old child who comes into school with no such clear distinction in mind.

For the baby and toddler, play is work. It is the means by which he finds out about his surroundings and about the people he encounters. Interactions between mothers (or primary carers) and infants are characterized by playfulness. Mothers smile, tickle, and talk to their babies, and babies learn to respond with smiles and gurgles. 'Games' and 'jokes' (often involving noses, ears, or tummies) develop between them as a vocabulary of play is established long before the introduction of toys, and long before language develops.

The following extract from an infant observation (Youell, 2007) may serve to illustrate the way in which learning and playing are inextricably linked from the earliest stages of life. Timothy was ten months old at the time of this observation. He had been sitting on the floor whilst his two older brothers (aged eight and ten) watched TV and played around with a recorder. When their mother came in, they asked permission to go out, and rushed past their baby brother, who looked put out. His mother saw the look and invited him to come to her.

> Timothy crawled over and climbed on to his mother's lap, grinning as she pulled him towards her for a cuddle. He wriggled free and down on to the floor again. He reached out for the red plastic recorder his brother had dropped. He looked at it closely and tried various bits of it in his mouth before dropping it and going instead for a plastic rattle and a card baby book. He took each in turn and examined them in detail before tossing them up in the air, his arms flapping forcefully against his sides. He played contentedly for a few moments before noticing that his mother was absent-mindedly fingering the recorder. Seeing that he was looking at her, she put it to her mouth and played

a single note. Timothy smiled with pleasure and reached out for the instrument. His mother gave it to him and he put it to his mouth, exploring both ends and the rounded surface in between. A few moments later, the recorder made a clear sound. Timothy pulled it away from his mouth, looking startled and his face began to crumple. Then he looked towards his mother who was exclaiming that he had played a note and his face broke into a huge smile. He put the mouthpiece back in his mouth and repeated the performance. He was soon filling his cheeks with air before blowing, and the sounds were getting longer and louder. His mother was delighted and congratulated him, commenting that he was blowing deliberately … he had learned what to do. She did not think either of his older brothers could have done the same at that age. Timothy was enjoying himself, but after a while seemed to become aware that his achievement was no longer a cause for celebration, and he went over to the bookshelf. He reached towards the books and then paused, looking over his shoulder at his mother before putting just one finger on a book, grinning provocatively. She said 'no' quite firmly but his grin was infectious and she was soon smiling too. She repeated her command and he continued to grin at her, now spreading two hands across the books on the top shelf. He looked as if he would pull the books down in spite of her, and I felt I had become part of his audience. I (the observer) looked away to hide my amusement and his mother managed to use a tone of voice which he understood really was a 'no' and then she distracted him with another activity.

The links with learning are clear in this sequence of play. Timothy is learning a skill by imitation and trial and error, but is not doing so in isolation. He is confident that his mother is aware of what he is doing and that he can engage her interest when he needs to do so. This is reinforced by her response to his making a sound with the recorder. He had been watching with wrapped attention whilst his older brothers were playing the instrument, and was spurred on by a real desire to do what they could do. He is delighted by the praise he receives, and this sustains him for a few minutes whilst he consolidates the learning by repetition. When he begins to feel alone with his play, he finds another way to engage his mother, and there is a playful interaction over his threat to pull down the books. This ends in his having to accept (learn) that she is the one who makes the rules, and that he can only go so far with his provocation.

In this sequence of playful interaction, Timothy learns something about playing a recorder. However, he learns much more about how he can impress and amuse his mother, how far he can go in provoking her, and what might be the consequences if he goes too far. The example which follows is taken from an observation of a Year Five (Key Stage 2) numeracy lesson. When looked at from a particular perspective, it is possible to see some parallels with the observation of Timothy.

> The class was asked to sit on the carpet while the teacher recapped on yesterday's lesson and explained the task of today. The children were to work in pairs, conducting their own simple survey and plotting their results on a bar graph. They were given a few ideas as to what question they might ask of their fellow classmates. The teacher suggested they could find out about each other's favourite foods, colours, lessons, pets, football teams, and so on. The buzz of excitement and competition grew as she talked, most of the children looking around and whispering loudly to claim their preferred partner. Many jumped up and began to shift chairs and grab pen pots. The teacher had to call them back to check that they knew what to do, and then she had to sort out the many small skirmishes which had erupted about who was working with whom. Predictably, perhaps, most of the boys opted to ask a question about football teams, while the girls chose to ask about favourite pets. The classroom became a hive of activity as the children drew their tally charts and began to ask each other their questions. They rushed around the room, falling over furniture and each other as if it were a race. It quickly became obvious that the boys were heavily invested in making sure that their own favourite football team got the most votes. In short, they cheated, but they did so in an entirely open, and often witty way. Once they knew what the teacher would say (West Ham), they either avoided asking her or asked her several times! They offered inducements to people who would say 'Chelsea' or got on their knees to beg a small timid newcomer (who could speak

little English) to utter 'Man U'. The girl pairings were almost as passionate about the animals; one pair cheering each time somebody voted 'dog'. Another tried to persuade everyone to say 'rabbit', insisting that dogs were dirty and dangerous. The boys tried to sabotage the girls' work by giving ridiculous answers such as 'snake' and 'kangaroo'.

The teacher asked them to keep the noise down, but decided to be flexible about time because she had rarely seen such enthusiasm. As anticipated, the graphs were inaccurate, with absolutely no consensus amongst the groups as to the results. However, the lesson had been fun, and the class had grasped the basic principles of conducting surveys. The teacher said she would return to the topic of graphs the next day.

This lesson would probably not have scored very highly on a standardized measure of learning outcomes, and the observer was alarmed by the noise levels and by some of the physical hazards created by fallen chairs and so on. However, the group went out to the playground buzzing with ideas about the lesson, unwilling to give up their particular campaign. It was clear that it had been a valuable learning experience for the whole group. Not unlike Timothy and the recorder, they had been able to enjoy grappling with a new activity. They had taken their cues from the teacher and from each other, testing out their capacity to impress, amuse, and persuade. They were pleased with their graphs, and the teacher was generous enough not to dent their pleasure by criticizing them at this point. Building on the learning could wait until the next day.

As discussed elsewhere in this book, there is some recognition amongst policy makers that young children need to play. There has been a slight relaxing in the 'testing' regime for early-years classes, with some acknowledgment that children learn through playing. The current government's enthusiasm for 'parenting classes' is, in part, recognition of the fact that many parents struggle with the tasks involved in bringing up a family. The emphasis in these courses is very often on behaviour management, with clear limit-setting, and reward and punishment strategies, but there is also a belief that it is important to teach parents to play with their children. Again, there can be no argument with that, but the problem is often that this is seen as a simple matter. In reality, play activities can be taught, but *playfulness* is a state of mind, and as such, cannot be *taught* or *learned* in the ordinary sense of those words. It takes time and skill to foster playfulness in a parent–child interaction.

There is a point to be made here about 'aggressive marketing' of sophisticated mechanical and electronic substitutes for some parental functions (e.g. electrically operated baby chairs which begin to rock in response to a child's cry). However, these 'aids' will only be adopted by parents if they feel themselves to be too depressed, busy, preoccupied, anxious, or lacking in confidence to enjoy playing with their babies. Parents whose own patterns of play are impoverished will not necessarily feel able to engage playfully with their children. They may be all too willing to believe that their child will be just as happy with a brightly coloured, all-singing, all-dancing mobile, or a TV screen. If they are also led to believe that exposing the child to 'educational' toys as early as possible is good for their future learning, the scene is set for an early experience which privileges 'work' and downgrades 'play'.

The current media debate on play rumbles along on a very superficial level. Are computer games good or bad for children? Do children watch too much television? Do violent games breed violent children? Should there be more facilities for outdoor play? Is obesity in children becoming more common because children aren't encouraged to play? Should sport be part of the school curriculum? Much of what gets air time is based on the assumption that all children are the same, and therefore one social policy or educational practice fits all.

In a recent article in *The Times* newspaper, Guy Clapperton (2007) claimed that the popular view of computer games is wrong, and that they are positive influences on children's development and learning. The article itemized what they could teach. The underlying assumption was that children can discern a good game from a bad game; that they can engage with implicit ethical dilemmas, absorb the lessons of history, develop entrepreneurial skills, learn to manage success and failure, take reasonable risks, and become adept at making choices under pressure. All of this may be possible for some well endowed and well supported children, provided the time spent at the computer is balanced with other, more people-centred activities. However, all the evidence would suggest that there are many children, possibly a majority, for whom this kind of learning is not possible. There are many children who are likely to become highly anxious or over-excited, and at risk of becoming addicted to the over-excitement. The debate tends to look at the content of the game and not at the psychological make-up of the player. This particular article seemed to have a view of all children as future contestants on 'The Apprentice'!

I have written elsewhere (Youell, 2002, 2005, 2007) about the huge discrepancies which exist in children's capacity to play. The experience of working in a family centre, conducting assessments for the family courts, led me to become preoccupied with the links between relationships, play, and learning. Children whose early relationships have been characterized by deprivation and neglect, or whose parents have been actively abusive, very often reach school age with severely inhibited patterns of play. In writing for teachers and social workers, I have drawn attention to the way in which play can look like play, whilst being devoid of any creativity, symbolic meaning, or sense of playfulness. Toddlers can be busy with toys and can giggle obligingly when tickled, but an open-minded, reflective, detailed observation will reveal the lack of substance in the play, the lack of progression, and the total absence of imagination. Children who have been traumatized often have difficulty with symbolic thinking, and are likely to confuse reality and fantasy.

I would want to argue, further, that children who cannot play (in the full sense of the word) are at a disadvantage when it comes to making relationships, and to tackling new learning tasks. If early relationships have not introduced the child to ideas of playfulness and shared humour, these elements will be missing in later attempts to make connections with people. Similarly, if early learning has not included an element of playfulness, the child will be likely to approach new tasks with an unmanageable degree of anxiety. Groups of older children, adolescents, and adults are often told to 'play around with an idea' as part of a task. For children who do not know how to play, this is a frightening notion, and is enough to send many children into a flurry of disruptive or avoidant behaviour. It is well documented that children in the 'looked-after' system, who have difficulty with making relationships with the adults who care for them, are the same children who have difficulties with learning and behaviour in school.

My ideas in this field were consolidated when I made a visit to an orphanage in Kenya, taking a supply of toys for a newly appointed teacher to use with the children. Observations of the ways in which the children used the toys over a two-day period were very revealing. Some children could do little more than make towers of bricks. Others made accurate representations of aspects of their immediate surroundings, such as a queue of Duplo children lining up, just as the orphanage children did at meal times. The older children, who attended schools outside the orphanage, chose the board games; keen to demonstrate their knowledge of draughts, and snakes and ladders.

Very few children used the toys in ways which might be described as imaginative or truly symbolic. What was significant, however, was that these were the same children who actively sought a response from the adults; they wanted to show us what they had done, and looked eagerly for our reaction. One six-year old 'flew' a car/plane around our hire car, clearly taken up by an idea of travel. A ten-year old girl made a 'shamba' (homestead) with fences and a few animals. Most striking, perhaps, was a five-year old boy who gathered the necessary items for a shamba in an upturned Frisbee, and carried it away on the back of a tricycle. When we sought information about these different children, we discovered that the children with the most impoverished play were the ones who had been abandoned at the orphanage at birth. The children who were more creative and playful, and who looked to the adults for approval, were those who had spent their early months or years with their families.

This chapter has been concerned with the idea that play and playfulness in a child's early relationships is of crucial importance in the development of what I might call *a good internal object* and which others might call *a secure sense of self* or *self esteem, secure attachment,* or *resilience.* These are not the same thing, but have much in common. Psychoanalytic psychotherapy with young children is based on the play technique pioneered by Melanie Klein. It differs in important ways from play therapy, in that the central focus is the relationship with the therapist rather than the play itself. Play in a therapy session may be cathartic, it may be expressive; it may be that a child is working through something through symbolic re-enactment, but the point about psychoanalytic psychotherapy is that the child is playing in the presence of a mindful adult, within a relationship (cf. Ricky Emanuel's Chapter 6, this volume). The child is communicating something about his or her experience, about his or her internal world to another, who is receptive and thoughtful. It is not cosy or cuddly; it is robust and challenging.

Deprived or traumatized children have impoverished patterns of play, and these, for the most part, are the children who come to see child psychotherapists. In recent years, I have become fascinated by the very high incidence of one particular game in the therapy of children who are 'looked after' or adopted. I could quote a dozen or more cases, my own and those I hear about in supervisions, where weeks and sometimes months of weekly or thrice-weekly sessions are characterized by seemingly endless games of Hide and Seek. Very young children whose early experience has been disrupted play rudimentary games of peek-a-boo with their therapists. Older children become completely absorbed in repeated games of hide and seek, constructing elaborate hiding places behind or underneath items of furniture. In small, relatively simple, sparsely furnished therapy rooms, children whose cognitive capacities would tell them that they could not possibly hide become very excited as the counting to 20 reaches 18. They often shout 'ready', somehow convinced that their therapist could not possibly locate them, from the direction of the sound of their voice. They crawl under the therapist's chair as if the fact that they are pushing up on the seat from below would not be noticed.

I once had a twelve-year old patient, a hardened, street-wise boy, insist that there were still plenty of places to hide in my tiny office. He was head and shoulders taller than any of my furniture! Children of all ages giggle expectantly as the therapist makes a show of looking for them and exclaims on finding them. A ten-year old adopted boy told me recently that he likes hiding, but most of all just loves being found. A thirteen-year old girl rather sadly announced after nearly two years' work that she thought it was probably a bit silly to try to hide herself in the room, but asked earnestly whether the therapist would go on playing if they agreed to hide a small teddy instead; a significant moment in terms of this girls' capacity to use symbols.

Of course, there are many ways in which the hide-and-seek game might be seen to have significant meaning for children who are separated from their birth parents, and who desperately want their families, or a new family, to seek them out and claim them. It is easy to see that they are desperate to exert some control over their lives; to know that the person they are with will look for them, will find them, and will be pleased to do so. These are generalizations, and the exact meaning will be different in each case; but what I find compelling is the way the game recurs, and the way the children suspend their ordinary senses, their awareness of reality, in order to enjoy the game. Some are looking to repeat an experience they had long ago and cannot consciously remember, while others are trying something out for the first time. For many, it is a courageous experiment in relatedness; the kind of experience which is the basis for the development of more sophisticated forms of play and playfulness. I will conclude by quoting a section of a chapter on play from the Tavistock Clinic publication *Talking Cure* (Taylor, 1999). Here, the author is describing the place of 'Peep-Boo!' in the development of the baby's capacity to tolerate 'small amounts of being alone'.

> 'Peep-Boo!', one of the very earliest games, is about a disappearance and a return. It gives us an interesting and significant idea of one of the functions of play. The timing of the mother's hiding her face before allowing it to reappear, often not quite where expected, is absolutely crucial. Too brief and too predictable, and the baby will quickly become bored. Too long and too unexpected will make the baby's capacity to play break down and be replaced by real anxiety about the whereabouts of the mother. ... The idea that there is a 'just right' length of time for the baby to be left with mother's vanished face amounts to a rule. All games have rules, even one this simple. This rule amounts to a structure, one which appears to control the baby's anxiety and allows fears of being abandoned, a precursor of the fear of death itself, to be made safe.

A brief extract from an observation of a thirteen-month old toddler will perhaps best illustrate the point.

> Jerome goes to the side of the kitchen where there is a big table and a glass cupboard. His mother tells me that this is where he goes to beat his hands on the cupboard, but he knows he shouldn't, and when he sees that she's coming, he runs away. Now he has stopped behind a chair and she says he is waiting for her to go and play. She goes up to him, asking, 'Is there a little

baby here?'. I hear Jerome laughing, but I can't see him until he appears in front of his mother. She says playfully, 'Booo. ...!' He shudders, and for a moment I am not sure whether his expression is one of fear or joy, but his face breaks into a smile and he laughs loudly. He goes back behind the chair and again his mother asks 'Where's the little monkey gone?'. She walks round the table and when they come face to face, he laughs and she takes him into her arms and kisses him.

Conclusion

In summary, the point I have sought to emphasize in this chapter is that each individual's capacity for playful exploration of ideas, when playing alone or with others, is dependent on his earlier experience of playful interaction with the adults who care for him. Although environmental factors play a significant part in the promotion or otherwise of 'healthy' play opportunities, playfulness is a state of mind, and one which is established within a relationship. Teaching children or adults to play when they have not had satisfying experiences in their early years is no simple task.

References

Clapperton, G. (2007). Computer games are good for you. *The Times* Newspaper, 18 October.

Edwards, J. (1999). Kings, queens and factors: the latency period revisited. In: D. Hindle & M. Vaciago Smith (Eds.), *Personality Development: A Psychoanalytic Perspective* (pp. 71–92). London: Routledge.

Erikson, E.H. (1950). *Childhood and Society.* New York: Norton.

Taylor, D. (Ed.) (1999). *Talking Cure: Mind and Method of the Tavistock Clinic.* London: Duckworth.

Youell, B. (2002). The relevance of infant and young child observation in multi-disciplinary assessments for the family courts. In: A. Briggs (Ed.), *Surviving Space: Infant Observation and Other Papers: Essays on Mrs Bick's Centenary* (pp. 117–135). London: Karnac.

Youell, B. (2005). Observation in social work practice. In: M. Bower (Ed.), *Psychoanalysis and Social Work Practice* (pp. 47–58). London: Routledge.

Youell, B. (2007). *The Learning Relationship: Psychoanalytic Thinking in Education.* London: Karnac.

CHAPTER THIRTEEN

Everyday play activities as therapeutic and pedagogical encounters*

Elizabeth Wood

Introduction

I am not a play therapist, nor am I knowledgeable about the discipline and practice of play therapy. My field of scholarship is education, and my research focuses predominantly on play in early childhood, and in education settings (Wood & Attfield, 2005; Wood, 2007a, b; 2008a, b). However, I have a lifelong interest in play, and spend a great deal of time observing people at play whenever and wherever play occurs. I am a skilled player, and I have a firm belief that life-long playing is as important as lifelong learning. So why should I be writing a chapter that focuses on everyday play activities as therapeutic encounters?

The chapter emerges from a paper I gave at a conference at Roehampton University in October 2007, which brought together professionals from diverse fields, with a focus on educational and therapeutic play. Whilst both fields have well-established traditions,

*An earlier version of this chapter appeared in the *European Journal of Psychotherapy & Counselling*, 10, 2008: 111–120; reproduced here by kind permission of Routledge publishers.

with respect to play their disciplinary boundaries are permeable. Although play scholarship is a serious business, I began with some playful thinking around the ideas of play as therapy, and therapy as play, and the similarities between therapeutic and pedagogical encounters. Looking to the dictionary for definitions of these concepts, I found a dual meaning for the word 'therapeutic':

- of or relating to the treatment of disease; curative
- serving or performing to maintain health.

(*Collins English Dictionary*, 1994, p. 1599)

The word 'therapy' comes from the Greek *therapeia* meaning attendance, which led to my next act of definition. Attendance involves being present, giving care, ministering, listening, paying attention to, devoting one's time, applying oneself, to escort, to accompany. It derives from the Latin *attendere*, to stretch towards. And it was at this point that I began to formulate some ideas about the ways in which everyday play activities can provide therapeutic encounters between people, by creating inter-subjective, relational spaces in which people attend to, or 'stretch towards', each other, and to the affordances within the play environment. Indeed, it is often the absence of attendance, in all its definitions, that contributes to the need for structured play-therapy interventions for children and families (Chazan, 2002; Emanuel, 2006).

The notion of therapeutic encounters also connects with my own research on play and pedagogy (Wood, 2008a, b), particularly the need for playfulness and playful orientations to education, for adults as well as for children. In the continental European model of social pedagogy, the emphasis is on co-construction, dialogue, and mutual engagement and understanding. Teachers-as-learners continually learn about the people with whom they work and play, and use their knowledge to inform their provision and practice, including everyday playful interactions as well as formal pedagogical routines. Learners-as-teachers continually test and refine their knowledge and skills, and may act as capable and knowledgeable others with peers and adults.

I also recognize that the processes of attendance and 'stretching towards' may not always serve positive or pro-social purposes.

In Sutton-Smith's (1997) scholarly analysis of the theory, rhetoric, and ambiguity of play, he discusses the characteristics of 'dark play' and 'cruel play' in which play may be used to disturb and disrupt the social order, and may cause intentional (or unintentional) harm to others. In the following section I outline some of the eclectic theories that aim to explain what play is, and what purposes it serves. This is followed by observations and narratives of play to illustrate contrasting theoretical perspectives, focusing on the importance of co-construction and inter-subjectivity in play activities. I then discuss the concepts of dark and cruel play, not least because these are all too often omitted from the more romantic and idealized accounts of play. The conclusion draws together some ideas about the future of play, and the fusion of play as therapeutic and pedagogical encounters.

Play in theory—the multi-headed hydra

The field of play scholarship is theoretically and methodologically eclectic, drawing on a wide range of disciplines, including philosophical and spiritual literatures. In the fields of psychology and education, research has provided substantial evidence to support the role of play in communication, language, and literacy learning; emotional and social development, including social competence and peer group affiliation; spatial and mathematical learning; creativity; the development of positive learning dispositions and orientations; and the formation of identity (Broadhead, 2004; Frost et al., 2005; Johnson et al., 2005; Wood & Attfield, 2005). Emerging evidence on the neurophysiological development of the brain also indicates the importance of children making connections between areas of learning and experience through play, exploration, and experimentation, and through collaborative, reciprocal relationships (Gopnik et al., 1999).

Whilst play is typically valued in early childhood, there is a broad consensus that play and playfulness are sustained in many different forms across the lifespan, from highly structured activities such as chess and Olympic sports, to more informal activities such as carnivals, festivals, beauty pageants, and drinking games (Sutton-Smith, 1997). The new forms of play that are being created by popular culture and new media technologies offer extended affordances for interactivity, meaning-making, and representation (Marsh, 2005; Salen & Zimmerman, 2004; Yelland, 2007). Being playful involves engaging in typical play activities, as well as being in a playful state of mind where the spirit or essence of play infuses other activities (which may be classed as non-play, or even work). Thus, in contemporary play scholarship, play is regarded as essential to lifelong learning, creativity, and well-being.

Sutton-Smith (1997) argues that although play is seldom the only determinant of any of the important forms of learning that occur in children, play in childhood is progressive, and may facilitate transfer of knowledge and skills between different contexts. Children's play development moves along paths of increasing social, physical, affective, and cognitive complexity, which involves using signs and symbols; sustaining episodes of imaginative play; creating rules, roles, and play scenarios; and controlling behaviour, mood states, and actions. Play typically becomes more organized and industrious, more rule-bound, and focused on ends as well as means. As children become skilled players, their play also becomes more sustained and more complex, with increased attention to structures, problem-solving, intentional activities, and outcomes (Broadhead, 2004). In play, children often display the positive attributes and dispositions that are considered essential to lifelong learning, such as planning and organization, problem-creating and problem-solving, concentration, engagement, involvement, participation, and meta-cognitive capabilities (Wood & Attfield, 2005). However, in school contexts, time for sustained play is reduced, and work takes centre stage. Constraining play beyond early childhood may therefore deny its many benefits, including opportunities for children to become master players, and to develop emotional resilience.

Proving the developmental and educational potential *of* play is not the only justification *for* play. For children, play is not merely a preparation for adulthood, just as for adults it is not a preparation for the next phase of life. Play is much more complex than that, because it is about the here and now, the driving interests, fascinations, motivations that people have to make sense of, and find their place in, their social and cultural worlds. From a play-therapy perspective, Chazan regards play as an ongoing component of all creative life processes:

> Playing and growing are synonymous with life itself. Playfulness bespeaks creativity and action, change and possibility of

transformation. Play activity thus reflects the very existence of the self, that part of the organism that exists both independently and interdependently, that can reflect upon itself and be aware of its own existence. In being playful the child attains a degree of autonomy sustained by representations of his inner and outer world.

(2002, p. 198)

The concept of inner and outer worlds is common to psychological and psychodynamic theories of play. Winnicott (1971) describes the transitional spaces within which play occurs as the pivotal realm between reality and fantasy. It is in such spaces that the 'what if and as if' dimensions of play are informed and enriched by children's knowledge and experiences in their everyday social and cultural worlds. Chazan (2002) argues that these spaces contain powerful affective content where children can play with positive as well as negative emotions (such as anger, anxiety, jealousy, fear, shame, indifference, dread, aggression, protest, humiliation). Attachment bonds are essential for extending the safe arena of play and the child's repertoire of play activities. Chazan provides detailed clinical case studies that show how transitions between such powerful affective states can be smooth or abrupt, depending on the child's own affective state, resilience and coping abilities.

Within the therapeutic disciplines, play, the creative arts, and meaningful work all have many benefits, particularly for children who have experienced dislocation through wars, natural disasters, and genocide; those who experience accidents, long-term illnesses, family break-up, self-harm, and aggression (for example, bullying, anti-social gang behaviours, social exclusion). Resilience and coping abilities stem from the capacity to develop a coherent narrative of the experience, to create meaning, and to make sense of traumatic events, transitions, and dislocations. So for therapists, and for educators, the processes of attendance and 'stretching towards' will involve encounters with difficult experiences, but will also provide the promise of healing, recovery, and resilience.

For Vygotsky (1978), play is revolutionary activity because play activities hold transformative potential in the playing and meaning-making process. Transformative processes can include symbolic activity; creative use of rules, materials, resources; transformations in thinking and action, and in the ways in which people think about themselves. Play is always located within the social, historical, and cultural structures of families, communities, and societies, but at the same time may be in opposition to those structures. In stretching towards play, children and adults may also be pulling away from reality, and may use play to subvert or challenge dominant forms of power and control. Therefore, it is the revolutionary nature of play that makes it difficult to accommodate in education settings. This is particularly salient in pure play, or purely free play, which takes place outside the realms of adult control, and generates emergent and unpredictable processes and outcomes. Children may reveal multiple identities and take up positions in which they act more knowledgeably, and more powerfully than in adult-controlled contexts (Wood, 2008a).

As the foregoing discussion reveals, the field of play scholarship is immensely complex. In contrast, Western traditions of rational, scientific thought position play as trivial, as having less value and status than work (Wood & Attfield, 2005). This is because play is often ephemeral, transitory, and may not result in immediate, tangible, or measurable outcomes that can be mapped against defined curriculum goals. Play, imagination, and pretence are, therefore, less credible, and are easily dismissed when people have to devote attention to the real business of life. However, the distinctions between play and work, or play and not play, are not clearly delineated in all cultures. Sutton-Smith (1997, p. 56) points out that within Hindu metaphysics, play is seen as one of multiple realities, all of which are transformable into each other. Imagination is more complex than pretence (which is often dismissed as merely making things up), for it involves image-making—calling images into mind, and transforming them into meaning and activity (a cardboard box becomes a spaceship, a stick becomes a magic light sabre). Huizinga (1955) also takes a metaphysical view:

> ...play is more than a mere physiological phenomenon or a psychological reflex. It goes beyond the confines of purely physical or purely biological activity. It is a significant function—that is to say, there is some sense to it. In play there is something

'at play' which transcends the immediate needs of life, and imparts meaning to action. All play means something.

(1955, p. 446)

Cohen and MacKeith (1991) use the evocative term 'world-weavers' to describe the imaginative worlds created by children, as well as adults, which may be ephemeral or sustained over a lifetime. The potential for world-weaving has been enhanced considerably by information and communication technologies, computer games, and virtual worlds where people can create their own multiple realities. Technological play spaces have infinite transformational possibilities, whether players experience the representation of something known and familiar or fantastically imaginative (Salen & Zimmerman, 2004).

In summary, the construct of play as everyday therapeutic and pedagogical encounters draws on powerful theories about the transformative, transcendent, and revolutionary qualities of play. In the following section, some of these ideas are illustrated in the context of two narratives of play.

Narratives of play

Joshua is seventeen months old; he is a confident walker and loves to be outdoors. In the summer months, he showed persistent interest in his grandfather's garden tools, particularly the long rake and the wheelbarrow. Much effort was focused on trying to push the barrow, and he had learned that the best strategy (for the time being at least) was for him to stand in front of Tony, and for them to push together with both sets of hands helping to steer. Because this is one of Joshua's favourite garden activities, his Mum and Dad had bought him a set of plastic garden tools, with a small barrow, which were well within his capabilities to manipulate and manoeuvre.

It is October, he is in the garden with his grandfather, and they are raking the leaves, and piling them into the big barrow. Joshua watches intently. Tony puts some leaves into Joshua's small barrow, and shows him how to empty them into the big bag. Joshua has other ideas. He tips the leaves out of his barrow and scatters them with his hands, laughing. Then he heaves on the big rake, trying to gather them in again. He falls over but is not daunted by the task. Tony again encourages him to use his plastic rake and pile leaves into the small barrow. Joshua again tips them out. After this happens a few more times, Joshua piles the plastic tools into the small barrow, and confidently trundles over to the shed, where he hides them, with a big smile on his face. He returns triumphantly to his main task, which is to use the big rake, and the big barrow, like his granddad. Tony helps him and they work together pulling the rake. He shows Joshua how to pull the leaves from the forks of the rake, and Joshua works seriously and intently on these tasks. Joshua stands between the handles of the wheelbarrow and stretches out to grasp them, but he is too small. He accepts a compromise—he grasps one handle, Tony grasps the other, and they both push the barrow. Then he returns to play mode, picking up handfuls of leaves from the barrow, throwing them in the air, and scattering them back over the grass. He laughs and claps his hands with excitement as his granddad joins in with his exuberance.

Pieter is seven years old and has recently arrived in the UK from Poland. He has joined a Year 2 class in an inner-city primary school, and speaks no English. The school has a very diverse population, with 87 per cent of the children from minority ethnic groups, and around 18 community languages spoken. Mohammad has been assigned to look after Pieter, a task that he accepts willingly. He is a mature and caring boy, a confident speaker of Punjabi and English, and is learning some Arabic at the mosque school. At play time, Pieter seems overwhelmed, but Mohammad sticks close by. He holds up Pieter's hands for him and they begin a clapping game, with Mohammad chanting a Punjabi rhyme. He does this three times, then holds up his own hands, chanting the rhyme whilst Pieter performs the rhythmic clapping. They continue repeating the game, each time getting faster, until they both collapse in a fit of giggles. When the whistle goes, they walk to the line with

> their arms around each other's shoulders, laughing and smiling. Mohammad stands behind Pieter in the line, with his hands on his shoulders, ready to steer him back to the classroom. Mohammad reports to the teacher that he played with Pieter and taught him a new game.

In relation to the Greek and Latin meanings stated in the introduction, these episodes reveal how 'attendance' and 'stretching towards' begin from infancy and continue throughout life. Play requires the players to be present in the shared activity, not least because play is fluid and open to change of pace and direction. In both narratives, there was a flow between play and not play, and between the physical, emotional, cognitive, and spiritual dimensions of play. Joshua reveals his developing understanding of theory of mind: by hiding the plastic toys, he signals his intention to master the real gardening tools, and exerts some agency in the activity. Tony's real task of clearing the autumn leaves becomes subordinated to Joshua's play, and to nurturing a powerful inter-generational relationship.

Whilst Tony and Joshua had an intimate family relationship, Mohammad and Pieter's narrative shows the power of instant play as a means of social inclusion, connectedness, and belonging, as well as Mohammad modelling how to navigate the complexities of the school day. Clapping games are a familiar playtime activity in this school, where children from different cultures exchange their own versions and rituals, as well as creating new ones. The clapping play enables them to cross boundaries of language, meaning, and culture. Indeed, play has its own symbolic language and culture, which can be readily understood by players. Mohammad recognizes clapping games as an inter-subjective space, which provides fun, pleasure, and engagement. In both narratives, the stretching towards is a dynamic two-way process. The players are present, paying attention, giving care, applying themselves to the flow of the play, and devoting time to play. There is ministering, escorting, and accompanying, and a meeting of minds.

Both narratives reveal that play is a serious business. Being a good player involves watching and listening, because the flow is reliant on the inter-subjective attunement of the players. In an age when literacy is defined in the English National Curriculum as 'speaking, listening, reading, and writing', it is easy to forget that communication is multi-modal and multi-faceted. Being in a state of play involves body language, facial expressions, gestures, signs, and symbolization. So maintaining a state of being present, paying attention, and stretching towards all help to sustain meaningful play.

These everyday play activities have therapeutic and pedagogical purposes, because they serve to maintain health and well-

204   CHILDHOOD, WELL-BEING AND A THERAPEUTIC ETHOS

being, in the sense of positive relationships, positive sense of self, connectedness, and belonging. However, play is not always used for pro-social purposes, and the dark side of play is explored in the following section.

The dark side of play

Sutton-Smith (1997, p. 151) makes the point that in Western culture, children (who are supposed to be the players among us) are allowed much less freedom for irrational, wild, dark, or deep play than are adults. These issues warrant some deeper analysis. Many forms of play involve, risk, hazard, and challenge, as well as promise. This may be seen in a simple game of chance such as 'snakes and ladders', where the promise is winning and the risk is losing. In more complex forms of play, risk and promise may involve higher stakes, such as position in a hierarchy, self-esteem and identity, and ego maintenance. So irrational, wild, deep, or dark play may involve different forms of risk and promise, according to the players and to the context. Wild play may include exuberant play that is characterized by high energy and deep involvement such as rough and tumble, play-fighting, war games, extreme sports, and raves.

Engagement in wild play therefore requires specific forms of attendance, especially where there is potential risk, hazard, and challenge, which is part of the 'wildness'. Attendance may take different forms—looking out for your co-players, checking their safety, stretching towards them to help them through a tough patch or learn a new skill. Alternatively, attendance can take the form of competition, where the stretching towards involves checking out whether one is winning or losing, where one is in the play, gaining advantage, possibly cheating if the stakes or rewards are high. Indeed, the competitive drive may compromise or destroy the spirit of play, for example when a footballer makes a deliberately damaging tackle that may take out a player from the game, and possibly from his or her career.

Dark or cruel play may include extreme contact sports and animal contests (such as cock-fighting, dog-fighting, bull-fighting) where there is a high risk of injury and death. Cruel play can also include 'mind play' such as teasing, joking, hazing, pranks, telling tales, playing tricks, gossip, blogging, and social-networking activities such as posting videos that involve violence and humiliation. Cruel play may also have sadistic elements which may be consensual (for example, sexual play including bondage and role play), or non-consensual, such as bullying and social aggression. The boundaries of cruel or dark play are likely to vary according to the mood, and affective and psychological state of the player. Teasing can easily be interpreted as bullying, just as flirting can be interpreted as sexual harassment. Maintaining or transgressing those boundaries is dependent on who is playing, the context of the play, the intentions of the players, and the mutual understanding of acting in or out of the 'what if' and 'as if' modes that distinguish play and not play, real and not real, actual and pretend.

These play forms can be viewed through different lenses. Biesty (2003) argues that crossing or pushing boundaries may be a way of grappling with the gravity of life:

> For example, insulting and debasing other players may be a test of inclusion rather than actual dismissal, and handling those insults may, in fact, be a way to grow into membership as well as a means of gaining social interaction skills.
>
> (2003, p. 54)

A counter-argument to this position is that not all children (or indeed adults) have the psychological and emotional capability or resilience to cross (or be pushed across) these boundaries. Whether cruel play is verbal or physical, the perpetrator may be able to get off the hook by spinning the defence 'I didn't mean it, I was only playing'. However, cruel or dark play may take some people into zones that are unsafe physically, psychologically, emotionally, and socially. And with the growth of new media and communication technologies, potentially unsafe spaces are opening up all the time, for example the use of social networking sites by paedophiles for grooming young people, and the use of messaging via mobile phones for the purposes of bullying, social exclusion, and intimidation. The pace of technological change demands from children incredible plasticity, adaptability, creativity, and flexibility. The nature of such change also demands that, as a society, we attend to the implications of new technologies, including their potential for pro- and anti-social play.

From a Kleinian perspective (e.g., Klein, 1953), one way of accounting for, or making sense of, dark play might be in terms of young children finding ways to manage and contain their own (natural) feelings of hate, rather than simply 'acting them out' in overt behaviour. Accordingly, it might be important for some children to have an enabling 'transitional space' (Winnicott, 1971), whether it be in a therapeutic or an educational setting, where they can use their play as a vehicle for assimilating and integrating such feelings, typically in an 'as if' way. As Klein maintained, these processes may enable children to move from what she referred to as a relatively immature 'paranoid-schizoid' position into a more mature, so-called 'depressive-position' mode of functioning and relating. To embrace some kind of psychoanalytic understanding of childhood experience requires that we stay open to the possibility that dynamically unconscious forces may well be at work in children's play (for example, in dark play). This means that teachers and parents should stay as open as possible to these deeper understandings, rather than settling for superficial interpretations of, and attitudes to, children's play. Adults need to attend to what is most important in children's play, and most important to the players.

Conclusion

In making the case for play activities as therapeutic and pedagogical encounters, I have drawn on a range of disciplinary and theoretical positions, and have offered some contrasting perspectives on play forms, and the multiple purposes that play serves. The common threads that join these positions include play as attendance (in all its definitions) and 'stretching towards' others in order to create relational spaces in which children and young people can develop their potential. In the twenty-first century, the pace of social, economic, and technological change is rapid, with far-reaching impacts on children's play lives. However, such changes continue to demand playful engagement with and in the world, and for the world to be a playful place in which humans can learn and develop. We all need time to develop the ludic intelligence and capability that enables us to be master players, and lifelong players. A shared responsibility (within all spheres of life) is to continue to develop a sense of what it means to be playful human beings.

Play is indeed a very serious business.

References

Biesty, P. (2003). Where is play? In: D.E. Lytle (Ed.), *Play and Educational Theory and Practice. Play and Culture Studies, Vol. 5* (pp. 43–55). Westport, CT: Praeger.

Broadhead, P. (2004). *Early Years Play and Learning: Developing Social Skills and Cooperation*. London: Routledge.

Chazan, S.E. (2002). *Profiles of Play: Observing Structure and Process in Play Therapy*. London: Jessica Kingsley.

Cohen, D. & Mackeith, S.A. (1991). *The Development of Imagination: The Private Worlds of Childhood*. London: Routledge.

Emanuel, R. (2006). Asking the right questions. Paper presented to the Childhood, Well-being and a Therapeutic Ethos Conference, Roehampton University, 14 December 2006; reprinted as Chapter 6, this volume.

Frost, J., Wortham, S., & Reifel, S. (2005). *Play and Child Development*. New Jersey: Merrill/Prentice Hall.

Gopnik, A., Meltzoff, A.N., & Kuhl, P.K. (1999). *The Scientist in the Crib: Minds, Brains and How Children Learn*. New York: William Morrow.

Huizinga, J. (1955). *Homo Ludens: A Study of the Play Element in Culture*. Boston: Beacon Press.

Johnson, J.E., Christie, J.F., & Wardle, F. (2005). *Play, Development and Early Education*. Boston, MA: Pearson Education.

Klein, M. (1953). *Love, Hate and Reparation*. London: Hogarth Press.

Marsh, J. (Ed.) (2005). *Popular Culture, New Media and Digital Literacy in Early Childhood*. London: RoutledgeFalmer.

Salen, K., & Zimmerman, E. (2004). *Rules of Play, Game Design Fundamentals*. Cambridge, MA: MIT Press.

Sutton-Smith, B. (1997). *The Ambiguity of Play*. Cambridge, MA: Harvard University Press.

Vygotsky, L. (1978). *Mind in Society: The Development of Higher Psychological Processes*. Cambridge, MA: Harvard University Press.

Winnicott, D.W. (1971). *Playing and Reality*. New York: Basic Books.

Wood, E. (2007a). Re-conceptualising child-centred education. *Forum*, 49(1): 121–136.

Wood, E. (2007b). New directions in play: consensus or collision? *Education 3–13*, 35: 309–320.

Wood, E. (2008a). Conceptualising a pedagogy of play: international perspectives from theory, policy and practice. In: D. Kuschner (Ed.), *From Children to Red Hatters: Diverse Images and Issues of Play*. Lanham, MD: University Press of America.

Wood, E. (2008b). Developing a pedagogy of play for the 21st century. In: A. Anning, J. Cullen, & M. Fleer (Eds.), *Early Childhood Education, Society and Culture*, 2nd edition (pp. 27–38). London: Sage.

Wood, E., & Attfield, J. (2005). *Play, Learning and the Early Childhood Curriculum*, 2nd edition. London: Paul Chapman.

Yelland, N. (2007). *Shift to the Future—Rethinking Learning with New Technologies*. London: Routledge.

CHAPTER FOURTEEN

From playing to thinking: How the Kindergarten provides a foundation for scientific understanding*

Eugene Schwartz

This chapter draws upon Rudolf Steiner's understanding of child development to show how the Waldorf Kindergarten (for children up to age 6) creates a space in which, through play and natural day-to-day activities, the necessary foundations are laid for future (more cognitive) learning. In this holistic ontology, the children's Kindergarten experiences, on the somatic level, percolate through the life of their feelings for seven or eight years, and are then ready to 'bubble up' in the form of thoughts in seventh grade. The archetypal movements and rhythms that underlie activities like sweeping, stirring, kneading, and washing, gestures which have formed the bodies and wills of human beings for countless generations, are rapidly disappearing in the lives of modern children. The Waldorf Kindergarten fosters an atmosphere akin to that of the 'home and hearth', where the child who plays creatively in those formative first seven years of life will have the potential

---

*An earlier version of this chapter appeared in the *European Journal of Psychotherapy & Counselling*, 10, 2008: 137–146; reproduced here by kind permission of Routledge publishers.

for a far more '*inner*' and living grasp of (for example) the laws of physics than a child who was little more than a passive observer in that period of life.

How do we educate the child in accordance with principles that ask us to honour and work with the soul and spiritual nature of the youngster? Must teachers be 'intuitive' in order to be certain that they are teaching in the proper way? Intuition is helpful, but we can go far with faculties that we often use without being aware that we *are* using them. For example, a mother can always tell when her child is not feeling well; with some experience, she can usually tell *in what way* the child is not feeling well. And every teacher knows the 'glow' radiated by a child who is healthy and, as we say, 'full of life'. Many of these judgments may be based on perceptions of the activities of what Rudolf Steiner, the originator of Waldorf education, termed the child's 'etheric body'.

What is essential here is that we are dealing with *activities*, with processes, rather than with 'products'. To understand the etheric body is to begin to understand those forces usually termed 'creative' in the world and in the human being. Our etheric body is active in a way that our physical body is not. We go through life as physical beings in an inert, 'cause and effect' manner. The etheric body works to reverse those effects suffered by the physical body in the course of daily life; it is a body of renewal and regeneration. In relation to the physical body we could also say that the etheric body works as an architect and sculptor. One need only watch children at play in the sandbox or at the seashore to see this sculptural–architectural power unconsciously at work. In later years, some individuals find themselves gifted with a surplus of etheric forces, and are naturally drawn, as architects, to form majestic 'bodies' in which thousands of people can worship or live, or, as sculptors, to continue to replicate their bodily form in endless permutations.

In its capacity as the 'body of formative forces', the etheric body holds the *memory* of the form of our physical body, so that we retain a recognizable physical identity throughout our life. In spite of aging and the vicissitudes of life, fingerprints and blood types and certain facets of our body chemistry remain the same, a 'signature' of the form-creating and form-maintaining activity of the etheric body. It is this particular aspect of the etheric body which goes through an important transformation after the first seven-year period in life.

As the etheric body is released from its intensive and ceaseless work upon the formation of the physical body; as that body's growth (when compared, for example, to its growth in the womb, or in the first three years of life) slows down, etheric forces are 'freed' to be utilized as our power of memory.

Rudolf Steiner's description of the etheric formative forces at this time in the child's life is intriguing. The very same forces that 'member' us, that place our heart and lungs and liver in relation to one another, that 'organ'ize us into a decidedly human form, are now released to re-member, and to 'organize' our life of memory. We could say that the forces of memory are at their most powerful in the first seven years of life, but Steiner is at pains to stress that they are not meant to be accessed for the purposes of memorization. In these first years of life, these forces are meant to serve the child's growth, pure and simple. It is certainly possible to divert these forces in order to teach a young child to memorize the alphabet, or to memorize a simple reading vocabulary, or to memorize times tables. Once diverted, however, these etheric forces no longer serve their primary mission, and the membering and organization of the child's body—the foundation for its health and vitality in later years—will be less perfect than if those forces had been allowed to go their own way. It is its recognition of the sacredness of these health-giving, creative forces that live in the child that gives the Waldorf Kindergarten its unique character.

The paradigm of education that has developed in the course of the past hundred years is intellectual and didactic. In this model, the teacher, and, especially in the last few years, the parent as well, is always supposed to be imparting information to the child. Much of this imparting is actually 'correcting,' adjusting the child's imperfect *understanding* of the world in the light of modern knowledge, and particularly modern scientific knowledge. This approach is so pervasive as to be almost invisible. How few toys are left that do not profess to be 'educational toys'? How much software is sold for young consumers that is not advertised as 'educational software'? Parents are encouraged to create environments for even the youngest child in which letters and numbers, abstract geometrical shapes (in mobiles or puzzles), and dolls depicting endangered species of animals will 'educate' the child, even when an adult is not in the room. The spectre of Generation One, the worship of the one-sided

Intellect who whispers that 'Knowledge is Power,' haunts the Kindergarten classroom, the theme park, and even the nursery.

The atmosphere of the Waldorf Kindergarten appears, at first, to be devoid of any of 'educational' accoutrements. The Kindergarten teacher Charlotte Comeras describes a typical Waldorf setting:

> The room is warm and homelike and the teacher is busy doing one of the many tasks involved in the life of the Kindergarten. If there is another adult in the room, he or she also will be occupied with something or other—maybe carding wool to make a puppet, or mending a torn play-cloth. Around the room are baskets filled with pieces of wood, fircones or large pebbles from the beach. Others are piled high with play-cloths or pieces of muslin in beautiful soft colors, all neatly folded and waiting to become whatever the children need them to be: the roof or wall of the house, the sea, pasture for sheep to graze, a shawl for a baby or a veil for a queen. The possibilities are limitless. On a shelf stand many puppets: a prince, a farmer and his wife, a child, a wise old woman. ... They can bring a castle to life or make a farm, re-enact a scene of human activity or be used to tell a story. These are just a few of the many things that the children will see when they come into the Kindergarten.[1]

Of no less significance than what is in the Kindergarten room is what is not in the Kindergarten room: there are no 'educational toys' (there are very few objects that could be construed as 'toys' at all), there are no books, no posters, no bulletin boards, no computers. There is none of the hardware issued by the Industrial-Educational Complex, and there is no software (unless we want to count soft dolls of wool and cotton as 'software'). For eyes accustomed to the Generation One model of mainstream education, there is nothing recognizably 'educative' about such a space; pedagogically speaking, it would appear to be something of a Black Hole. It is no wonder that a respected independent school headmaster, serving on an accreditation committee that was visiting Green Meadow Waldorf School in New York State, remarked after his initial visit to the Kindergarten, 'This room is like something out of the nineteenth century!'.

Unlike the assertively educational objects and spaces that fill a mainstream Kindergarten room, the environs of a Waldorf

Kindergarten take on meaning only when there are children present who can *imbue* them with meaning:

> ...the children will each find their own way in their own time. Some, drawn to the adults and whatever they are doing, will want to do it too, or to help; whilst others, possibly the very youngest, will be happy to watch silently, taking in every detail, every movement. Other children will know exactly what they want to do: build huge suspension bridges with planks, logs and bits of woolen rope, or make a house for themselves, using clothes horses and colored play-cloths. It may take a while for the children to sort themselves out and find their playmates. Sometimes a little unobtrusive adult-guidance is needed to bring this about, but as much as possible the adults carry on with their own work, yet, at the same time being aware of everything going on in the room.[2]

The 'play-cloth', mentioned often by Comeras, is the 'archetypal plaything' of the Waldorf Kindergarten. This is a large cloth of cotton (or cotton gauze, or sometimes silk) which has been dyed with natural plant colours. Compared to a plastic action figure, it is soft and devoid of form; compared to an 'educational' pull-toy, it is immobile, has no parts, and so specific function. The play-cloth is as close to a non-thing as a child can come; it is almost nothing; but, as Faust tells Mephistopheles, 'Within that Nothing I will find my All!' Even Mary Sheedy Kurcinka, in discussing choices made by 'spirited' children among the predominantly plastic educational toys available in a completely conventional setting, observes that

> most spirited kids like toys that allow them to use their imagination. Items such as little toy people, blocks, Legos, Fisher-Price play houses, musical and story tapes, and dress-up clothes are favorites. These are all toys that can be used in many different ways. There isn't one correct answer. Most spirited kids won't look twice at toys that have one 'right' way to play with them. This includes puzzles, many board games, cards, and peg boards. If your spirited children enjoy puzzles, watch how they actually use them. In most cases the pieces are being employed as pretend food, space ships, and other inventive creations![3]

Following a lecture given to an audience of parents unfamiliar with Waldorf educational ideas, I visited the home of a family I'll call the Smiths. As we sat and talked, little Cynthia Smith, a vital and awake 2½ year-old, who has already opened her front gate and taken walks (on her own) quite some distance from home, was exploring an even stranger world—that of educational toys. She had come upon a toy composed of several sections of plastic pipe. Each section had a 'male' and 'female' end, as they say. Cynthia had taken the sections apart and was now attempting to put them back together. For some time, she tried to place two male ends together, undoubtedly perceiving that since they looked alike, they must 'belong' together. She tried, and tried, and tried again, but the sections fell apart. Finally, she matched a male end to a female end, and the sections slid smoothly together. Repeating what she had just learned, Cynthia was able to reassemble the whole pipe; once that task was done, she moved on to something else.

A child psychologist would probably proclaim Cynthia's discovery to be a 'developmental step', or 'a watershed in growth'; one school of psychology might even assert that she had gained some *understanding* of human sexuality through her interaction with those male and female endings. But in learning that there is *only one way* in which to combine those sections of pipe, Cynthia had also accepted a contraction in her realm of possibilities, a cramping of her creative potential. One pipe-fitting does not make for a prison cell, of course, and Cynthia soon found her way to a formless and yielding pile of leaves in which she played happily by the hour. Yet toy after toy, 'educational experience' after educational experience, slowly but surely teaches the malleable soul of the child, so filled with *possibilities*, that life is but a series of one-way streets which never converge and have no destination.

The play-cloths and other objects found in the Waldorf Kindergarten are deliberately 'incomplete' in nature. A lot of room is left for the child's active imagination to 'finish' the plaything, but that process of completion is never dictated by the object itself. The etheric forces of the child (referred to earlier), engaged in ceaselessly imbuing the child with life, are mobile enough to imbue any object to which the child turns her attention with 'life' as well. If the object broadly suggests a human or animal form—and we need think only of the venerable rag dolls and wooden hobby horses of childhood past (they are still to be found in the Waldorf Kindergarten!) —the child is well able to give the plaything a voice, a personality, moods, and appetites.

A Kindergarten teacher who had been trained in both the Montessori and Waldorf approaches took a leave from teaching in order to raise her own family. After several years, she started a home play-group for children of nursery and Kindergarten age. Since she still had the supplies and accoutrements gathered during her years of practising both approaches, she set up two rooms in her house as a 'Waldorf Room' and a 'Montessori Room'. She learned that whenever a newcomer joined the playgroup, the experienced children would point to the Waldorf Room and say, 'That's the room where you're allowed to pretend', and then point to the Montessori Room and say, 'And that's the room where you're not'.

Toys that are already formed to provide an exact semblance of physical life, e.g. dolls that are 'anatomically correct' (a beloved educational tool), whose eyes open and close, whose innards contain synthesized 'cries' and 'voices,' or 'action figures' whose hard limbs are encased in futuristic armour, etc., leave the child with little or nothing to add. Play with such toys is merely physical, for the life-forces have no outlet when confronted with a finished product. Boredom sets in easily, and the only solution appears to be buying yet *another* toy to add to the collection. The Kindergartener is already learning how to become a consumer, rather than a creator.

In the past, children played with their toys; today, we might say that the toys do the playing, and the child watches. Television, of course, heightens this experience. Within the tube, people (or their cartoon equivalents) are running, dancing, juggling, flying, swimming, and, of course, wielding very powerful weapons. Outside the tube, the child is sitting, or reclining, moving only his eyes. Children are fast losing their instinctive sense for play. Learning how to play must become an essential element in the life of the Kindergarten. Charlotte Comeras describes the children's activities:

> We use the word creative, but really, what they are doing for a large part of the time is recreating. They play house, cooking, cleaning, taking care of babies, or they make a shop with everything carefully laid out for the customers to come and buy. Children visit friends in other houses and sit drinking cups of tea and

they will all leave their houses to ride on a bus or train that is just about to leave the station. All these things are part of their daily lives and now they re-enact what they have seen the grown-ups doing and thereby enter into the activities in their own way.

For the young child there is no separation between work and play—all play is work and all work is play. ... We see how strong is the necessity, in each child's own being, to imitate what they experience around them and thereby find their relationship to the world. Through this recreative play, they start to gain a healthy orientation to life, and through this process of learning, and understanding their environment, they can feel more secure and at home in it.[4]

One of the more popular attractions on the Waldorf Kindergarten playground is the seesaw or teeter-totter (many Kindergartens have an indoor equivalent for rainy days, as well). This is an eminently social plaything; each child depends on her companion, at the other end, to shift the balance sufficiently so that she can rise or descend. Now and then, a mischievous child will discover that, by leaning back when he is on the ground, he can keep his counterpart up in the air, or that by crawling along the plank towards its centre-point, he can make it very difficult for his friend to lift him up. Such a playground experience offers many lessons about the 'give-and-take' of social situations, in the Kindergarten and beyond. These are lessons which go more deeply than the best-intentioned teacher's imprecations to 'please share with your friends, please wait for others to go first, please be considerate of those around you!'. The teeter-totter works on the non-verbal, pre-intellectual 'visceral' level, which is the most active component of the Kindergartener's nature; through her *will*, the child embodies a relationship to the world which will only later awaken in her feeling life and still later in her conscious life of thoughts.

Several years later, many of the same children return to the Kindergarten playground with their seventh grade teacher. She allows them to play freely for a few minutes, and then has them gather around the seesaw. Now she directs them to observe carefully what happens as two seventh-graders, equal in size, sit at opposite ends of the plank and move each other up and down. Two youngsters then sit at one end: can they be lifted by one child? What has to change for this to happen? Is anything altered when youngsters sit at different places on the plank? The next day, a stump and a long four-by-eight plank are used to create a much larger seesaw with a moveable centre point, and on the third day groups of seventh graders are working in the classroom with calibrated 'New York balances' to reproduce their outdoor experiments, with accurate measurements and corroboration from their classmates. Now the algebra that they have recently learned is put into service, and they learn the Law of the Lever:

Effort times Effort Arm Distance equals Weight times Weight Arm Distance

or

$$E(ED) = W(WD)$$

The children's Kindergarten experiences on the somatic level of will have percolated through the life of their feelings for seven or eight years, and are now ready to 'bubble up' in the form of thoughts in seventh grade. The highly abstract equation which expresses the Law of the Lever is nothing but an abstraction for all too many of today's American children, who have had little experience interacting through active play. For a child who spent two or three years in a Waldorf Kindergarten, $E(ED) = W(WD)$ is nothing less than the expression of a rich store of memories that live on in the youngster's etheric/physical nature. Indeed, we might say that the child who plays creatively in those formative first seven years of life will have the potential for a far more *'inner'* and living grasp of the laws of physics than a child who was little more than a passive observer in that period of life.

The importance of play as an element in scientific understanding—indeed, as an essential part of scientific *discovery*—is powerfully illustrated by an incident in the life of the physicist and Nobel laureate Richard Feynman. In his autobiographical collection, *Surely You're Joking, Mr. Feynman!*, he describes a period in his life when he found himself at an impasse concerning his research work:

> Then I had another thought: Physics disgusts me a little bit now, but I used to enjoy doing physics. Why did I enjoy it? I used to play with it. I used to do whatever I felt like doing—it didn't have to do with whether it was important for the development of nuclear physics, but whether it was interesting and amusing for me to play with. ... I'd invent things and play with things for my own entertainment.

So I got this new attitude. Now that I am burned out and I'll never accomplish anything, ... I'm going to play with physics, whenever I want to, without worrying about any importance whatsoever.

Within a week I was in the cafeteria and some guy, fooling around, throws a plate in the air. As the plate went up in the air I saw it wobble, and I noticed the red medallion of Cornell on the plate going around. It was pretty obvious to me that the medallion went around faster than the wobbling. ...

Feynman then describes the extensive research in which he engaged in order to understand the wobbling phenomenon:

It was effortless. It was easy to play with these things. It was like uncorking a bottle: Everything flowed out effortlessly. I almost tried to resist it! There was no importance to what I was doing, but ultimately there was. The diagrams and the whole business that I got the Nobel Prize for came from that piddling around with the wobbling plate.[5]

The neurologist Oliver Sacks has enumerated the rich variety of experiences that can be had by the child or adult in swimming, as the human will encounters the classical 'element' of water:

Duns Scotus, in the thirteenth century, spoke of 'condelectari sibi', the will finding delight in its own exercise. ... There is an essential rightness about swimming, as about all such flowing, and, so to speak, *musical* activities. And then there is the wonder of buoyancy, of being suspended in the thick, transparent medium that supports and embraces us. One can move in water, play with it, in a way that has no analogue in the air. One can explore its dynamics, its flow, this way and that; one can move one's hands like propellers or direct them like little rudders; one can become a little hydroplane or submarine, investigating the physics of flow with one's own body.[6]

The passive attitude encouraged by toys that do everything for the child, but nothing *with* him, is further exacerbated by the prevailing urban and suburban modern life-style in which there is no longer time for chores to be learned and performed. As time seems to accelerate and socio-economic pressures lead to two-career families, the many hours a week that it would take to teach a child to help prepare a soup or wash the dishes are given over to homework, or 'recreation' in front of the TV or stereo. As mechanical and electronic 'servants' appear to bear most of the burden of cooking and cleaning, the young child has no human model to imitate in relation to the simplest tasks of life. The archetypal movements and rhythms that underlie such activities as sweeping, stirring, kneading, and washing, gestures which have formed the bodies and wills of human beings for countless generations, are rapidly disappearing in the lives of American children. The Millennial Child, who carries such powerful will impulses, is provided with little that can tame and form and heal them.

For this reason the Waldorf Kindergarten fosters an atmosphere akin to that of the 'home and hearth' that is fast disappearing from American family life. Every day of the week is devoted to a different cooking or baking task (Monday is 'Bread-Baking Day,' Tuesday is 'Vegetable Soup-Cooking Day,' etc.) taken up by the teachers. For the most part, children are not asked to help; the teachers know that as they begin to slice the vegetables or knead the dough, the children's curiosity, imitativeness, and, above all, their playful *love* of work, will lead to ask if they can help. And so they learn to slice vegetables evenly, to see, and smell, and taste their transformation as they are stirred and boiled up—and seven or eight years later, as they study the phenomena of organic chemistry, the powerful sensory experiences of Kindergarten will arise and foster the adolescent's ability to grasp them on a conceptual level.

By first educating the will through providing the child with experiences of playing and doing, the Waldorf Kindergarten gives the Millennial Child the physical and etheric foundation for her future development. By respecting the work of the etheric 'life' forces upon the physical body, the Kindergarten teacher assures that all that the child learns in these years will be alive and will have a relation to 'real life'. It is not a matter of 'teaching morality' to young children, but rather helping the child imitatively to develop habits which awaken her to the powerful forces of will that she possesses as a birthright. By recognizing that in this first seven-year period, the child is predominantly a being of *will*, we can understand that the Kindergarten she attends is not only responsible for nurturing her health, but for *cultivating her future relationship to her own deeds*. Thus, creative play and the cultivation of meaningful habits can become the foundation for moral action in later years.

It is ironic that many observers of the Waldorf Kindergarten, such as the headmaster referred to above, initially perceive it as a 'sheltered' situation. To a degree, this is true: during the school day, Waldorf Kindergartners are protected from the media, electronic devices, synthetic noises, and processed foods. On the other hand, unlike most urban and suburban preschoolers, Waldorf Kindergar-teners are exposed to a great deal as well: the realities of food prepa-ration, the wind, the rain, warmth and cold, brambles and briars (on their daily walks); in some settings, they encounter sheep and goats, chickens and ponies, birds and fish, in all their raw reality, uncaged and unlabelled. (Encountering animals who are unaccompanied by explanatory labels or animated software may not be 'educational,' but such meetings are memorable and very *real*.) So which child is the 'sheltered' one, and which is the child who is really meeting *life*? Returning to the independent school headmaster I quoted earlier, I will note what he said on the *last* day of his visit:

> When I first saw the Waldorf Kindergarten room, I thought to myself, 'This room is like something out of the nineteenth cen-tury!' But after spending a week on your campus, watching the little children play and watching the older kids learn, I realize now that this school is providing education for the twenty-first century![7]

Notes and References

1. Charlotte Comeras, Creative play in the Kindergarten. *Child and Man*, 25 (2), July 1991: 10.
2. Ibid.
3. Mary Sheedy Kurcinka, *Raising Your Spirited Child*. New York: Harper, 1991, p. 266.
4. Op. cit., p. 11.
5. Richard Feynman, *Surely You're Joking, Mr. Feynman!* New York: Norton, 1985, pp. 173–174.
6. Oliver Sacks, Water babies. *The New Yorker*, 26 May, 1997: 45.
7. In conversation, member of NYSAIS Accreditation Visiting Com-mittee for Green Meadow Waldorf School, 1988.

CHAPTER FIFTEEN

Play—excerpts from *They F*** You Up* and *Affluenza*

Oliver James

The importance of play

In his book *Playing and Reality*, Donald Winnicott (1971) shows that children's play is not just a method for exorcizing fears and conflicts; it also exists as a joyful activity, in and of itself, vital to emotional well-being in adulthood. As adults, we have a strong tendency to become excessively concerned with our internal states, such as our instinct-driven desires for sex or food. Equally, we are very liable to become swamped with the external, such as the need to meet deadlines or to conform with social pressures. In Winnicott's account of play, we are combining inner and outer—but not to achieve some preordained goal, whether instinctive or external.

The loss of our capacity to be playful at work or at home is a dreadful impoverishment, yet finding a way to combine the demands of a busy adult life with personal needs in a playful manner is not easy. Some aspects of modern life, like our freedom from strict morality or greater opportunity to choose careers, should make it more possible, but there are a great many countervailing pressures. For example, being able to work as a freelance, as the name suggests, offers liberty; yet that very freedom can become oppressive if the freelance is overburdened by a sense that he is not doing as well as his contemporaries. The insecurity of the freelance about getting work is not a bad metaphor for the Modern Man or Woman—someone who is always worried about how to succeed in their personal as well as professional life, obsessively and enviously comparing themselves with others, never satisfied with what they have got. If we live our lives beyond hierarchies, there is a danger of creating new ones that are even more totalitarian. As a result, for too many of us the simple enjoyment of a playful life is not possible for much of the time.

A simple test of our aliveness is provided by the ways we go about responding to everyday requests for information about our state of mind and recent experience. Asked 'How are you?' by a friend, most people do not give an honest reply. 'Fine', we say, omitting to mention the blazing row we just had with our partner, or the pall of gloom that descended when reading our bank statement over breakfast. Of course, when people ask after your well-being they rarely want an honest answer, and rarely would it be appropriate. But there are different ways of going about representing our mental state, even in this trivial exchange. It is one thing to offer a lively 'Fine' with enough spin to indicate to the observant listener that you mean nothing of the kind, quite another simply to go through the motions. Even more significant is the way you go about accounting for your life to strangers when you are introduced. Asked 'What do you do?', you can engage in an empty ritual, flatly describing the facts of your professional life, or you can attempt to bring it alive each time, connecting each narrative to the particular person with whom you are communicating. Indeed, half the battle of living a playful life lies in committing yourself to authentic communication. The fun of engagement with others soon follows.

One playful application is to try and make sense of other people by understanding the past in their present. This is a whole lot easier than analysing ourselves—and who does not enjoy analysing someone else? Apart from being fun, it can be very practical. For example, if we have a boss who is so pernickety that he drives all his staff mad, we can ease the burden of dealing with him by paying close attention to how he makes us feel. Very often, what he is doing is using us as a place to deposit his own unwanted feelings, so if *we* feel unaccountably humiliated or angry or fearful, it may well be that this is really how *he* is feeling. Merely grasping that this is what is happening will be surprisingly soothing. Should we happen to get to know him better and he tells us something of his childhood, we will soon see what he is re-creating in his dealings with us.

I witnessed a particularly creative use of this technique at the hands of a consultant who was advising a team of health professionals who had an unusually disturbed and disturbing boss. The consultant asked the team to tell him how they felt after spending time with their boss. One member said she felt stupid, another inferior, and yet another reported a sense of empty futility. When they had finished, the consultant asked them to picture the daily experience of being the person who was their boss. After envisaging a tremendously insecure, lonely man, they were able to see that the boss himself felt what he was making them feel. After that, although they continued to have to cope with his destructiveness, at least they were able to avoid confusing his problems with their own. They became adept at trying to work out what was wrong with him on a particular day from examining how he made them feel.

Playfulness is the cornerstone of emotional fulfilment, a key to insight and volition. It can be activated by any kind of everyday task, from gardening to washing up. Although we need to earn a living, and although there are many practical tasks we have to perform, living as playfully as possible makes our existence infinitely more worthwhile.

Sanity, creativity, and schizophrenia

The idea that there are sharp divisions between sanity and madness is doubtful. Rather, there is a spectrum, ranging from super-realism at one extreme, via average realism, minor illness, and Personality Disorder, to major delusion at the other extreme.

At one end is the most realistic kind of adult, whose perceptions of the world are as undistorted as is possible for a human being. Not many of us are like that. Next is where the average person lives, with a perception largely unclouded by depression or neurosis. Then come people suffering from minor mental illnesses, and after them, veering at times towards the delusional, are people with Personality Disorders or the eating disorder anorexia. At the delusional end of the spectrum are those in the grip of manic depression, major depression, and schizophrenia. There are large grey areas, such as that between many Personality Disordered people, with their sub-personalities and dissociation, and the fully-fledged delusions of the schizophrenic. A very startling parallel can be drawn between schizophrenia and the normal thinking of small children.

At the age of four we engage in plentiful magical thinking, making all manner of playful connections between things that are actually not connected. I was recently playing with a lively girl of this age, my niece Lydia. Speaking of her older brother, she said, 'Jack has gone away for a year and he told me he will only return when the weather changes'. When quizzed in more detail as to the likely reality of this, she simply elaborated the fantasy to accommodate any inconvenient facts. Since I knew that Jack was actually at home with Lydia's parents, and since I knew that she knew that I knew this, I asked what sort of weather would get Jack back. Pointing at the blue sky, she replied, 'Jack said he won't come back while the sky is blue'.

Many of Lydia's comments were surreal non sequiturs, such as 'Jack is sixteen and he has six fishes and eight videos'. She adores puns and word play, so that her current favourite joke goes, 'What's the favourite food of a monkey in space? An astronut.' She likes to carry a doll around with her called Fizz, and gave me regular bulletins about Fizz's feelings which, on many occasions, you did not need to be a psychoanalyst to realize were very thinly veiled accounts of herself. When it was time for Lydia to go to bed, as if apropos of nothing, she reported that Fizz was not feeling tired. She was possessive of what happened to Fizz, resisting suggestions that I knew anything about her. She had invented the idea that it was Fizz's eleventh birthday the next day, and when I said that I could make her a birthday cake she immediately said, 'Oh no, it's not Fizz's birthday'. Fizz was clearly a useful character for feeling in control.

There are interesting parallels between Lydia's play and the work of creating literary or other artistic fictions, sheer pleasure in creation being only one. The novelist knows his characters are not real, but at the moment of creation he believes in their reality, just as the reader does when reading the eventual book. Lydia knows at one level that Fizz is not a real person, and any attempt to expose the connection between what Lydia and Fizz feel is not pleasing to Lydia. Anyone who has tried suggesting to a novelist that their fiction is 'really' about them usually gets equally short shrift. It spoils the pleasure and seeks to undermine a satisfying defensive activity. Whether it be child or novelist, their fictions are often a way of working out uncomfortable realities, recasting them in more tolerable form, or living them out second hand. Of course, neither children's play nor artistic work should be reduced purely to these functions, but they do show the proximity of normality to schizophrenia.

There is a thin line between a child believing in its imaginary friends, a novelist locked into the fictional lives of characters, and a schizophrenic conviction that the plot of your life has developed in such a way that you have become a spy. Every bit as much as the child or the novelist, the schizophrenic is inventing a character and believing in its reality; but the character is himself rather than someone else. So, in people with a weak sense of self, schizophrenia can be viewed as a regression to the childish stage of development as an escape from unbearable adult realities.

Playfulness versus game-playing

In English-speaking work-places, there has been a strong tendency to prohibit play or to exploit it through faux 'fun', like that satirized in David Brent's *The Office*. The modern office also provides abundant opportunity for charlatans, charmers, machiaevels, and Marketing Characters to employ playfulness as a method for self-advancement. Such game-playing perverts a fundamental human need, but fortunately, this perversion is not global.

Everywhere you go in Moscow you encounter a humorous undercurrent, often—though by no means always—coloured by a black dye. During the Soviet era the populace would cheer themselves up with jokes about the grotesque actions of their leaders, and today the people still gain considerable amusement from the outrages perpetrated in their name by President Putin (Humphrey, 1995). They talk about them with a long-suffering, dry sarcasm. Serena is a woman in her fifties who, although a direct descendant of the Romanovs, the Russian royal family, is still a passionate believer in Communism. She is certainly earnest, severe, and venomous in her criticisms of modern Russia, but for much of the time she spoke in a humorous, playful way. She railed against the impact of the financial 'shock therapy' in the early 1990s ('Shock therapy? Shock murder, more like!'), but with a rueful smile never far from her lips. 'How many times did we suffer an economic depression under the Soviets after 1953? None at all. We had calamities before that, but during my life there had been none. Then, in the 1990s, we lived through the equivalent of the United States' Great Depression—twice. All the savings of the whole nation were wiped out overnight, twice. You try going home now, going to bed and waking up to find you have no money whatsoever. Try to imagine that.' With bleak chuckles, she told me about the privatized electricity supply: 'On the news only yesterday there was a report that a whole city had been disconnected and their sewers now don't work, so doctors have to distribute pills against typhoid. How can they do that? Where's our government?' You could not help being reminded of Michael Moore: 'Dude, where's my country?'

Of course, Americans also have a strong tradition of jokes about their ruling elite, nowadays whizzed around by email. But all too often, the telling of these jokes is done competitively, with the hidden objective that the cleverness of the joke will raise the status of the sender. In the case of Michael Moore, for example, his narcissism is legendary amongst friends of mine who were involved in his British TV series. Although the funniest situation comedies are often now American, there is rarely anything more significant to them than the exploitation of our enjoyment of humour to make the producers, authors, and actors rich and famous (*The Simpsons* being the honourable satirical exception). In Russia, the point of the sardonic bleakness is not 'look how clever I am', so much as 'what a bunch of shits are running our country'.

Although various attempts have been made to elevate playfulness in the pecking order of Western culture's desirable character traits (by far the most influential being that of Winnicott, 1971), none have been successful. Writing at the end of the eighteenth century, the poet Schiller stressed its importance as an antidote to the earnestness of duty and destiny, and went as far as to offer it up as man's truest being (Trilling, 1971): 'Man only plays when he is in the fullest sense of the word a human being, and he is only fully a human being when he plays.' Unfortunately, he has gone unheeded. The best way to understand the value of playfulness to adults is by examining its purpose amongst children.

In their fantasy play (Winnicott, 1971), children use imagination to convert the seemingly mundane into the magical, enthralling, and amusing. For example, yesterday our daughter corralled four teddies into a game as pupils, with her and me as the teachers. Two teddies were singled out as having been naughty and deserving a smacking (corporal punishment, I hasten to add, has played no part in her nurture, so I don't know where this idea comes from). These miscreants have devised the idea of putting books down their trousers to prevent pain. However, our daughter has spotted their ruse. They are now to be subjected to a fantastical 'smacking machine'. Using sticks, she makes circular movements on the wall to start the machine, then smacks (more like batters to death) the naughty children with a coal spade. I let out shrill squeals of pain on their behalf to indicate that this is getting a bit bloodthirsty, but she says, 'Don't worry, it's only pretend, dada', speaking as if I must be very thick to have failed to grasp this basic point.

The game is repeated, as necessary, until our daughter decides that it's time to set fire to the bears. She rubs the sticks together 'like how fire was in olden days', gets me to imitate her, then we poke the bears with the burning sticks, setting fire to them. Again I shriek on their behalf, again our daughter reassures me that it's only pretend, repeating this several times as if to reassure herself as well as me. Now she employs magic to set the sticks alight, banging a drumstick on a plastic toy and casting a spell with the words 'abracadabra-fire-comes *now*'. More burning ensues, more reassurance from her that it's only pretend, and finally it's time for bed.

Perhaps I shall pay a heavy price for regaling you with this story. When our adult daughter comes up in court charged with arson and torture, you will be able to testify against me for having encouraged her. However, the likely consequences or meaning of this play are a matter of debate, for, as our daughter was at some pains to point out, she was only pretending. Some psychoanalysts (most notably, Anna Freud, 1965; Klein, 1932) interpret such play as a method for exorcising anxieties and forbidden impulses, of enacting them harmlessly; and to my mind there is little doubt that it can serve this purpose. For example, when our daughter was aged two years and eight months, my wife, heavily pregnant with our son, went off for a hard-earned ten-day residential yoga retreat. At that age, her mother's disappearance was not too great a problem for our daughter, but she used a fantasy to express the degree of annoyance she did feel about it.

On the second morning after my wife had left, we set off to visit my sister, and as we passed over a speed-bump she began talking about a hole in the road, and the need for me to call Mr Builder to repair it—'You call Mr Builder on your teffone'. Having got Mr Builder to the hole, she said, 'Mama's in the gweat big hole and she's covered in mud. What happens now?' I suggested that Mr B would get her out, but that particular plot development was disallowed, so that mama was left there in a 'serves her jolly well right' sort of way. The story of the gweat big hole was returned to again and again over the next few days. Thankfully, as her anger towards mama decreased, mama was allowed to be rescued. Indeed, it was our daughter, rather than Mr Builder, who eventually came to the rescue. (Subsequently it was Bear-Bear who was in the hole; for much of that time, Bear-Bear was her baby rather than her solace, being cradled and put in a toy push-chair. She was very aware of her forthcoming sibling, wanting to watch the episode of Pingu the penguin in which his younger sister is born out of an egg, over and over again.) You do not have to be Sigmund Freud to see that our daughter's chucking of her mama into the hole was a way of expressing rage towards her, and there can be little doubt that some portion of the fantasies children enjoy are serving a similar sorts of purpose.

Some psychoanalysts take this further, connecting children's play with art and artists (for the definitive critique of this position, see Storr, 1972; see also James, 2003, Chapter 6). The adult artist's working life is portrayed as an attempt to deal with anxiety or suppressed wishes, and the resultant art as technically indistinguishable from neurotic symptoms. Just as some people develop a fear of cars or an obsession with dirt, an artist may deal with the underlying feelings that these symptoms symbolize by painting pictures of cars or of clean rooms.

Although this theory is not completely unfounded, it does leave a great deal out. The English psychoanalyst Donald Winnicott (along with Schiller) regarded both art and play primarily as sources of joy in our lives, a way of Being with its own justification, more than a container for anxieties, and distinct from dreams and neurotic symptoms. In this view, an adult may infuse their work or leisure time with playfulness simply in order to make it fun, not just for catharsis. Winnicott's non-cathartic play has no goals beyond this—it is designed neither to achieve any practical end nor to express suppressed conflict. Rather it is a temporary exit from normal reality into the world of imagination, with all the freedom that brings from social convention and the laws of physics and chemistry, a place where pigs can fly. I can enter a transitional mental space, expressing both myself and what is out there, a place that is neither me nor not-me, where I am neither seeking to impose myself on the world nor aping its dictates.

A primitive, childish example of playfulness is the full-throated laughter that comes from our daughter if I subvert an expectation. When I sing 'Twinkle, Twinkle Little Star', she finds it hilarious if I begin the next verse 'Baa-Baa Black Sheep'. Obviously, children and most artists are cut a great deal more imaginative slack than adults with conventional occupations, but it is only a matter of degree. Playfulness is possible in the execution of all social roles, be they professional or otherwise. Putting on funny voices, making odd facial expressions and gestures, or using strange ideas or forms of words—all of these can and are employed in playfulness in even the most serious of contexts, including during births, weddings, and funerals. Whether cathartic or not, what distinguishes this as play, as opposed to manipulation or game-playing or being charming or entertaining to further your interests, is that it has no self-aggrandizing goal, nor is it an attempt to control the outside world. This distinction is subtle. If you imitate another person's dialect or eccentric use of language when talking about them to a mutual friend, it may seem playful to a stranger who happens to overhear it. But without knowing the precise details of your motives, it would be impossible to tell, because motive is all.

In the Marketing Society, politicians and business people frequently impersonate both playfulness and authenticity in order to convince. Exploitation of play is rife, whether in advertising products, closing deals, seducing sexual partners, or marketing one's self. Disentangling the real from the false can be difficult, and is made ever more so by the immense complexity of modern culture and its history.

In England at the end of the nineteenth century (Trilling, 1971, pp. 118–120), there was a wave of revulsion by some artists and thinkers in response to the moral and social earnestness of Victorian society. Oscar Wilde was the greatest exponent of pretence, both as an antidote to being 'proper' and as a paradoxical route to authenticity. 'The first duty in life is to be as artificial as possible. What the second duty is no one has yet discovered', he famously wrote. Even more explicitly, he penned the epigram 'Man is least himself when he talks in his own person. Give him a mask and he will tell you the truth.' With reference to art, he wrote that 'all bad poetry springs from genuine feeling'. This amusing love of not taking anything too seriously became a lynchpin of upper-class English culture, enshrined in the characters of P.G. Wodehouse, and more contemporaneously evident in the life and work of Stephen Fry (James, 2003). Fry has commented that 'Oscar Wilde teaches one to take the serious things in life trivially and the trivial things seriously. That's ultimately my attitude.' During a TV interview in 1988 (Channel 4 Television, 1988) he told me that 'A fiction is the best way to be true' and, at least at that time, he rarely if ever stopped assuming personae, paradoxically feeling most real when pretending to be someone else. That may have been what lay behind his confession to me that his greatest fear is 'being found out—most men live in fear of a nameless "being found out"'.

In fact, most men feel nothing of the sort. There is a world of difference between our daughter acting the role of Peppa the Pig, and Fry's kind of imposture. Whereas it is true that all of us probably sometimes feel more real through fictions of one sort of another, that is not our main source of authenticity.

I can recall shedding tears at the end of the film *Casablanca*, because I had recently broken up with a girlfriend and was upset at the thought of a relationship ending. The fiction briefly gave me access to my true feelings, but that is not the same as living most of my life as if I am someone else. The actual relationship with the real girlfriend lasted rather longer than the film and my subsequent tears. Through social roles, certainly, as well as through consuming or creating art, we can play and achieve authenticity, but we can be manipulative, deadened, and deadening in these roles as well. Having sat through dozens of best man's and bridegroom's speeches, I have noted the authentic ingenuity of play in some, and the inauthentic emptiness of overcontrived, uncomfortably self-referential artifice in others.

The second-hand living that afflicted Stephen Fry is fuelled, particularly in America and England, by an addiction to irony: saying one thing when another is meant, in order to establish a disconnection between the speaker and his listener, or between the speaker and that which is being spoken about, or even between the speaker and himself. This particular species of second-hand living is not restricted to a highly educated elite of the literary-minded: it is found widely in the upper echelons of British society, such as merchant banks or commercial law firms, where irony is used as a method for putting people down in office politics, or as a device for being charming during financial negotiations rather than to achieve entertaining or artistic ends. Unfortunately, it is not only the elites who suffer second-hand living: less complex forms are widespread.

Studies show that the mental state we enter whilst watching TV is a passive, floating, vicarious consciousness (Sigman, 2005, Chapter 3). The emotional and sometimes visible animation of a person attending live theatre or ballet or opera, or when watching a deeply moving film, or when reading a great novel, are very rarely present. Occasionally television does achieve this effect in viewers. During exceptional sporting events, such as the 2005 Ashes cricket matches, it can happen. It can, too, at high points in soap operas, as in the programme with the highest-ever TV audience in Britain, the powerful episode of *EastEnders* in which Den announced that he was leaving Angie, and she trumped him by claiming to have cancer.

The doublethink-named 'reality TV' shows (which are nothing of the kind because heavily edited: even when broadcast live, there is a lot of editing in choice of camera shots, and actual censorship of what the contributors say) very occasionally achieve the same, such as 'Nasty Nick's' exposure as a machiavel in the first series of *Big Brother*. But for the vast majority of the time, watching TV is a form of dead, second-hand living. Increasingly, to save money, broadcasters are exploiting the greater availability of cheap video cameras to bring together our lumpen need for low-grade TV with our desire to record our lives rather than simply live them. Viewer-as-programme-material is found not just on shows compiled from clips of 'hilarious' misfortunes (increasingly contrived to get them onto the small screen)—dogs falling into swimming pools and dads banging their heads on sharp edges—there is also greater use of it in documentaries, with contributors asked to keep video diaries of their experiences. As we find ourselves scrabbling to switch on the digital camera or mobile phone in time to catch our child's first steps, the having of the authentic experience is increasingly supplanted by the need to make a record of it, and as the activities we record are increasingly modified by us and our children to correspond to a desired end. Never mind 'say cheese'—our children are becoming alert at ever younger ages to the need to perform for the camera. The urge to use home footage to gain 15 seconds of fame on TV is rampant amongst young people in England and America, millions of whom have now prepared brief videos of themselves to send to TV companies as applications for a shot at fame in a reality TV show.

Significant numbers dream of being famous, of having others fantasizing about them. In England, 16 per cent of 16–19 year-olds truly believe that they will become famous (Learning and Skills Council, 2006); and 11 per cent would abandon their education for a stab at fame on a reality Television show, even though the victors of such contests seldom remain in the public eye.

Fascination with the famous amongst the young has mushroomed. A substantial number of English and American studies in the last five years suggest that about three-quarters of young people report having had a strong attraction to a celebrity at some stage in their life (see, for example, in England's case, Maltby et al., 2004; and for America, see Boon et al., 2001). In itself, this is a form of virtual relationship, of second-hand living, a fantasy relationship with a stranger. For 7 per cent of 18–47 year-olds (see Maltby et al., 2004), the relationship becomes obsessive and worshipful. People with such attachments to celebrities (Maltby et al., 2006) are also prone to emotional distress. Adolescents with weak attachment to parents (Giles et al., 2004), or who are exceptionally reliant on peers for their sense of status and well-being, are at greater risk of becoming obsessive.

Despite these and the many other atrocities committed in the name of Selfish Capitalist, Neoliberal Thatcherism in this country and throughout the English-Speaking world, playfulness can never be completely subdued. That our young people's liveliness has been so sadly expropriated in order to make a few billionaires richer is regrettable. But in the end, our will to play is always greater than the desire to exploit it. We can get by without the fruits of that exploitation; we cannot find reasons to live without play.

Acknowledgements

Thanks are due to the respective publishers for granting kind permission to reproduce the foregoing excerpts from Oliver James's two books, *They F*** You up: How to Survive Family Life*, London: Bloomsbury, 2003 (2nd revised edition, 2007); and *Affluenza*, London: Vermillion, 2007.

References

Boon, S.D., & Lomore, C.D. (2001). Admirer–celebrity relationships among young adults: explaining perceptions of celebrity influence on identity. *Human Communication Research*, 27: 432–465.

Channel 4 Television (1988). *Room 113*.

Freud, A. (1965). *Normality and Pathology in Childhood*. London: Hogarth.

Giles, D.C., & Maltby, J. (2004). The role of media figures in adolescent development: relations between autonomy, attachment, and interest in celebrities. *Personality and Individual Differences*, 36: 813–822.

Humphrey, C. (1995). Creating a culture of disillusionment: consumption in Moscow, a chronicle of changing times. In: D. Miller (Ed.), *Worlds Apart: Modernity though the Prism of the Local* (pp. 43–68). London: Routledge.

James, O. (2003). *They F*** You up: How to Survive Family Life*. London: Bloomsbury, 2nd edition 2007.

James, O. (2007). *Affluenza*. London: Vermillion.

Klein, M. (1932). *The Psychoanalysis of Children*. London: Hogarth.

Learning and Skills Council (LSC) (2006). Kids seeking reality TV fame instead of exam passes. London: Press release, Learning and Skills Council.

Maltby, J., Day, L., McCutcheon, L.E., Gillett, R., Houran, J., & Ashe, D.D. (2004). Personality and coping: a context for examining celebrity worship and mental health. *British Journal of Psychology*, 95: 411–428.

Maltby, J., Day, L., McCutcheon, L.E., Houran, J., & Ashe, D. (2006). Extreme celebrity worship, fantasy proneness and dissociation: developing the measurement and understanding of celebrity worship within a clinical personality context. *Personality and Individual Differences*, 40: 273–283.

Sigman, A. (2005). *Remotely Controlled: How Television is Damaging our Lives and what We Can Do about It*. London: Vermillion.

Storr, A. (1972). *The Dynamics of Creation*. Harmondsworth: Penguin.

Trilling, L. (1971). *Sincerity and Authenticity*. Oxford: Oxford University Press.

Winnicott, D.W. (1971). *Playing and Reality*. Harmondsworth: Penguin.

CHAPTER SIXTEEN

Editorial conclusion: *Therapeia* today (re-instating the soul in human experience)

Del Loewenthal and Richard House

If we allow Plato to speak, he will suggest that the question before us is whether we shall shrivel on the positivistic vine, or with him, plumb again the resources of the human soul and so recover ...

(Cushman, 2002, p. xvi)

Materialistic learning ... dominates education .... Education has become an institution whose purpose ... is not to make culture, not to serve the living cosmos, but to harness humankind to the dead forces of materialism. Education, as we know it, from pre-school through graduate school, damages the soul.

(Robert Sardello, 1992: *passim*)

So where do this book's diverse conversations, centred on the vicissitudes of modern childhood, leave us? The psychological therapies can certainly help as a vehicle for learning again through a different kind and quality of relational experience (Rose, Loewenthal & Greenwood 2005), but in a preventive sense, what may be even more vital is for the quality of educational experience *in general* to be addressed, through home, school, and our wider culture. For such concern for the soul as is entailed in psychotherapy and education to effectively enhance our well-being, Plato's argument is that the focus has to be more on dialogue. How can we minimize being corrupted? Plato argues that *virtue* is a precondition for knowledge (cf. Sardello, 2004), and that well-being is inaccessible to corrupt minds. This well-being evolves from an ethos which requires an appropriate balance of affection within the soul. But what is this appropriate balance, and can we facilitate this and enable people to come away from what may be corrupting?

How can we 'wise up' and give technical thinking (with its detrimental impact on personal meaning) a secondary place? For Plato, the truth of all things always resides in our soul (quoted in Cushman, 2002, p. 91). One does not necessarily have to go along with Plato completely to sense that he may well be on to something very important, even essential. This book is for those who are concerned that we are doing too much that is wrong for both the well-being of our children and ourselves. The very ground that we move on in the post-postmodern world increasingly appears less solidly our own, whilst paradoxically, more and more people really seem to believe in the individualist rhetoric of 'I did it my way'.

So how might we define and embrace a therapeutic ethos that enhances the well-being of childhood? Can virtue be imparted and acquired through the psychological therapies? And perhaps far more importantly, is there the necessary political will to impart it more generally in our societies? If we want to work for the good, then to what extent do we at times have to, as individuals and therapists, stay with the bad?—referring to both the bad in ourselves and the bad in the wider society. Such approaches would be in direct contrast to those which might take our minds off anything which causes us to be anxious or depressed. Approaches like cognitive behaviour therapy (CBT) can, of course, be helpful to some individuals (House & Loewenthal, 2008). But if taken up too much and too uncritically in or by modern culture, it can quickly become the equivalent of burying our heads (and more tragically, our souls) in the arid sand of a soulless technocracy, thereby generating unnecessary further momentum towards cultural catastrophe.

There is a further question in relation to the training of psychological therapists, regarding the extent to which a more explicitly *psycho-social* dimension to education might be more helpful. In such an educational approach, our values could be explored in terms of changing political, economic, social, and technological contexts. However, most importantly, it has been argued that Therapeutic Education needs to include both societal and 'local' perspectives. We need, for example, to be able to return to a situation where our sexuality does not frighten us to the extent that we can no longer spend embodied and engaging time with children, and through this enhance our own lives as well as theirs. For those who still require a 'quality assurance indicator' to show at least some 'green shoots' of rediscovering a therapeutic ethos for the good, then we could start by allowing teachers to again be alone in the classroom with a child without our erotic fantasies, or our uncontained fears of them, getting in the way of, and compromising, the quality of our relational experience.

We believe that *Childhood, Well-being, and a Therapeutic Ethos* is the first putatively academic book to have addressed in a thorough-going way the 'toxic childhood' phenomenon that Sue Palmer brought to public awareness so effectively in her seminal book in 2006. But the current book is far more than a detached academic treatise, for as we wrote in the introduction to our Chapter 1, the book is also replete with opinion, assertion, empassioned argument, ideology-critique, cultural critique, and campaigning zeal—but all, we hope, with its own rigour. And given the nature of the subject-matter, we certainly make no apology for that, as the concept of the 'objective', apolitically disinterested academic is one that we feel is open to re-examination (House, 2007).

Our contributors have looked closely at various themes implicated in childhood's alleged (but by some, disputed) toxicity, being instances of the kinds of arguments that critics of so-called 'toxic childhood' have been developing in recent years. *Play and playfulness* have certainly held a place of particular prominence in the book, not least because play constitutes a key nexus at which therapeutic and eductional interests intersect, therefore constituting a key site on which any mature notion of 'Therapeutic Education' would be expected to play itself out.

As has been argued at times throughout this book, one grave danger is that the various symptoms of the toxic-childhood syndrome perpetrate a kind of violence to the soul; to the very values and ways of being which are of most importance in defining quality, subtlety, and *heart* in early learning and therapeutic healing encounters. And these latter are critically important if an effective creative space is to be preserved in which children's playing, for example, in all its richness and imaginative elaboration, can truly flourish, and in which troubled adults can themselves re-discover the 'genius' and wonder of play (Jenkinson, 2001). One is also reminded of Rudolf Steiner's prophetic statement of almost a century ago, that any educational experience should contain within it a seamlessly integrated *healing ethos*, through the very way in which the learning milieu is sensitively and imaginatively created, and with children's developmentally appropriate experience being placed at the forefront. In short, on this view, education at its best is seen as being an *intrinsically* healing force for the child—and sometimes for the teacher, parents and community too.

In stark contrast, the relentless preparation of children for the audit culture, for unrelenting consumerism and acquisitiveness, and for what Marx termed 'capitalist social relations of production' (e.g. Althusser, 1971; Bowles & Gintus, 1976) must necessarily produce an educational milieu that is very different from that envisaged here by Steiner, Sardello, and others; and it is these kinds of values that we should all surely strive to uphold and work with in both therapeutic and educational milieux—values which increasing numbers of mainstream practitioners are now realizing must be reclaimed and reaffirmed at all costs, as the arid 'managerialism' of Late Modernity's auditing juggernaut blunders on through human sensibilities and sensitivities (see, for example, Alexander, 2009).

In short, early-childhood practitioners and psychotherapists alike, therefore, surely have *a shared ethical professional responsibility* to do all they can to protect the children in their charge from the intrusively poisonous, low-trust values that the audit culture at its worst represents and actively cultivates; and to the extent that they fail, there promises to be a veritable army of clients/patients queuing up at the door of the psychotherapist for years to come. Though turkeys do rarely vote for an early Christmas, this is certainly one grotesquely inadvertent job-creation scheme that we hope all therapists and educationalists can unite in subverting and opposing with every fibre of their being.

It is important to acknowledge that the chapters in this book by no means cover all of the themes in the 'toxic childhood' debate. Not least, the issue of information technologies (ICT) and the impact of an increasingly all-pervading televisual culture on people's (and particularly children's) lives (Greenfield, 2008; House, 2009; Sigman, 2005; Winn, 2002) have not been extensively considered (though see Oliver James's Chapter 15). The kinds of potentially devastating critiques of technological modernity developed by commentators like Martin Heidegger (1977; see also Zimmerman, 1990), Jean-François Lyotard (1992; see also Sim, 2001), and Neil Postman (1992) are certainly ones that must play a key role in the unfolding and urgent cultural conversation to which this book imperfectly is attempting to contribute.

We could do far worse than end this book with a quotation from one of the great thinkers of any epoch, Ludwig Wittgenstein, who wrote:

> Getting hold of the difficulty *deep down* is what is hard. Because if it is grasped near the surface it simply remains the difficulty it was. It has to be pulled out by the roots; and that involves our beginning to think about these changes in a new way ... . The new way of thinking is what is hard to establish.
>
> (Ludwig Wittgenstein, quoted in Newman, 1995,
> p. 85, original emphasis)

It is indeed a new kind of thinking that may well be required if we are going to achieve any effective insight into, the diverse modern phenomena that fall under the less than discriminating but, rhetorically, extraordinarily effective term, 'toxic childhood'.

References

Alexander, R. (2009). *Children, Their World, Their Education: Final Report and Recommendations of the Primary Review*. London: Routledge.

Althusser, L. (1971). Ideology and the Ideological State Apparatus. In: his *Lenin and Philosophy and Other Essays*, (pp. 127–186). London: New Left Books.

Bowles, S. & Gintus. H. (1976). *Schooling and Capitalist America: Educational Reform and the Contradictions of Economic Life*. New York: Basic Books, 2nd edition, 1999.

Cushman, P. (2002). *Therapeia: Plato's Conception of Philosophy*. New Brunswick/London: Transaction Publishers.

Greenfield, S. (2008). *ID: The Quest for Identity in the 21st Century*. London: Sceptre.

Heidegger, M. (1977). *The Question Concerning Technology and Other Essays*. New York: Harper Torchbook.

House, R. (2007). Schooling, the State, and children's psychological well-being: a psychosocial critique. *Journal of Psychosocial Research*, 2 (2): 49–62.

House, R. (2009). Television in/and the worlds of today's children: a mounting cultural controversy. *Teacher's College Record*, 23 March; retrievable at: http://www.tcrecord.org/Content.asp?ContentId=15594

House, R., & Loewenthal, D. (Eds.) (2008). *Against and For CBT: Towards a Constructive Dialogue?* Ross-on-Wye: PCCS Books.

Jenkinson, S. (2001). *The Genius of Play*. Stroud: Hawthorn Press (new edition, 2007).

Lyotard, J.-F. (1992). *The Inhuman, Reflections on Time*. Oxford: Blackwell.

Newman, A. (1995). *Non-Compliance in Winnicott's Words: A Companion to the Writings and Work of D.W. Winnicott*. London: Free Association Books.

Postman, N. (1992). *Technopoly: The Surrender of Culture to Technology*. New York: A.A. Knopf.

Rose, T., Loewenthal, D., & Greenwood, D. (2005). Counselling and psychotherapy as a form of learning: some implications for practice. *British Journal for Guidance and Counselling*, 33: 441–456.

Sardello, R. (1992). *Facing the World with Soul: The Reimagination of Modern Life*, Great Barrington, MA: Lindisfarne Press, new edition, 2004.

Sardello, R. (2004). *Power of Soul: Living the Twelve Virtues*, Charlottesville, VA: Hampton Roads Publishing Co.

Sigman, A. (2005). *Remotely Controlled: How Television is Damaging Our Lives*. London: Vermillion.

Sim, S. (2001). *Lyotard and the Inhuman*. Cambridge: Icon Books.

Winn, M. (2002). *The Plug-in Drug: Television, Computers, and Family Life*. New York: Penguin, special anniversary edition.

Zimmerman, M.E. (1990). *Heidegger's Confrontation with Modernity: Technology, Politics, and Art*. Bloomington: Indiana University Press.

INDEX